CIVIL PROCEDURE

CIVIL PROCEDURE

MODEL PROBLEMS AND

OUTSTANDING ANSWERS

Second Edition

Scott Dodson

OXFORD
UNIVERSITY PRESS

UNIVERSITY PRESS

Oxford University Press is a department of the University of Oxford. It furthers the University's objective of excellence in research, scholarship, and education by publishing worldwide.

Oxford   New York

Auckland   Cape Town   Dar es Salaam   Hong Kong   Karachi   Kuala Lumpur   Madrid
Melbourne   Mexico City   Nairobi   New Delhi   Shanghai   Taipei   Toronto

With offices in

Argentina   Austria   Brazil   Chile   Czech Republic   France   Greece   Guatemala   Hungary
Italy   Japan   Poland   Portugal   Singapore   South Korea   Switzerland   Thailand
Turkey   Ukraine   Vietnam

Oxford is a registered trade mark of Oxford University Press in the UK and certain other countries.

Published in the United States of America by
Oxford University Press
198 Madison Avenue, New York, NY 10016

© Oxford University Press 2013

Library of Congress Cataloging-in-Publication Data
Dodson, Scott.
   Civil procedure : model problems and outstanding answers / Scott Dodson.—Second edition.
      pages cm
   ISBN 978-0-19-996522-9 (pbk.)
1. Civil procedure—United States—Examinations, questions, etc. I. Title.
   KF8841.D63 2013
   347.73'5076—dc23
                                                                                    2012022949

Printed in the United States of America on acid-free paper

Note to Readers
This publication is designed to provide accurate and authoritative information in regard to the subject matter covered. It is based upon sources believed to be accurate and reliable and is intended to be current as of the time it was written. It is sold with the understanding that the publisher is not engaged in rendering legal, accounting, or other professional services. If legal advice or other expert assistance is required, the services of a competent professional person should be sought. Also, to confirm that the information has not been affected or changed by recent developments, traditional legal research techniques should be used, including checking primary sources where appropriate.

*(Based on the Declaration of Principles jointly adopted by a Committee of the
American Bar Association and a Committee of Publishers and Associations.)*

You may order this or any other Oxford University Press publication
by visiting the Oxford University Press website at www.oup.com

TABLE OF CONTENTS

ABOUT THE AUTHOR

Scott Dodson is a Professor of Law at University of California Hastings College of the Law. He is a graduate of Duke Law School, where he was an editor of *Duke Law Journal*. After law school, Professor Dodson clerked for Judge Nicholas G. Garaufis in the Eastern District of New York. Before becoming a law professor, Professor Dodson practiced law in private practice in Houston and Washington, D.C., where he also worked as an attorney for the U.S. Department of Commerce. He also taught at Duke Law School, William & Mary Law School, and University of Arkansas School of Law. He is the author of *Slamming the Federal Courthouse Doors: New Pleading in the Twenty-First Century* (Oxford Univ. Press). He also has written over 20 articles on jurisdiction and procedure, appearing in such journals as *Stanford Law Review, Michigan Law Review, California Law Review, University of Pennsylvania Law Review, Virginia Law Review,* and *Northwestern University Law Review.*

ACKNOWLEDGMENTS

This book would not have been possible without the assistance of many people, and I want to take a moment here to acknowledge that assistance and express my deep gratitude for it. My former colleagues at the University of Arkansas supported and mentored my development as a law professor and civil procedure scholar in myriad ways, and I am grateful for their interest in my success and encouragement. I also have become close to many—too many to name individually—scholars in my field who have contributed to my development, knowledge, and appreciation for the wonder that is civil procedure. Many thanks to Steve Sheppard for inviting me to write this book, to the terrific editorial staff at Oxford University Press who helped make the book the best it could be, and to the outside reviewers for detailed and insightful comments. I also thank Aaron Bruhl for personally reviewing several chapters and identifying much-needed improvements. William & Mary Law School provided a research grant that enabled me to work on this book over the summer of 2009. And several research assistants were invaluable in formatting the book, checking the citations, and giving me several additional pairs of eyes from a student's perspective: Samantha Leflar, Chris Cantrall, and Matt Beard. Finally, I am eternally grateful to my wife, Ami, without whose love and support this book would not exist.

INTRODUCTION TO THE BOOK

Students often deem Civil Procedure the hardest class in their first year (and perhaps even their entire law school career). There are several reasons. The first is that the doctrine usually taught at the outset—personal jurisdiction—is extremely opaque. The second is that the policies and values underlying the rules of civil procedure are latent and difficult to pin down. The third is that the course is a hybrid of common law reasoning, rule and statutory analysis, and constitutional doctrine. Combine all of these, and one gets an extremely challenging course, particularly for a student who has just matriculated into law school.

Just as often, however, students deem Civil Procedure the most useful and important doctrinal class in their first year (and even in law school). For litigators, the class is crucial. Having a working knowledge of the rules and doctrines is essential even in summer jobs during law school. For non-litigators or for criminal attorneys, the course can still be useful, if only to provide a comparative or analogous perspective. For all lawyers, the procedural thinking and reasoning that a student learns in the course is simply invaluable, regardless of what career path the future holds.

This book strives to assist in achieving those goals in a format that will (hopefully) make civil procedure both easier and interesting. I separated chapters by their natural breaks in topics, breaks that generally correspond with major topics treated in most civil procedure courses. In U.S. law schools, civil procedure can be as short as a single semester, three-credit course, or as a long as a two-semester, six-credit course. I have erred on the side of inclusion rather than exclusion. As a result, students in shorter courses may find topics in this book, such as Class Actions, which they are not covering in their course. (No matter. Perhaps they will have use for the book again when they take Advanced Civil Procedure or Complex Litigation!) But in any case, the fundamentals are all here.

I also have attempted to design the problems to have separate components so that a student in a course that covers a particular topic, say, *Erie*, deeply will have a rich chapter in this book to explore those issues. At the same time, a student in a shorter course that touches on *Erie* but does not expect such depth will still be able to use components of the problem to explore the fundamental basis of the doctrine.

The problems also have some easy answers and some more difficult ones. In the Tools sections, I have identified which are particularly difficult and which are easier so that you can better appreciate those distinctions and provide more meaningful self-evaluation. The Tools sections are, perhaps, the best part of the book, and in those sections I have attempted to explain carefully how one gets from the hypothetical to the answer in a way that is satisfactory to yourself and (hopefully) your professor.

This second edition has been updated to incorporate new paradigm cases, including *Wal-Mart*, *Goodyear*, and *McIntyre*. It also reflects the new rule and statutory amendments that have taken effect since the printing of the first edition, including the Federal Courts Jurisdiction and Venue Clarification Act of 2011.

I hope that you enjoy learning from the book as much as I enjoyed writing it.

Scott Dodson
San Francisco, CA
December 1, 2012

CIVIL PROCEDURE

PERSONAL JURISDICTION

1

OPENING REMARKS

The doctrine of personal jurisdiction likely has scared more law students than any other legal doctrine. The antiquated and difficult case of *Pennoyer v. Neff* is often the first case assigned on the first day of many civil procedure courses. Later developments have provided some, though by no means complete, clarity. And the lack of a concrete statute or rule—other than the vagaries of "due process" and "state sovereignty"—leaves many students bewildered.

In a nutshell, personal jurisdiction is the power of a court over a party. A judgment against a defendant issued by a court that lacked personal jurisdiction over that defendant is unenforceable. Traditionally, personal jurisdiction was circumscribed by state borders; a court in Texas could not exercise jurisdiction over an unconsenting defendant not found in Texas. With the modernization of a mobile society, the reduced emphasis on territorial limits of state authority, and the increasing attention to notions of justice and fairness, that rigid test has been broadened to reflect the flexible nature of its source: the Due Process Clause of the Fourteenth Amendment to the U.S. Constitution.

That constitutional source sets the outer bounds of personal jurisdiction, but states are free to impose additional limitations on the reach of their courts. Many such "long-arm statutes" extend to the limits of the Due Process Clause and therefore collapse the personal jurisdiction analysis into a single inquiry. Other states impose additional restrictions on the extraterritorial reach of the courts under their purview. In short, different states have different notions about how far their courts' extraterritorial reach should extend.

Personal jurisdiction is not all about the power of the court, however. Its modernization has led to a recharacterization of personal jurisdiction as primarily—though not exclusively—a personal right of a defendant. Accordingly, a defendant can waive or forfeit that right and consent to suit, even if a court otherwise would lack personal jurisdiction over her.

HYPOTHETICAL

You have just passed the bar exam and have started working as an associate at the law firm Larry, Curly, & Moe LLP. Mr. Moe comes into your office on Friday at 4:00 p.m. and says, "You took Professor Dodson's civil procedure class, so you must know everything there is to know about civil procedure. We need some analysis of the law of personal jurisdiction for our client, Paul Pennington. We decided to sue in Fayetteville, Arkansas, because the juries are better for us there, but now I'm not so sure we can get personal jurisdiction in Arkansas. I'll need a memo with your analysis in two hours."

You open the case file and realize that the complaint has already been filed and served. The complaint contains the following allegations:

Paul Pennington is a resident of Tulsa, Oklahoma. He has a cabin in the Arkansas Ozarks, which he visits every fall to do some hiking.

Last fall, Pennington visited his cabin and brought with him a new pair of hiking boots with a new tread called "Ozark Tread," manufactured and sold by a small footwear store in Tulsa called Deff Footwear. He specifically bought the boots because a sales associate at Deff told him the tread on the boots was specifically designed for the kinds of hiking trails found in the Arkansas Ozarks.

On one of his treks, however, Pennington stumbled. The ankle support on his right hiking boot was less sturdy than on his left boot, and, as a result, he twisted his right ankle and fell. Pennington now walks with a permanent limp and can no longer hike.

Pennington sued Deff Footwear for his injuries in Arkansas state court. Deff specially appeared for the sole purpose of challenging personal jurisdiction. The court ordered limited discovery on the personal jurisdiction issue and, in a deposition, a Deff representative testified as follows:

Deff, a partnership organized under the laws of Oklahoma, is a small footwear store with a single location in Tulsa. Its two general partners are lifelong residents of Oklahoma and, with one exception mentioned below, have never been to Arkansas.

Deff currently does not market or advertise its products in other states and, in fact, does not even ship orders out of state. Rather, it sells shoes only to customers who physically enter the store. It does not do business in Arkansas, does not have a registered agent there, and has no office or employees there.

However, Deff admitted that, in developing the "Ozark Tread," Deff's assistant manager, using the Tulsa store's computer, downloaded maps of and information on Arkansas terrain from the Fayetteville Public Library. In addition, although Deff does not know where its customers take its shoes, Deff does know that Arkansas customers have purchased shoes with Ozark Tread in the past. Deff plans to open another shoe store in Fayetteville.

In furtherance of those plans, Deff sent one of its two general partners to Arkansas to secure preapproval for a commercial loan from Arvest Bank, a local Arkansas bank, and to sign an agreement with some Arkansas developers to develop commercial real estate in Arkansas. Deff has not yet purchased any land or set up any business operations in Arkansas. Except for that one trip to meet with the bank and the developers, no employee, agent, or partner of Deff has ever set foot in Arkansas.

Pennington personally served Deff by handing the partner the summons and complaint in Arkansas while the partner was at Arvest Bank to secure preapproval for the commercial loan. Assume that under Arkansas law, personal service on any general partner is effective service on the partnership, and partnerships may sue or be sued in their own name. Deff has waived any objection to service and is challenging only personal jurisdiction.

In your research, you discover that Arkansas's long-arm statute extends to the full reach of the Constitution's Due Process Clause. You also learn that Tulsa and Fayetteville are approximately 90 miles apart, with the Arkansas-Oklahoma border directly between them.

Please draft a memo analyzing whether Arkansas may assert personal jurisdiction over Deff. Assume that Deff has not consented to suit or otherwise waived or forfeited its objection to personal jurisdiction. Also assume that neither Arkansas nor the Eighth Circuit has expanded upon the Supreme Court's case law of personal jurisdiction. In your answer, a separate recitation of the facts is unnecessary—simply incorporate the relevant facts into your analysis.

SUGGESTED READINGS

U.S. Const. amend. XIV, § 1
Pennoyer v. Neff, 95 U.S. (5 Otto) 714, 714–36 (1877)
Int'l Shoe Co. v. Washington, 326 U.S. 310, 310–22 (1945)
World-Wide Volkswagen Corp. v. Woodson, 444 U.S. 286, 286–312 (1980)
Burger King Corp. v. Rudzewicz, 471 U.S. 462, 462–87 (1985)
Asahi Metal Industry Co. v. Superior Ct. of Cal., 480 U.S. 102, 102–22 (1987)
J. McIntyre Machinery, Ltd. v. Nicastro, 564 U.S. _ (2011)
Goodyear Dunlop Tires Operations, S.A. v. Brown, 564 U.S. __ (2011)
Burnham v. Superior Ct. of Cal., 495 U.S. 604, 604–40 (1990)

SAMPLE ESSAY

MEMORANDUM

To: Mr. Moe
From: Me
Re: Personal Jurisdiction in *Pennington v. Deff Footwear*

ISSUE
Does the Arkansas court have personal jurisdiction over Deff Footwear?

SHORT ANSWER
Probably. The Arkansas court likely has specific jurisdiction over Deff based on minimum contacts. There also is a colorable argument for transient jurisdiction based on the service of Deff's general partner in Arkansas.

DISCUSSION
For a court to have personal jurisdiction over a defendant, the court's jurisdiction must be authorized by both the state's long-arm statute and the Constitution's Due Process Clause. Arkansas's long-arm statute authorizes the assertion of jurisdiction to the full extent of the Due Process Clause. Therefore, the only issue here is whether Arkansas's assertion of jurisdiction over Deff comports with the Due Process Clause.

There are two possible ways to satisfy the Due Process Clause on these facts. The first is under the "transient jurisdiction" doctrine of *Burnham*—serving the defendant when physically present in the state. The second is under the "minimum contacts" test of *International Shoe*—showing that the defendant has sufficient minimum contacts with the state such that jurisdiction would not offend traditional notions of fair play and substantial justice. Both are possibilities here.

A. Transient Jurisdiction

In *Burnham*, all of the justices agreed that a state had personal jurisdiction over a nonresident individual defendant who was personally served while voluntarily in the state. Justice Scalia and Justice White relied upon the historical and traditional acceptance of in-state service as a ground for personal jurisdiction. Justice Brennan, however, reasoned that it was fair and reasonable to subject such a defendant to jurisdiction because the in-state presence of the defendant gives rise to the privileges and benefits of that state's laws and because the in-state presence suggests that it would not be burdensome for the defendant to litigate in that state.

Here, the question is whether a partner who is served while voluntarily in the state for partnership business is the partnership for purposes of transient jurisdiction. *Burnham*, on its face, applies only to individuals, not business associations. Thus, the question is whether *Burnham* ought to apply to partners of a partnership defendant and, if so, under what circumstances.

Justice Brennan's concurring opinion in *Burnham* may provide some guidance. He justified transient jurisdiction as a quid pro quo for the concomitant receipt of the benefits and privileges of the forum state's laws and on the assumption that the burden on the defendant to travel to the forum state was not undue. These justifications have some application to a defendant partnership—after all, a business entity can only act through its agents, and, as *International Shoe* made clear, the "presence" of a corporation can be found by the activities of its agents. Thus, the presence in a state of a partner, so long as he is on partnership business, can provide the partnership with benefits and privileges of that state, including the right to do business, the protection of business interests, and the right to sue to enforce business transactions made in that state. It is true that the individual also receives personal benefits unrelated to the partnership business, and that it may be difficult to disaggregate the personal benefits from the partnership benefits, but that does not mean that there are no partnership benefits and privileges. In sum, there is a strong argument that a partnership defendant reaps benefits and privileges of a state's laws by sending into that state a representative wielding agency power of the partnership.

The second part of Justice Brennan's rationale, that an individual's presence gives rise to the assumption that litigating there is not burdensome, also applies to partnership defendants. A partnership defendant's burden should not necessarily be more than an individual's, and, in fact, possibly could be much less, particularly if a high-level agent such as a partner is already found in the state. As a result, Justice Brennan's *Burnham* concurrence may provide a justifiable rationale for extending transient jurisdiction to the partnership context.

One obstacle to transferring Justice Brennan's rationale to the partnership context is *International Shoe*. There, the corporate defendant's sales agent was personally served in-state, and it is at least arguable that Justice Brennan's rationale ought to have justified transient jurisdiction over the corporation in that context. Yet the Court did not undertake a transient jurisdiction analysis but instead focused on minimum contacts. That focus suggests that service on a low-level employee such as a sales agent is insufficient to give rise to transient jurisdiction over a corporation. But, of course, *International Shoe* did not involve partnerships, and it could be argued that partners represent the presence of the partnership better than officers represent the presence of the corporation.

Another obstacle to transferring transient jurisdiction to the partnership context may be Justice Scalia's rationale in *Burnham* that transient jurisdiction over individuals had a long and unbroken historical acceptance. It is unclear what historical acceptance transient jurisdiction has with respect to partnerships, but if it is less extensive or uniform than that for individuals, then extending transient jurisdiction to partnerships may be undermined by Justice Scalia's opinion in *Burnham*.

In the absence of controlling law, there is at least an argument (which would be strengthened by the existence of a long historical acceptance of such exercise of personal jurisdiction) that transient jurisdiction should be exercised over a partnership defendant whose general partner is served in a state while acting as a partnership agent.

B. Minimum Contacts Test

The minimum contacts test has two parts. First, the defendant must have sufficient minimum contacts with the forum state. Second, the exercise of personal jurisdiction must comport with fair play and substantial justice. The Court in *Burger King* suggested that these two components work together such that the strength of one can overcome the weakness of the other.

1. MINIMUM CONTACTS

"Minimum contacts" requires that the defendant purposefully avail himself of benefits and privileges of the forum state such that the defendant could reasonably foresee being haled into court there. There are two relevant ways to satisfy the minimum contacts part of the test: specific jurisdiction and general jurisdiction.

A. GENERAL JURISDICTION

A defendant's contacts with the forum state satisfy general jurisdiction if they are "continuous and systematic," a more difficult test than for specific jurisdiction. However, unlike the test for specific jurisdiction, the general jurisdiction analysis takes into consideration all of the defendant's contacts with the state, not just those giving rise to (or possibly relating to) the cause of action.

In *Goodyear v. Brown*, the most recent general jurisdiction case, the Court characterized general jurisdiction as where the defendant was "home" and illustrated using the "paradigm" examples of a corporation's state of incorporation and principal place of business. Because in *Goodyear* the defendants' only connection to the forum state was that the defendants enabled their products to reach the state, and because the defendants otherwise had no other connections to the forum state, the Court concluded that the defendants were not home in the forum state and thus not subject to general jurisdiction there.

Here, it is unlikely that Deff would meet the general jurisdiction test for minimum contacts. Deff does not do business in Arkansas, has no operations there, does not market its products there, and does not sell its products there. Deff's preliminary activity—to engage in more substantial activity in Arkansas—probably is insufficient at this time to establish general jurisdiction. The extent of that activity comprises (1) Internet research by Deff's assistant manager on Arkansas terrain and the downloading of information from Arkansas servers, (2) the securing of preapproval for a commercial loan from an Arkansas bank, (3) the accompanying trip of a partner to secure that loan, and (4) the signing of an agreement with Arkansas developers to develop land in Arkansas. It could be argued that Deff has purposefully availed itself of the benefits and privileges of doing business in Arkansas such that it could reasonably foresee being haled into court there under a specific jurisdiction analysis (e.g., breaching the developer's agreement). And perhaps in the future, if Deff's Ozark business becomes its dominant business and its presence in Arkansas becomes its dominant operations, then Deff might be more amenable to general jurisdiction in Arkansas. At this time, however, because no firm plans have been made and no business activity there has yet commenced, these contacts, like those in *Goodyear*, fall short of the level of continuous and systematic. Further, the plaintiff's connections to the forum state, while perhaps relevant to specific jurisdiction, are not relevant to the general jurisdiction analysis. It is therefore unlikely that a court would find Deff to be home in Arkansas for purposes of general jurisdiction.

B. SPECIFIC JURISDICTION

A defendant's contacts with a forum satisfy specific jurisdiction if they give rise to (or perhaps relate to) the cause of action, and if they were the product of purposeful availment by the defendant of the benefits and privileges of that state's laws (rather than unilateral action of a third party) such that the defendant could reasonably foresee being haled into court there. Importantly, the defendant's own actions must establish purposeful contacts with the state rather than through a third party's unilateral or fortuitous actions.

Here, it is possible that an Arkansas court can assert specific jurisdiction over Deff. The cause of action did arise in Arkansas while Pennington was hiking in the Ozarks wearing Deff's shoes. The critical question is whether that connection between Deff and Arkansas was the result of unilateral or fortuitous activity of Pennington or whether it was the result of some purposeful availment by Deff of the benefits and privileges of Arkansas laws such that Deff could reasonably foresee being haled into court there.

World-Wide Volkswagen is informative as a case with contrasting facts. There, the defendant's contact with the forum state was the single, isolated, and fortuitous accident that occurred there. That a defective car sold in New York could cause injury in Oklahoma was foreseeable, but it was not reasonably foreseeable such that World-Wide could expect to be haled into court there. World-Wide did not purposefully avail itself of the benefits and privileges of Oklahoma, other than the fact that interstate roads connecting New York to Oklahoma made it possible for car purchasers to drive to such distant states. Instead, this was just the unilateral activity of the purchaser. In addition, the Court said that the very marginal increase of revenue from the fact that the cars sold could be used in Oklahoma is insignificant and its cause attenuated.

Deff's contacts are more substantial than those in *World-Wide*. Deff had additional contacts with Arkansas, including Internet research into Arkansas for the purposes of developing Ozark Tread. In addition, the name "Ozark Tread" suggests an attempt to market the shoes for use in Arkansas. Indeed, Deff's own employees specifically recommended them for use in Arkansas. Finally, the proximity of Oklahoma, a flat plains state, to Arkansas, where the Ozarks are, suggests a closer tie between Deff and Arkansas than between World-Wide and Oklahoma. Pennington's activity was not merely "unilateral" because Pennington bought the shoes based on Deff's marketing of them as specifically designed for use in Arkansas. It might have been mere unilateral activity if Pennington had taken the shoes to New Mexico. But, instead, he did exactly what Deff told and expected him to do—take the shoes to Arkansas. Together, these contacts suggest that Deff purposefully directed its commercial activities into Arkansas, targeting the state and its residents and visitors, and making it reasonably foreseeable that Deff's shoes would end up in Arkansas and that Deff could be haled into court there.

Although distinguishable as stream-of-commerce cases in which business intermediaries deliver the products to the forum state, *Asahi* and *McIntyre* both support specific jurisdiction over Deff. Justice Brennan's concurrence in *Asahi* would have held that knowledge that a company's products regularly ended up in a state and could cause injury there is sufficient to establish minimum contacts. Justice O'Connor's principal opinion in *Asahi* would have required some additional purposeful activity directed at the forum state, such as designing the product for use in that state. Thus, both opinions recognized that specific jurisdiction could cover stream-of-commerce facts if the defendant purposefully targeted the forum state. And the opinions in *McIntyre* do not disturb this principle of specific jurisdiction derived from *Asahi*. This principle supports jurisdiction over Deff because Deff knew that its products were likely being used in Arkansas and, in fact, purposefully targeted Arkansas by designing Ozark Tread specifically for use in that state.

There are counterarguments. Deff could invoke the plurality opinion from *McIntyre* proposing a strict consent-based theory of minimum contacts and argue that none of its relevant contacts availed it of the benefits and protections of Arkansas laws sufficient to manifest an intent to be subject to personal jurisdiction there. But the plurality's reasoning in *McIntyre* did not command a majority vote of the Court (indeed, five justices expressly disagreed with that reasoning). Further, Deff's conduct is distinguishable from the defendant's conduct in *McIntyre* in that Deff specifically targeted Arkansas. Finding personal jurisdiction over Deff in Arkansas for this particular lawsuit would not open Deff up to liability in such faraway states as Alaska because Deff's own conduct targeting Arkansas limits its submission of jurisdiction only to that state. In sum, even if the plurality opinion in *McIntyre* controlled, personal jurisdiction might still be proper.

For all these reasons, it appears likely that Deff has minimum contacts with Arkansas under specific jurisdiction principles.

2. FAIR PLAY AND SUBSTANTIAL JUSTICE

The minimum contacts test includes a component of "fair play and substantial justice." These factors can either raise or lower the bar for satisfying minimum contacts. Several factors inform this inquiry: (1) the burden on the defendant, (2) the interests of the forum state in hearing the dispute, (3) the interests of the plaintiff in convenient and effective relief, and (4) the shared interstate interest in efficient resolution of controversies and in furthering substantive social policies. Here, these factors probably neither raise nor lower the bar for acquiring jurisdiction over Deff.

Because of its small size and local nature, Deff may experience some burden in defending the lawsuit in Arkansas. Nevertheless, that burden is ameliorated by ease of travel generally; technological advancements; and the close distance between Tulsa and Fayetteville, a shorter distance than between Tulsa and many other courts within Oklahoma. It is unlikely that the cost of travel would be so burdensome as to prejudice Deff's defense (indeed, a Deff partner has already traveled to Arkansas before) or that witnesses or evidence would be unobtainable in Arkansas. On balance, this factor only slightly undermines Arkansas's exercise of jurisdiction over Deff.

Arkansas does have some interest in resolving the dispute with Deff because the injury caused by Deff's shoe occurred in Arkansas and is likely to be repeated because of Deff's targeted marketing of Arkansas. Thus, Arkansas courts have an interest in providing a forum for redress for Arkansas citizens that may be harmed by that conduct in that state. Here, however, Pennington is from Oklahoma and was just visiting Arkansas. Although the injury occurred in Arkansas, none of the parties is located in Arkansas. As a result, Arkansas may not have a substantial interest in adjudicating this dispute against Deff. Accordingly, this factor only slightly supports Arkansas's exercise of jurisdiction.

The interest of Pennington in the Arkansas forum is not strong. Pennington is from Oklahoma, not Arkansas, and it would seem that Pennington could obtain more convenient relief in Oklahoma. The sole reason for bringing suit in Arkansas is the strategic reason of increasing the likelihood of a favorable jury. Thus, this factor only slightly supports Arkansas's exercise of jurisdiction.

Efficiency would tend to undermine jurisdiction in Arkansas. Both Deff and Pennington reside in Oklahoma, and it is likely that most of the witnesses will come from Oklahoma. Nevertheless, Oklahoma is not far from Fayetteville, and so this factor only slightly undermines Arkansas's exercise of jurisdiction.

On balance, then, these factors likely cancel each other out, neither raising nor lowering the bar for establishing minimum contacts.

TOOLS FOR SELF-CRITICISM

The facts noted that Pennington was a resident of Oklahoma but had a cabin in Arkansas. Did you think this fact relevant to the personal jurisdiction analysis? Generally speaking, in a case like this one, the *plaintiff*'s residence and contacts are irrelevant. The inquiry instead focuses on the *defendant*'s contacts with the forum state. After all, the personal jurisdiction inquiry primarily exists to protect the due process rights of defendants. The plaintiff, on the other hand, is master of the claim and gets to file where he wishes and thus does not generally need the due process protection of personal jurisdiction. Indeed, when the plaintiff does so, he effectively consents to personal jurisdiction in that state.

The facts state that Pennington bought the boots because Deff told him the treads were designed for Ozark hiking. Did you recognize that this was an important fact because it is evidence that Deff is intentionally targeting Arkansas markets? Did you understand that this fact is legally important because of *Asahi*?

Did you address the implications of Deff's plans to expand into Arkansas? The fact is significant because it reduces the need to protect Deff from defending in an inconvenient forum. On the other hand, Deff's plans are not yet complete. That is an important limitation of the fact's legal significance. You should discuss this tension and attempt to resolve it.

The two major issues in this question—transient jurisdiction and minimum contacts—present different opportunities for analysis. The minimum contacts issue presents an opportunity to synthesize existing precedent and apply it to the facts, comparing and contrasting the various cases along the way. The transient jurisdiction issue, on the other hand, presents an opportunity to explore normative and doctrinal justifications for extending or cabining the law. Both are important skills. With which did you feel most comfortable? On which do you think you performed better?

What level of objectivity did you maintain? The assignment called for an objective analysis, not an advocacy piece. That does not mean you should avoid giving an answer or reaching a conclusion—to the contrary, you must do so. However, in an objective assessment, you should determine which way the law points, even if that direction is unfavorable to your client. Mr. Moe asked for an honest answer—you should give him one. Did you maintain impartiality, or did you slant your answer in favor of Pennington?

The final paragraph of the question narrowed its focus to personal jurisdiction issues. You were not asked to address subject-matter jurisdiction, venue, or service. You were to assume that the defendant did not consent to suit or otherwise waive or forfeit its objection to personal jurisdiction. Did you nevertheless address any of these issues or discuss in detail the law pertaining to consent or waiver? In particular, did you address the fact that the federal rules prohibit parties like Pennington from serving process themselves, even though Deff waived any objections to service? If so, you wasted time doing so and may even have cost yourself points in your answer. Be careful of red herrings.

By contrast, did you analyze the relevant issues deeply enough? Because personal jurisdiction issues are highly fact dependent, and because there were many relevant facts in the question, your answer should spend considerable time using those facts in the analysis and comparing them closely with the facts of the relevant cases. A good answer will address each relevant issue thoroughly, using all relevant facts in the analysis.

Compare your organization to the sample answer above. Note how issues are embedded in each other. Personal jurisdiction requires both satisfaction of the long-arm statute and due process. Due process may be met through specific jurisdiction, general jurisdiction, or in-state service. Does your answer reflect the proper doctrinal structure of personal jurisdiction?

How strong were your conclusions? Note that, in the sample answer, the conclusion with respect to specific jurisdiction is fairly certain, whereas the conclusion with respect to transient jurisdiction is less certain. At times, the outcome of the application of law to facts is difficult to predict because the doctrines are unclear or are generalized. The doctrine of transient jurisdiction, as set forth in *Burnham*, is fairly constrained by that case's facts. Accordingly, extending it to partnerships necessarily requires charting uncertain waters and evaluating the relative merits of different lines of reasoning. In such cases, it may be appropriate to point out that the law is unclear and may lead to different results depending upon what doctrinal reasoning the court decides to follow.

Did you grasp which parts of the case law were controlling and which were not? *Asahi*, *McIntyre*, and *Burnham* are all non-majority opinions. Did you gauge the precedential value of each opinion correctly, and were you able to justify which lines of reasoning you used? For more on the precedential value of non-majority opinions, see Marks v. United States, 430 U.S. 188, 193–94 (1977) (stating that the concurrence with the narrowest rationale controls). In the same vein, how comfortable were you relying on non-majority opinions as opposed to firmer precedent like *World-Wide*?

Did you address *Burger King*? That case found specific jurisdiction over a breach of contract action based primarily on the existence of a long-term contract with a party in the forum state. The cause of action in that case is so tied to the contact that *Burger King* may not be as useful for answering this essay as the other cases discussed in the sample answer. If you used *Burger King*, how did you resolve its distinguishing facts, and do you think your answer could have been better without it? Remember that not all cases are important to a fact pattern—some will best be distinguished in your answer as *not* useful. Many students tend to throw everything into an answer, but a good answer will explain why one case is appropriate support and why another is not.

Consider the practical issues at stake and whether they are relevant. Mr. Moe asserted that the reason the lawsuit was filed in Arkansas was to increase the potential for obtaining a plaintiff-friendly jury. Suing in a forum with favorable juries is a common and accepted litigation strategy. It is irrelevant for personal jurisdiction purposes, however. How did you address this issue?

VARIATIONS ON THE THEME

What if Paul Pennington were a resident of Arkansas instead of Oklahoma? What if he were a resident of Alaska? Would either of these changes to his residency have changed your analysis? In particular, you may wish to think about the changes to the "fair play and substantial justice" factors.

What if Pennington had bought the shoes in Arkansas instead of Oklahoma by, for example, ordering them over the phone? What if he had bought them in Arkansas but was then injured in Oklahoma? How might these changes have affected your analysis?

What if Deff were a corporation rather than a partnership, and the person served in Arkansas had been Deff's president and CEO? Before *International Shoe*, the general rule was that in-state service of a corporate officer does not confer personal jurisdiction over a corporation not doing business in that state. *See, e.g.*, James-Dickinson Farm Mortgage v. Harry, 273 U.S. 119, 122 (1927) ("Jurisdiction over a corporation of one state cannot be acquired in another state or district in which it has no place of business and is not found, merely by serving process upon an executive officer temporarily therein, even if he is there on business of the company."). However, the Supreme Court has not so held since *International Shoe*, and a few lower courts, which are in a small minority, recently have suggested that transient jurisdiction might constitutionally be applied to corporations. *See, e.g.*, N. Light Tech., Inc. v. N. Lights Club, 236 F.3d 57, 62, 64 n.10 (1st Cir. 2001); Amusement Equip., Inc. v. Mordelt, 779 F.2d 264, 270 (5th Cir. 1985); Oyuela v. SEACOR Marine (Nigeria), Inc., 290 F. Supp. 2d 713 (E.D. La. 2003). What do you think the right answer is?

What if Deff were a Mexican business with its principal place of business in Mexico? Would you have answered differently? Why or why not? For some guidance, see FED. R. CIV. P. 4(k)(2); Peter Hay, Comment, *Transient Jurisdiction, Especially Over International Defendants: Critical Comments on* Burnham v. Superior Court of California, 1990 U. ILL. L. REV. 593, 602–03 (1990).

What if Mr. Moe had asked for a brief in opposition to Deff's motion to dismiss? How might you change your answer to an advocacy piece as opposed to an objective piece, while still maintaining credibility with the court?

Note that the hypothetical was artificially constrained by proposing that neither Arkansas nor the Eighth Circuit had expanded upon the Supreme Court's personal jurisdiction jurisprudence. That artificial constraint was necessary in this book to make the problem appealing to a wide audience already familiar with the crucial Supreme Court cases. In a real-world situation, of course, an attorney would amass a much broader set of research materials from the lower federal courts and from state courts. What if the Eighth Circuit had extended *Burnham* to corporate officers, but the Arkansas Supreme Court had limited it to individuals? Would it matter which decision had been decided first?

OPTIONAL READINGS

Should transient jurisdiction be extended beyond individual defendants? Most courts and commentators believe not. *See, e.g.*, RESTATEMENT (SECOND) OF CONFLICT OF LAWS § 40 cmt. b (1971) ("The mere presence of one of the partners or members in the state is not a sufficient basis for the exercise of judicial jurisdiction over the partnership or association."). *But see* First Am. Corp. v. Price Waterhouse LLP, 154 F.3d 16, 19–21 (2d Cir. 1998) (extending transient jurisdiction to a foreign partnership when a partner was served in-state); Nutri-West v. Gibson, 764 P.2d 693, 696 (Wyo. 1988) ("The general rule appears to be that personal service upon one partner who is present in the forum state confers jurisdiction over the partnership, particularly when, as in this case, the partner's presence in the jurisdiction is related to partnership activity.").

The problem above involved an issue of the relevant time period for establishing minimum contacts. For a survey of the uncertainty in the law in this area and a solution, see Todd David Peterson, *The Timing of Minimum Contacts*, 80 GEO. WASH. L. REV. 202 (2010).

2

NOTICE

OPENING REMARKS

Generally, due process requires notice and an opportunity to be heard. It also requires a reasonable attempt to inform the person of the pending action with sufficient details and time to prepare meaningful objections. The notice component thus encompasses both the method and the content of the notice. However, there is a subtle difference between method and content! The method is the way in which the notice (usually a physical, verbal, or electronic communication) is delivered to the recipient. Mail, e-mail, phone calls, and billboards are all examples of a method of communication. The method must be a reasonable attempt, under the circumstances, of getting the message to the intended recipient. Content is what is contained in the communication. If the message does not, for example, disclose when or where the hearing is to be held, then the content is insufficient even if the method was sufficient.

What constitutes reasonable notice depends upon the circumstances. Thus, notice to a single individual of known residence might reasonably require a method different than notice to a host of persons of unknown location. The touchstone is what, under all of the circumstances, reasonably would be calculated to provide actual notice. Actual notice may not matter if the method chosen was unreasonable.

Constitutional notice is different than service. The service rules of Rules 4 and 5 of the Federal Rules of Civil Procedure are not necessarily required by due process; rather, they are the technical requirements to perfect service within the confines of constitutional due process. You will have an opportunity to explore the nuances of service later, in Chapter 10.

Importantly, notice applies not only to formal lawsuits but also to proceedings for provisional remedies, such as attachment or garnishment or temporary restraining orders. It also applies to nonjudicial deprivations by the government of life, liberty, or property. This next problem is set within the context of the latter.

HYPOTHETICAL

Thirty years ago, the state of Calizona built 100 low-income public housing apartment buildings along its coast, each with 1,500 apartment units. The building common areas (such as the roofs) are owned, maintained, and paid for by the State, but the individual apartments were sold as real property sales to residents at a fraction of fair market value. The deeds forbid sales and rentals to persons who earned more than a certain income level. Every unit is now privately owned and occupied by either a renter or an owner. Approximately 50 percent of the units are rentals.

Employees of the Calizona Land Planning and Development Commission act as building managers for each of the properties. Aside from fire escapes, each building has only one entryway, which passes by the building manager's desk.

The desk is staffed from 8 a.m. to 6 p.m., Monday through Saturday. The building managers know the names of each apartment owner and renter of record. They also maintain a list of addresses of all nonresident owners, though it is up to the nonresident owner to update his or her address in the event of any changes.

During a recent renovation of the buildings, the State donated refurbished desktop computers to each unit and agreed to provide wireless Internet service. In the process, the State also provided an Intranet system that allows computers within a building to send instant messages to each other. The instant messaging system can be disabled by individual users. If not disabled, an instant message that is sent will pop up on screen as long as the computer is on. If the messaging system is disabled on a particular computer, that computer will send an instant message to the original sender, notifying the sender that the recipient had disabled the functionality and did not receive the message. If the receiving computer enables instant messaging but is not on, however, the instant message simply waits to appear until the next time the computer is turned on.

The Intranet also houses a contact list (including name, unit number, and e-mail) that can be filled in by residents. There are approximately 1000 names on each building's list. The building managers can access the Intranet address lists, but only the residents may fill in and modify them.

Each building has a glass case in the front entryway next to the building manager's desk where residents can post paper messages to each other, such as organizing play dates for children or seeking pet sitters. The case is kept locked by the building manager, who has the only key. Residents who wish to post something can do so, but they must have the building manager open the case for them. Some postings include the e-mail address of the poster. In addition, because the mailboxes are accessible only by the U.S. Post Office and whoever holds the unit owner's mailbox key, deliveries that arrive by other means are left with the building manager, who, by custom, posts a list of unit numbers receiving packages in the glass case each day.

Last year, after a series of earthquakes, the Commission decided that the public housing apartments were in too dangerous of a location. Accordingly, the Commission has ordered that the public housing be demolished and relocated to a safer area. Because the Commission feared that a major earthquake could cause significant damage to the properties and injury to residents, the Commission also ordered that the evacuation begin as soon as possible.

You work in the Office of the General Counsel at the Commission. The Commissioner's position is that both residents and nonresident owners have a due process right to be notified. She has asked you to oversee all notices to appropriate owners and residents. She instructed you to give notice as cheaply as possible within the confines of due process. Please identify what method(s) of notice you will provide, and explain why you chose it (them) over others. Do not discuss details about the contents of the notice.

SUGGESTED READINGS

U.S. CONST. amend. XIV, § 1
Mullane v. Cent. Hanover Bank & Trust, 339 U.S. 306, 306–20 (1950)

Greene v. Lindsey, 456 U.S. 444, 444–60 (1982)

Dusenberry v. United States, 534 U.S. 161, 171–73 (2002)

Jones v. Flowers, 547 U.S. 220, 220–39 (2006)

SAMPLE ESSAY

Mullane is the principal judicial precedent on what notice is required under the Due Process Clause. Under *Mullane*, notice must be reasonably calculated, under all the circumstances, to apprise interested parties of the action and afford them a reasonable opportunity to object. The means employed must be such as one desirous of actually informing the absentee might reasonably adopt to accomplish it. As *Jones v. Flowers* suggests, however, knowledge that an attempt was unsuccessful can impose a duty to use a different method, even if the first attempt was reasonable when made.

There are several methods of notification to consider, including personal service, use of the mails, publication in a newspaper, posting on doors, posting in the glass case, e-mail, and Intranet instant messaging. The method of notification will be considered in the context of each of two categories of persons to be notified: (1) residents and (2) nonresident owners.

A. Residents

As for residents, the State knows their names and residential addresses (i.e., apartment units). The State may have additional information from information posted in the glass cases and from the Intranet list, to the extent those are accurate. In addition, the State knows that each unit likely contains a computer that is reachable via the Intranet instant message system, assuming that the computer is on and has not had its instant messaging functionality disabled.

Personal service might be the most effective approach. The building managers can simply knock on the residents' doors and hand them the notice. In the alternative, the building managers may see the residents as they enter or exit the building and can provide personal notice at that time. However, personal service may be quite burdensome for the State. Residents may not be at home at the time the building managers come knocking. They may enter or exit the building during the times that the front desk is unstaffed. Repeat attempts, even for a small number of residents, may become costly, in terms of both time and effort. Here, the total number of residents is at least 150,000, which could ultimately require many multiples of that number in terms of service attempts.

As *Mullane* noted, personal service is not always required. If conditions do not reasonably permit such notice, another reasonable form may be selected if not less likely to actually notify the recipient.

Posting a notice in each building's glass case probably is the most reasonable alternative. The glass cases are located in the only entryway to the building (besides fire escapes), making it likely that residents will see the posting. Further, residents are notified of packages via the glass case, and therefore they are likely to expect other important notifications to be posted there. In short, a posting in the glass cases is likely to be viewed by most residents.

The other methods probably are no more likely to give actual notice. E-mail may be rejected by spam filters, deleted unopened, deleted by other authorized users of the e-mail account, or never be received if the intended recipient does not check his e-mail account. Further, the e-mail addresses known by the State are of unknown accuracy—they may be incorrect, outdated, disabled, or unused. For these reasons, e-mail is probably a poor way to provide notice.

Publication via newspaper generally is disfavored when other reasonable means exist. As *Mullane* noted, small type on the back pages of a newspaper makes it unlikely to be received, except by chance. Publication is particularly unreasonable here, where addresses of the residents are known, and other methods of notifying them at their place of residence exist.

Posting notices on residents' doors is a potential alternative, but it is probably less likely to provide actual notice than posting in the glass case. As Justice Brennan reasoned in *Greene v. Lindsey*, postings can be torn down by other residents. Although there is no evidence that this has happened here, it did happen under similar situations in *Greene*. The glass case, by contrast, is locked and accessible only with the building manager's key. Thus, under the circumstances, posting in the glass case is likely more reasonable (and cheaper) than posting on residents' doors.

Similarly, use of the mails is a potential alternative but is inferior to posting in the glass case. As Justice O'Connor wrote in her *Greene* dissent, mail may be misdirected, lost, stolen, or delayed. Plus, it seems silly to send the notices to residents' mailboxes when those mailboxes are located next to the glass case. It would be far more direct (and cost effective) to place the notice in the glass case. Of course, if the mailboxes were accessible to the building manager via a slot, then the mails might be more reasonable. But that does not appear to be the case—the facts state that a key is needed to open them.

Perhaps the cheapest method would be via the Intranet instant messaging system. Such notice should reach all those persons who have their instant messaging system enabled, who have their computer on, and who are available to read their instant messages. Unfortunately, the State does not have any data on the numbers of residents who meet these three criteria. And, even if these criteria are met, a named resident might not receive the instant message if, for example, a child or visitor in his unit deletes the message without telling him, or if he is out of town for an extended period of time. Finally, for those whose system is disabled, the State will receive notification of that fact and will be required, under *Jones v. Flowers*, to employ a different methodology for those residents anyway, if a reasonable alternative exists (and the reasonable alternative of posting in the glass case does exist).

Nevertheless, the instant messaging system is very inexpensive and is likely to provide actual notice in a significant number of cases. Although perhaps unlikely to satisfy due process on its own, the State may combine that method with other reasonable efforts to increase the likelihood of complying with due process requirements.

Accordingly, I would recommend a three-pronged approach for notifying residents. First, send notice via each building's instant message system. Second, post a single copy of the notice in each building's glass case. Third, instruct building managers to remind those persons whose instant messaging system is disabled to check the glass case, assuming the building managers see such persons during the regular course of the day. Of course, *Dusenbery* makes clear that the availability of a particularly good method does not render other methods unconstitutional, and thus it could be argued that only one of the three approaches, for example, posting in the glass case, is required under the Due Process Clause. But whether that is correct or not is unclear; the State is on far firmer due process grounds using all three methods together. And given the low (rather than "heroic," as described in *Dusenbery*) cost in terms of time and effort that the three methods together impose, it might be unreasonable for the State not to.

B. Nonresident Owners

As for nonresident owners, the State knows their names, the apartment units they own, and the names of their renters. In addition, the State has their last known addresses.

Assuming residents are notified as suggested above, nonresident owners likely need additional notification. Three additional methods are possible: publication by newspaper, use of the mails, and personal service.

Notification by publication is cheap but unlikely to be successful, for the reasons described above and in *Mullane*. Use of the mails would be more expensive but more likely to achieve actual notice. Personal service provides the surest notification, but its cost is extremely high given the estimated 75,000 nonresident owners, some of whom may reside in distant states.

Mullane provides some guidance. There, the Court stated that the Due Process Clause strikes a balance between legitimate state interests and individual interests in receiving notice. The Court reasoned that personal service is not always required by that balance. Indeed, in *Mullane*, the Court held that personal service was not required because of the costs that personal service would entail and the availability of the mails to achieve reasonable notice to persons whose addresses were known. Here, personal service almost certainly would be unreasonably burdensome, given the sheer numbers involved.

It is true that publication plus posting on real estate often satisfies notice requirements for proceedings in rem. However, here, notice to nonresident owners is akin to that in *Mullane*, in which the property was in the hands of the party proceeding against the property and in which, as a result, more notice for known beneficiaries was required. As in *Mullane*, the State is in control of the management of the property and is the party wishing to adversely affect it. Thus, nonresident owners whose addresses are known deserve more effective notification. Nevertheless, *Mullane* sanctions notice by publication if addresses cannot be found after due diligence.

Deciding between publication and mail thus depends upon the confidence of the State in the accuracy of the address information on file for nonresident owners and upon the costs of verifying that information if the State's confidence level is low. It is possible that the information on file with the managers can be verified through due diligence, particularly if the information is accessible from the State's own information resources. In addition, the building manager might be able to ask tenants in the building for the contact information of their landlords. Or, perhaps the State's confidence level is high because nonresident owners regularly update their address information or respond to communications sent by the managers to the addresses on file. Thus, if nonresident owners' addresses can be verified without undue burden, then notice by the mail ought to be sufficient given the high cost of personal service on 75,000 nonresident owners. If not, then publication is the only feasible alternative.

In either case, though, the fact that some nonresident owners might not receive actual notice is ameliorated by two additional considerations. First, there is a strong possibility that the reasonable efforts to notify residents will actually notify most of the tenants, who then likely would alert their owners themselves. And, second, even if a number of nonresident owners never receive actual notice, these efforts likely will give actual notice to a significant number of affected persons whose interests are generally aligned with nonresident owners. In other words, if there is cause to object, the notification procedures implemented likely will give actual notice to persons with the incentive and means to do so.

TOOLS FOR SELF-CRITICISM

Note the difference between this problem and the first. This problem defined the issue for you and tested your analytic ability and creativity. The first one left the issues less defined to better test your issue-spotting skills. Did you approach the two questions differently as a result? With which were you more comfortable?

This problem presents several different ways to organize an answer. The sample answer structures the response in terms of residents and nonresidents. That makes sense because each of those two separate groups has shared notice-related characteristics within the group but very different characteristics as compared with the other group. As a result, identifying those two groups guided the organization of the answer. That is not to say that dividing the groups as this answer did is the sole way to respond to the question. For example, you might organize by method of notice. How did you organize your answer? Do you think that your organization was appropriate on the law and clean in structure?

Note that the flexibility of notice and the large number of factors and possibilities presented by this problem permit combining different methods. Combining methods of notice generally increases the burden of providing notice while also increasing the likelihood of giving actual notice. The prospect of combining methods also exponentially complicates the problem and organizational structure of the answer. How did you address the potential for combination? Note that if you simply addressed each form of notice alone, you missed the opportunity to think creatively and carefully about what methods of notice might exist and best fit the particular situation at hand.

What methods of notice did you identify? Remember that *Mullane* does not require the best notice or even the most accurate notice—just notice reasonably calculated to give actual notice. That standard could encompass a range of possible methods. Did you identify other methodological options not discussed in the sample answer?

Note also that the law does not necessarily require one particular reasonable notice over the other. It just prohibits notice not reasonably calculated to provide actual notice (and, under *Jones*, imposes a duty to supplement when reasonable to do so). It is possible that several different methods of notice in this problem would pass constitutional muster. If you so concluded, how did you balance the nonconstitutional values underlying the law of notice in order to give your client a recommendation? Was your balance affected by your client's interests? Should it have been? Here, you should have taken your client's interests of inexpensive methods into account, but you also have to remember that you, as the lawyer, are advising her about the constitutionality of the methods—it would be a disservice to pick a cheap but unconstitutional method of providing notice. In addition, as a lawyer, you are an officer of the court, and so you have an obligation to act within the ethical bounds even if they contravene your client's wishes.

How did you use *Greene*? Justice Brennan's opinion carried the day in *Greene*, but that does not mean that Justice O'Connor's dissent is valueless, particularly because notice issues are extremely fact dependent. Indeed, Justice O'Connor's dissent is relevant to the potential for notice by mail and notice by posting, and you should have discussed its important implications. Even though her opinion is nonprecedential and distinguishable, it may still provide a justifiable foundation for support.

How much did you incorporate your own understandings of the perils and potentials of various forms of notice, such as e-mail, into your answer? If you have experienced the loss of an incoming e-mail message because of a broad spam blocker, for example, you may have been more likely to mention spam blockers as a strike against e-mail notification in your answer. Or, if you never read the paper, you may have stressed the inadequacy of notice by newspaper publication. To what extent did your own biases and experiences affected your answer? That is not necessarily a criticism—after all, even the Supreme Court justices have done the same in the notice cases you have already read—but it is important to recognize and appreciate how much influence you personally incorporated into your answer and, where appropriate, to qualify it as such.

VARIATIONS ON THE THEME

Suppose the state-supplied Intranet instant messaging system could not be disabled. How would that affect your analysis for notifying residents? What if the instant messaging system could not be disabled, and the message could only be removed if a response was sent acknowledging receipt and understanding of the message?

Suppose the building management were contracted out to a private building management company whose employees were on-site. What if they were on-site at the front desk 24 hours a day, seven days a week?

How might your answer change if Calizona had good scientific evidence that another major earthquake was 80 percent likely to occur in the next few days?

The problem asked you not to address the contents of the notice. What if it had? Consider any legal notices you have received yourself, such as small type-font but long letters in the mail about class-action notices, or credit card fine print. In this hypothetical, what would your notice say, and how would it say it? Keep in mind your client's ultimate interest in eviction, the constitutional requirements of meaningful notice, and (perhaps) the moral imperatives at stake under these facts.

If the agency providing notice was a federal agency instead of a state agency, would the Due Process Clause of the Fourteenth Amendment still control? *See* U.S. Const. amend. V.

HEARING

3

OPENING REMARKS

The requirement to give notice is derivative of the due process requirement of an opportunity to be heard because, without proper notice, the opportunity to be heard does not exist. Thus, the primary due process protection is the opportunity to be heard before property or liberty is taken away. The idea is that a full and fair hearing is essential to protect against erroneous deprivations and to comport with procedural justice. As a result, nearly all deprivations require a pre-deprivation hearing. The precise nature of the hearing will depend upon what is "full and fair" under the circumstances and in light of the nature of the deprivation at stake.

There are notable exceptions to a pre-deprivation hearing requirement. Historically, provisional remedies were allowed without a hearing under certain circumstances because of the need for immediate deprivation. Such remedies included preliminary injunctions, temporary restraining orders, and pre-action attachments, garnishments, replevins, seizures, and sequestration. Other extraordinary and truly unusual situations may also justify pre-hearing deprivation, such as those critical to a U.S. war effort.

The Supreme Court has imposed tight standards on what circumstances can justify a pre-hearing deprivation. Although the inquiry is highly fact specific, due process generally requires a pre-hearing deprivation to contain adequate safeguards against wrongful deprivation that may be tighter or looser depending upon the need for immediacy and the nature of the plaintiff's and defendant's interests in the property or right affected.

HYPOTHETICAL

In 2005, after being married for 17 years, Dolly and Peter divorced in Calizona. They have two children together, Sam and Sarah, who are now 12 and 8, respectively. The divorce was amicable, with Dolly retaining custody of the children, Peter receiving significant visitation rights, and Peter paying child support to Dolly in the amount of $900 per week. Other assets were divided up by mutual agreement.

Peter is a partner in a small law firm. Partnership proceeds have been relatively consistent in the past, fluctuating between $100,000 and $200,000. In 2007, he purchased a BMW, worth approximately $50,000. He bought it outright with cash after a particularly good year in 2006. He sold his old car and now uses only the BMW for transportation. There is no public transportation available for him to get to and from work.

The year 2007 marked a significant decline in revenue for Peter based on market conditions beyond his control. He made only $75,000. And, he predicts that level of revenue to continue for the foreseeable future. Although he has tried his best, he has been unable to meet his child support obligations. For the last 10 weeks, he has paid Dolly only $500 per week.

Calizona's Deadbeat Parent Act allows a custodial parent to sue a noncustodial parent to enforce child support payments. The Act allows a custodial parent, in conjunction with such a lawsuit, to petition the state to seize and sell at a public auction a noncustodial parent's motor vehicle if the noncustodial parent's child support payments are at least eight weeks delinquent, and the delinquency exceeds $1,000. The Act allows for pre-hearing seizure of the motor vehicle if the custodial parent files a verified affidavit with the court attesting to the child support obligation and the delinquency. The custodial parent must attach a copy of the child support agreement or order and any other documentation that supports the existence of a delinquency. Only a judge may issue a pre-hearing seizure order, and then only after making a finding on the record that the custodial parent has shown "compelling evidence" of entitlement to seizure. Seizure is usually made at the time the complaint for delinquent child support payments is served. The sale may not take place until at least three days after seizure, and the noncustodial parent can immediately repossess the car and dissolve the seizure order by posting a bond in the amount of the child support delinquency. In addition, if the noncustodial parent prevails on the underlying child support lawsuit, the court can award damages for erroneous seizure. There is no requirement that the custodial parent post a bond or show that the vehicle is subject to concealment or removal beyond the jurisdiction of the court.

Dolly is not naturally a litigious person, but she relies on the child support, and the delinquency is affecting her ability to provide for the children. Accordingly, she files a complaint to enforce the child support obligations and simultaneously files a petition accompanied by a verified affidavit to seize Peter's BMW. She attaches copies of the 10 $500 checks, a copy of her bank statement showing that no other funds have been deposited in the last 10 weeks, and a copy of the child support agreement. A judge reviews the petition ex parte and orders seizure. Seizure is made contemporaneously with service of the complaint.

Peter does not post a bond for dissolution but instead files a motion for dissolution, arguing that the Act violates the Due Process Clause of the Constitution. You are the judge hearing the dissolution motion. Please resolve it and explain your rationale. You need not discuss any background facts or procedural history except to the extent necessary to resolve the case.

SUGGESTED READINGS

U.S. Const. amend. XIV, § 1
Fuentes v. Shevin, 407 U.S. 67, 67–87, 90–93 (1972)
Mitchell v. W.T. Grant, 416 U.S. 600, 600–20 (1974)
N. Ga. Finishing v. Di-Chem, 419 U.S. 601, 601–08 (1975)
Connecticut v. Doehr, 501 U.S. 1, 1–24 (1991)

SAMPLE ESSAY

DISTRICT COURT OF CALIZONA

Dolly

v.   Case No. 1000

Peter

MEMORANDUM ORDER

Peter has filed a motion to dissolve the seizure order, arguing that the pre-hearing seizure procedures violate due process. Due process requires a meaningful opportunity to be heard before permanent deprivation of property. On rare occasions, temporary deprivation of property, such as seizure, can occur before a hearing, but only if sufficient protections exist. What suffices depends upon the circumstances as informed by a series of Supreme Court decisions. Under these circumstances and based on the protections it provides, the Deadbeat Parent Act is constitutional. Accordingly, defendant's motion is DENIED.

I

In *Doehr*, the Court made clear that the *Matthews* factors test the constitutionality of a pre-hearing deprivation. The factors include consideration of (1) the interest affected; (2) the risk of erroneous deprivation and the probable value of additional or substitute safeguards; and (3) the attacher's interest in the attachment, with due regard for any ancillary interest the state may have in providing the procedure or foregoing the added burden of providing greater protections.

A

The first *Matthews* factor—the defendant's interest in the deprivation—undermines the statute's constitutionality. Generally, persons need possession of their motor vehicles. Unrestricted use is often essential to meet career, familial, and personal needs. Such is the case here, in which Peter's sole method of transportation to and from work appears to be his car. There may be situations in which a defendant owns multiple motor vehicles and in which the seizure of one will not adversely affect him substantially, but that likely is the rare case in child custody situations, and it certainly is not the case here. In addition, seizure is a complete deprivation. For all these reasons, seizure of a car is almost certainly more detrimental to a defendant than the imposition of a lien on a defendant's home, as was the case in *Doehr*. Thus, the first factor undermines the constitutionality of the Act.

B

The second factor, however—the risk of erroneous deprivation and the probable value of additional or substitute safeguards—undermines the defendant's motion. The Act is replete with safeguards for the defendant. Like in *Mitchell*, the Act requires the plaintiff to submit a verified affidavit with specific facts that lend themselves to clear documentary proof. The Act even goes further by requiring copies of documentary proof, if available. (And, because some documentary proof ought to be available, the unavailability of the proof likely would suggest to the judge that the affidavit is insufficient.) As a result, the concern of the Court, as expressed in *Doehr* and *North Georgia*—that allegations leading to deprivation are easily made but difficult to disprove—is unlikely to exist under the Act.

As an additional safeguard, a judge, rather than a court officer or clerk, makes the final determination as to whether the affidavit and documents rise to the level of "compelling evidence" of entitlement to seizure. This appears to be an evidentiary burden, rather than a mere pleading burden, and one that goes beyond mere good faith belief on the part of the plaintiff. Thus, the burden on the plaintiff to make her case before deprivation is more difficult than in *Doehr* and *North Georgia* or even than in *Mitchell*.

Like most of the cases above, the noncustodial parent can immediately repossess the car and dissolve the seizure order by posting a bond in the amount of the child support delinquency. This provides an additional safeguard allowing immediate repossession if the noncustodial parent actually does have the funds to satisfy any judgment.

Finally, as in *Mitchell*, if the noncustodial parent prevails on the underlying child support lawsuit, the court can award damages for erroneous seizure. This feature provides yet another protection against erroneous deprivation, for if the plaintiff's claims are unsuccessful, she may be subject to penalties for wrongful deprivation.

The Act does not require the custodial parent to post a bond to cover damages for erroneous deprivation. The Court has stressed that the posting of a bond is an important safeguard against erroneous deprivation, and cases like *Mitchell* and *Doehr* support the requirement. Here, however, requiring a bond is likely to be counterproductive. The Act specifically addresses the need to rectify child support delinquencies because of the adverse financial impact on the custodial parent. Custodial parents invoking the Act generally have limited funds—posting a bond may be impossible for them. As a result, requiring a bond may nullify the salutary existence of the Act for those instances in which its existence is most critical.

Fuentes, *Mitchell*, *North Georgia*, and *Doehr* do not hold to the contrary. Though they acknowledge the importance of a bond, each of those cases involved an applicant who readily could post a bond and whose financial woes were not assumed by the statute at issue. This case, therefore, presents a situation with respect to a bond requirement that was not addressed by those cases—whether a bond is required under a statute designed to ameliorate the financial hardship of the plaintiff. I conclude that, under these circumstances and based on the strong additional protections against erroneous deprivation, a bond would not add value as an additional safeguard and, in fact, would undermine the salutary benefits of the Act.

In sum, the Act's substantial safeguards, particularly the requirements on the custodial parent to prove her case, reduce the risk of erroneous deprivation to a minimal level even absent a bond requirement. Accordingly, this factor strongly supports the constitutionality of the Act.

C

The third *Matthews* factor is the plaintiff's interest in the property. A custodial parent generally has no preexisting interest in the noncustodial parent's car. Thus, this case is different from a creditor who retains some property rights in the target property, as was the case in *Fuentes* and *Mitchell*. It is more akin to *Doehr*, in which the plaintiff in an assault case has no real interest in obtaining an attachment of the defendant's home.

The Court's reasoning in *Doehr*, however, leads to a different analysis. There the Court reasoned that the assault claimant lacked an interest in the defendant's home because there were no allegations that the defendant could not satisfy judgment through his real estate or that he would transfer or encumber it to avoid judgment. Such allegations might be necessary for a home, which is immovable and difficult to conceal, remove, or waste.

A different situation arises with a car, the very purpose of which is mobility, and which would be easy to conceal, waste, or remove beyond the jurisdiction of the state. This feature of motor vehicles supports the plaintiff's interest in seizing the car and, as in *Mitchell*, supports the constitutionality of the statute.

It is true that, unlike in *Mitchell*, the Act does not require the custodial parent to allege or prove that the motor vehicle is concealable or removable. But that is inherent in the nature of a motor vehicle. Because the Act specifies that a "motor vehicle" can be seized, the natural assumption is that the motor vehicle may be concealed or removed to the detriment of the noncustodial parent. Of course, a counterargument is that if the defendant can show a critical and ongoing need for the car, then the likelihood that it would be removed out of state or sold becomes low and undermines the plaintiff's interest in securing it.

The rub of all of this is that the situation contemplated by the Act gives rise to some interest in the custodial parent of the noncustodial parent's vehicle. Because the custodial parent must make a convincing showing that the noncustodial parent's delinquency exceeds $1,000 and eight weeks, because a motor vehicle is an asset that is easily salable to satisfy the delinquency, and because a motor vehicle is easily hidden or driven out of the jurisdiction of the court by the possessor, the custodial parent has an interest in ensuring that the noncustodial parent's vehicle is available to satisfy any delinquency proved at trial.

II

Having applied the *Matthews* factors separately, I am faced with the task of integrating them into a resolution for this case. The first factor undermines the constitutionality of the Act, the second factor supports it strongly, and the third factor supports it moderately. On balance, I conclude that the *Matthews* factors support the constitutionality of the Act.

I remain particularly troubled, however, by the first factor, which strongly weighs against the constitutionality of the Act. As discussed above, the noncustodial parent's possessory interest in a motor vehicle often is strong, and it is particularly compelling in this case. Because notice cases are fact specific, no precedent directly controls this case, and, in my opinion, reasonable minds could differ as to its proper outcome based on the strong interest of the defendant. Thus, this is a close case, and I welcome the Court of Appeals to weigh in, if defendant here chooses to appeal.

But I must render a decision now. *Fuentes* made clear that pre-hearing deprivations are permitted only in extraordinary situations justifying prompt action. Under the circumstances, and given the strong protections that the Act supplies, I believe this is one of those situations. I am comforted somewhat by the fact that if Peter really had wanted to meet his child support obligations, he likely could have sold his relatively expensive BMW and bought a less expensive car that would have met his transportation needs while also netting him the liquidity needed to meet his child support obligations, at least in the short term. Accordingly, defendant's motion is DENIED.

SO ORDERED.

TOOLS FOR SELF-CRITICISM

Doehr synthesizes the preceding pre-hearing deprivation cases of *Fuentes*, *North Georgia*, and *Mitchell* and overlays them with the due process test set forth in *Matthews*. Thus, a good way to approach this problem is to correctly state and apply the *Matthews* factors as explained by *Doehr*. There may be other ways to approach it, though. Did you begin with the *Matthews* factors? If not, why not?

The sample answer then balances the three *Matthews* factors, as should you have done. The sample answer finds that the second and third factors outweigh the first factor, but that does not mean that you could not have balanced them differently. Did you find the first *Matthews* factor as compelling as the sample answer? If so, what facts or values did you use to support your position? If you addressed those raised by the sample answer, how did you acknowledge and deal with them? Did you find the first *Matthews* factor more compelling, such that it rendered the Act unconstitutional? If so, how did you address the potential that you might be wrong or that reasonable minds could differ? Always keep in mind the importance of acknowledging the other side.

Speaking of acknowledging the other side, did you find the third factor more compelling than the sample answer did? The state has a strong interest in providing for child support that has at least emotional appeal over a noncustodial parent's attempt to shirk financial responsibility for that child. A deadbeat parent driving a BMW is simply unsympathetic. There is a flavor of that in the conclusion of the sample answer, and there may be more to say about it.

The pre-hearing deprivation cases are highly fact specific. How did you use those cases to support your position? How did you distinguish or deal with those that undermine it? Might there have been other ways of characterizing the importance of various safeguards, and how did you select the method that you chose? The facts of this case fall somewhere between *Mitchell* and *Doehr*. There are significant safeguards akin to those in *Mitchell*. Yet there are significant repercussions from the deprivation, as there were in *Doehr*. Analysis by analogy should be a prominent feature of your answer.

Look closely at the third *Matthews* factor—the plaintiff's interest. Here, the plaintiff has no interest in the property itself; rather, the plaintiff has an interest in using the property as a means to secure a money judgment. Any property should suffice, not just the vehicle. How did you address this point? Did you make the assumptions that the sample answer did—that a vehicle is a particularly amenable property to secure a judgment because it is usually valuable enough to cover the delinquency and salable enough to convert it to cash? Did you note that, unlike a home, cars are meant to be driven, and the nature of a car makes it inherently removable? How might you dispute these assumptions? Might certain vehicles be deemed essentially unable to be hidden?

VARIATIONS ON THE THEME

Try drafting the opinion again under the assumption that the Act does not require any documentary proof but instead just the good faith belief of the custodial parent. Try again, but assume that the Act requires the judge only to find "probable cause" for the seizure. Would these change your answer?

What if the Act did not specify the noncustodial parent's motor vehicle but instead left the property description general? What if it specified attachment of his home? Would these new facts change your answer?

What if the Act is the same but the facts were different? Say the facts stated that, in this situation, the noncustodial parent had several luxury cars and was simply unwilling, rather than unable, to meet the child support obligations. Or, say that the custodial parent had recently inherited a large sum of money and thus was not financially strapped but nevertheless pursued remedies under the Act for other reasons. Would these facts change your analysis and conclusions?

Say Peter did not own his car free and clear but rather had a car loan. Would the car loan creditor have a say in whether its due process rights are implicated by the Act?

OPTIONAL READINGS

A few years after *Doehr*, the Second Circuit upheld the constitutionality of Connecticut's attachment statute when the plaintiff was a repair contractor suing in breach of contract to obtain payment for work done on the home. *See* Shaumyan v. O'Neill, 987 F.2d 122 (2d Cir. 1993).

For a summary of and commentary on the Court's hearing cases, see Comment, *Lis Pendens and Procedural Due Process: A Closer Look after* Connecticut v. Doehr, 51 MD. L. REV. 1054 (1992) (discussing the Court's hearing cases in the context of lis pendens).

4 FEDERAL-QUESTION JURISDICTION AND SUBJECT-MATTER JURISDICTION GENERALLY

OPENING REMARKS

Federal subject-matter jurisdiction differs from personal jurisdiction both in form and in function. Personal jurisdiction is power of a court over a particular party—it is tied to that party's due process rights under the Fifth or Fourteenth Amendment and therefore can be waived, consented to, or forfeited by the party. It asks, "Which states' courts can exert power over the parties?"

Subject-matter jurisdiction, by contrast, is the power of the court over the action. It is tied to underlying values that are independent of the parties' individual interests—federalism, docket control, and case allocation among judicial systems. As a result, subject-matter jurisdiction cannot be waived, consented to, or forfeited; it may be raised by any party or the court sua sponte any time before final judgment; and it is not subject to any equitable excuses for noncompliance. It asks, "Which judicial systems (usually between state or federal courts) can hear this case?"

In federal court, subject-matter jurisdiction derives from Article III of the U.S. Constitution. Article III sets forth nine jurisdictional authorizations, including federal-question jurisdiction and diversity jurisdiction, which are the two authorizations most commonly studied in the typical first-year civil procedure course. At the district court level, Article III is not self-executing, and so in addition to constitutional authorization, a federal district court needs congressional authorization to have subject-matter jurisdiction. Congress has provided federal-question jurisdiction in 28 U.S.C. § 1331 and diversity jurisdiction in 28 U.S.C. § 1332.

Note two important points. First, any one jurisdictional grant is sufficient to confer subject-matter jurisdiction—a case that lacks diversity jurisdiction, for example, may still be heard in federal court if it has federal-question jurisdiction. Second, the presence of federal subject-matter jurisdiction usually provides not *exclusive* jurisdiction in federal court but merely *authorization* for the federal court to hear the case; absent statutory language stripping state courts of jurisdiction (such as for bankruptcy or certain securities cases), state courts generally can hear any case that has federal subject-matter jurisdiction. In short, the plaintiff gets to choose the initial forum of state or federal court.

Original federal-question jurisdiction derives from the Article III "arising under" provision and § 1331. Its general purpose is to ensure that federal district courts are open to hear disputes involving federal issues. Although they have nearly identical language, the statutory grant has been interpreted far more narrowly than the constitutional grant. The following will test your knowledge and understanding of subject-matter jurisdiction generally and of federal-question jurisdiction in particular.

HYPOTHETICAL

Joe is employed by Redriver Contractors. Redriver contracts with the U.S. government to provide security services to support U.S. military operations overseas. Pursuant to a government contract, Joe was sent to Iraq. In Iraq, while on a security mission assigned by the U.S. Army, Joe accidentally shot and injured Mary, a civilian aid worker from the United States.

Mary sues Redriver in U.S. District Court under state tort law. She alleges that Redriver negligently failed to train Joe properly, as Redriver was obligated to do under the government contract. She also alleges that any defense of federal sovereign immunity is unavailable for private contractors. Mary and Redriver are citizens of the same state.

In its answer, Redriver asserts the defense of federal sovereign immunity and denies the negligence allegations. It concedes the existence of federal subject-matter jurisdiction. The district court grants summary judgment to Redriver based on the immunity defense. Mary appeals and, for the first time, argues that the district court lacked subject-matter jurisdiction. She urges the appellate court to vacate the district court's decision and order the district court to dismiss the case for lack of subject-matter jurisdiction.

Although federal law regulates the terms of government contracts, and the government contract at issue did, in fact, impose a duty on Redriver to train properly its employees like Joe, no federal law provides for a private right of action by a third party such as Mary who is not a party to the contract.

Did the District Court have constitutional "arising under" jurisdiction? Did the district court have statutory subject-matter jurisdiction under § 1331? What should the appellate court do, particularly in light of the fact that it was the plaintiff who invoked federal jurisdiction in the first place and who is now seeking to overturn an adverse judgment based on lack of subject-matter jurisdiction?

SUGGESTED READINGS

U.S. CONST. art. III § 2
28 U.S.C. § 1331
Osborn v. Bank of the U.S., 22 U.S. 738, 818–28 (1824)
Louisville & Nashville R.R. Co. v. Mottley, 211 U.S. 149, 152–54 (1908)
Grable & Sons Metal Prods., Inc. v. Darue Eng'g & Mfg., 545 U.S. 308, 310–20 (2005)
Empire HealthChoice Assurance, Inc. v. McVeigh, 547 U.S. 677, 680–92, 699–701 (2006)

SAMPLE ESSAY

The district court had constitutional subject-matter jurisdiction. Under *Osborn*, Article III "arising under" jurisdiction extends to a case in which federal law might form an "ingredient" in the case, even if the case is dominated by state law issues. The federal ingredient need not be actually disputed; it is enough if the federal ingredient might come up. In *Osborn*, the Bank of the United States sued under state law for restitution of state taxes that were collected in violation of a federal order. The fact that the Bank was chartered under federal law and could not act except as authorized under federal law injected a federal ingredient even into a state claim brought by the Bank.

Here, the existence of a government contract, the potential availability of federal sovereign immunity, and the presence of federal law governing government contracts all provide federal ingredients in the case sufficient to give rise to Article III "arising under" jurisdiction. In addition, the effect of the claims on a U.S. war effort, waged under Article II powers, likely provides another federal ingredient. All of these ingredients may arise as issues to be decided by a court. Accordingly, constitutional "arising under" jurisdiction exists.

The district court may have had statutory subject-matter jurisdiction. Although the constitutional grant of "arising under" jurisdiction is broad, and although 28 U.S.C. § 1331 uses identical language to Article III, the Supreme Court has interpreted the statutory grant to be much narrower.

Under *Mottley*, statutory "arising under" jurisdiction exists only if the federal issue appears in the plaintiff's well-pleaded complaint. In other words, the federal issue must not only appear in the complaint, but it must be a part of the plaintiff's claims. It may not arise solely by way of a defense or counterclaim, even if anticipated in the plaintiff's complaint. Rather, the federal issue must give rise to the plaintiff's affirmative claims.

In addition, the federal issue must be actually disputed and of substantial importance. *Grable*. This substantiality requirement supposes that substantial federal issues ought to be available to be heard by the court system with the experience, solicitude, and hope of uniformity appropriate to those issues. In *Grable*, for example, the proper construction of what method of service was required to be made by the IRS when foreclosing on a tax lien on real property was of sufficient importance to give rise to federal jurisdiction because of the need for uniformity on that question and the important federal interest in collecting taxes.

Finally, the exercise of federal jurisdiction must be consistent with the delicate balance of docket allocation struck by Congress. *Grable*. In *Grable*, for example, the Supreme Court found federal jurisdiction because the number of quiet title cases based upon the construction of the tax code's notice provision was likely to be so miniscule as to not affect the division of labor between the state and federal courts. This was so even though Congress had not provided for a private right of action under federal law for relief based on the method of service. Nevertheless, as *Grable* made clear, the absence of a private right of action may be evidence of the intent of Congress in allocating caseloads. The Court noted that the absence of a federal private right of action might be particularly compelling if allowing federal jurisdiction based on a particular federal issue would greatly expand the number of cases filed in federal court.

The most recent federal-jurisdiction case decided by the Supreme Court, *Empire HealthChoice Assurance v. McVeigh*, presents another overlay. There, a private insurer sued under state contract law for reimbursement of health care benefits paid to an insured under the Federal Employees Health Benefits Act. The employee had successfully recovered in an action against the responsible party directly, and so the insurer sought reimbursement required by the insurance contract. The Court stated that not all cases involving government contracts gave rise to federal jurisdiction and held that, there, no federal jurisdiction attached because the resolution of the case was fact specific, as opposed to a pure question of federal law covering numerous other cases as in *Grable*. In addition, *Empire* suggested that federal jurisdiction was appropriate in *Grable* because it involved the proper action of a federal agency under federal law (even if that agency was not a party to the lawsuit). *Empire* ultimately characterized the rule of *Grable* as covering only a special and small category of cases.

Here, two federal issues are implicated: federal sovereign immunity and the federal duty imposed by the government contract.

Federal sovereign immunity likely satisfies some of the "arising under" tests imposed by the Supreme Court. Whether private parties who contract with the federal government to provide security support to U.S. military efforts overseas are entitled to assert federal sovereign immunity in private tort claims is an important and substantial issue of federal law that likely would satisfy the *Grable* standard. That issue ought to be decided by the federal courts, which have the experience and solicitude to weigh the sensitive national policy interests involved. In addition, the need for uniformity on the issue is important, for if one state held immunity not to apply, then plaintiffs could seek out that particular state to circumvent immunity.

It is unclear just how many cases might be filed in (or removed to) federal court on this basis were federal jurisdiction allowed, but the number is likely more than the miniscule number suspected in *Grable*. If many such government contracts exist, then allowing federal jurisdiction over state claims based on the potential availability of a federal immunity defense may open the federal courthouse doors far wider than Congress intended. On the other hand, whether federal military contractors like Redriver are entitled to assert immunity is primarily (if perhaps not entirely) a question of law that may resolve many other similar cases.

Whether the federal immunity issue meets these tests is likely moot, however, because the affirmative defense of federal immunity likely is barred from serving as a basis for statutory "arising under" jurisdiction by *Mottley*'s well-pleaded complaint rule. Redriver's answer must be disregarded under *Mottley*'s rule, and therefore its assertions of federal immunity cannot satisfy *Mottley*. In addition, the plaintiff's anticipatory statements about federal immunity must also be disregarded under the well-pleaded complaint rule because they do not give rise to the plaintiff's claims. Thus, federal immunity likely cannot satisfy the *Mottley* standards for statutory "arising under" jurisdiction.

However, the plaintiff's claims do arise from an embedded federal issue—the duty imposed by the government contract on Redriver. That federal issue does give rise to plaintiff's claim and therefore meets *Mottley*'s well-pleaded complaint restrictions.

It also likely meets *Grable*'s substantiality requirement. The government has an interest in a uniform federal-court construction of the duties imposed by government contracts, particularly government contracts involving the duty of private security contractors supporting U.S. military combat operations. Arguments to the contrary are not without some merit; as *Empire* makes clear, not every issue involving construction of government contracts will give rise to federal jurisdiction. But it is likely, given the context of this government contract, that this is one that will, at least, meet the substantiality standard.

The more difficult question is whether the federal issue is consistent with the delicate balance of docket allocation struck by Congress. If many government contracts provide federal duties that can serve as the basis for third-party state law claims, then allowing those claims to be heard in federal court may greatly expand federal court caseloads. Particularly because Congress has not provided a federal cause of action for the kinds of claims asserted by Mary, any disruption in federal/state docket allocation likely will undermine the argument for federal jurisdiction.

In addition, whether Redriver actually breached its federal contractual duty is a highly fact-specific question. Unlike the pure question of law presented in *Grable* that implicated federal agency action, Mary's claims involve case-specific factual inquiries that implicate only private party action. For this reason, such claims may, as *Empire* cautioned, not be within the special and small category of cases described by *Grable*.

The appellate court should vacate and remand with instructions to the district court to dismiss for lack of subject-matter jurisdiction. At the outset, the fact that the plaintiff filed in federal court originally, thereby invoking federal jurisdiction, does not preclude the plaintiff from raising subject-matter jurisdiction defects for the first time on appeal. Nor does the defendants' consent to jurisdiction matter. Unlike personal jurisdiction, subject-matter jurisdiction cannot be waived, forfeited, or consented to. Although it may seem unfair and inefficient to allow a party who invokes federal jurisdiction and then loses on the merits to then seek to void that judgment on the basis of a jurisdictional defect that she herself caused, the underlying societal values of federalism and docket control outweigh that unfairness and inefficiency. Accordingly, because the above analysis suggests that the district court lacked subject-matter jurisdiction, the appellate court should vacate the judgment and remand with instructions to the district court to dismiss the case.

TOOLS FOR SELF-CRITICISM

There is no one right answer to this question. It is likely that reasonable minds could differ on the ultimate disposition. The sample answer gives one possible answer and justifies it but also necessarily acknowledges the uncertainty. For this question, the most important part of your answer will not be the ultimate outcome but rather the reasoning and analysis you undertook. Be sure to acknowledge the uncertainty and provide thoughtful analyses of the arguments against your conclusion.

As the Opening Remarks indicate, constitutional federal-question jurisdiction is very broad. Only statutory federal-question jurisdiction is narrower. Thus, the existence of a government contract and the potential availability of federal sovereign immunity make the constitutional "arising under" prong a no-brainer. It is the statutory component that will require more careful analysis. Did you spend a relatively inordinate amount of time analyzing the constitutional requirement? The sample answer spends two paragraphs on the issue mostly for explanatory reasons, but your answer could spend even less time on it.

The statutory prong requires a complicated synthesis of Supreme Court cases, particularly *Mottley*, *Grable*, and *Empire*. In some ways, they fit together clearly; in others, they do not. Did you synthesize the cases appropriately? You at least should have recognized the need for an actual federal issue, substantiality, and congressional intent. Consider going back and re-reading these cases in light of your experience with the hypothetical. Do they make more sense holistically upon a re-read? Do you think that you could answer an "arising under" question even better now?

This problem also requires a complicated application of the law to the facts, which are different from the factual scenarios presented by the cases. Did you analogize to the factual similarities in the cases? The key "arising under" issue in the hypothetical is the national scope of military combat efforts. Do those efforts necessarily arise under federal law? How are they different from, or similar to, railroads, federal taxes, and ERISA in the case law?

To what extent did you address underlying policy considerations of federal jurisdiction? The problem provides a nice forum for that discussion because it implicates matters of national security, a quintessentially federal issue. A complete answer would discuss in some detail the importance of uniformity and of federal experience on issues related to national defense.

The last question asked by the problem addresses the nature of subject-matter jurisdiction generally—that it cannot be waived or consented to. Did you grasp the underlying policy reasons?

VARIATIONS ON THE THEME

What if Congress, though still not providing for a private right of action in favor of third parties like Mary, nevertheless provided in a statute that private military contractors like Redriver could not assert any form of federal immunity for breaches of duties imposed by government contracts? Would that change the analysis of whether the federal duty gives rise to federal jurisdiction?

What if, before Mary filed, Redriver filed in federal court first under the Declaratory Judgment Act, seeking a judgment that federal immunity barred any claims against it? For the special issues implicated by declaratory judgments, see Skelly Oil Co. v. Phillips Petroleum Co., 339 U.S. 667 (1950) ("[I]f, but for the availability of the declaratory judgment procedure, the federal claim would arise only as a defense to a state created action, [federal] jurisdiction is lacking.").

OPTIONAL READINGS

The well-pleaded complaint rule is controversial. For more, compare Donald Doernberg, *There's No Reason for It; It's Just Our Policy: Why the Well-Pleaded Complaint Rule Sabotages the Purposes of Federal Question Jurisdiction*, 38 HASTINGS L.J. 597 (1987) (criticizing it), with Arthur R. Miller, *Artful Pleading: A Doctrine in Search of Definition*, 76 TEX. L. REV. 1781, 1783 (1998) (praising the rule for its bright line). For some cases routinely cited in the development of the rule, see Am. Well Works Co. v. Layne & Bowler Co., 241 U.S. 257 (1916); Smith v. Kan. City Title & Trust Co., 255 U.S. 180 (1921); Moore v. Chesapeake & Ohio Ry., 291 U.S. 205 (1934).

For recent district court cases struggling with applying *Grable* and *Empire* in national-security and government-contract contexts, see *In re* Nat'l Security Agency Telecommunications Records Litig., 483 F. Supp. 2d 934 (N.D. Cal. 2007) (upholding "arising under" jurisdiction over state-law claims that implicated the "state secrets" evidentiary privilege asserted by private-defendant telephone companies); HC Servs., Inc. v. Hiller Inv., Inc., No. 2:06cv160KS-MTP (S.D. Miss. Mar. 30, 2007) (refusing to allow federal jurisdiction over state-law claims that involved the construction of government supply contracts for the provision of fire extinguishment equipment); McMahon v. Presidential Airways, Inc., 410 F. Supp. 2d 1189 (S.D. Fla. 2006) (upholding federal jurisdiction over state-law wrongful-death actions by survivors of soldiers killed in a noncombat plane crash in Afghanistan where the plane operator was employed by the military, and the claim would implicate the construction of a government contract).

DIVERSITY JURISDICTION

5

OPENING REMARKS

Another form of subject-matter jurisdiction is diversity jurisdiction. Article III provides for federal jurisdiction when a controversy is between citizens of different states, even if the cause of action arises under state law rather than federal law. The reason why the Framers incorporated this provision is unclear, but the best guess, and the one the Supreme Court has sanctioned, is to provide an impartial federal forum when a state court might be biased against an out-of-state litigant.

State and federal courts are different. Their procedures vary. Jury pools are broader in federal courts (which pull from districts) than in state courts (which pull from counties). Federal judges, who are life tenured, may be less susceptible to local politics and local issues than state judges, who often are elected. Note, however, that under the *Erie* doctrine, which Chapter 8 will address, state substantive law will apply in diversity cases. Thus, generally speaking, federal diversity courts decide and apply state substantive law.

Of course, the diversity clause permits a plaintiff to invoke a federal forum even if she is the in-state litigant or for reasons other than anticipated state-court bias. Congress has attempted to limit diversity jurisdiction to its underlying purpose of avoiding state-court bias in the removal context, but it has not done so with respect to implementing original diversity jurisdiction under 28 U.S.C. § 1332(a), which tracks language in Article III.

Although the language in the statute is similar to that in Article III, there are two significant restrictions. The first is the amount-in-controversy requirement of § 1332, which requires that the amount exceed $75,000, exclusive of interest and costs. The second is the complete diversity rule, an interpretation by the Supreme Court of § 1332, which requires that no plaintiff be of the same state citizenship as any defendant.

Alienage jurisdiction, which is related to diversity jurisdiction, allows for federal jurisdiction over controversies between a citizen of a U.S. state and a foreign state or a citizen thereof. Section 1332(a) imposes the same amount-in-controversy requirement on alienage jurisdiction. Alienage jurisdiction avoids state bias against foreign litigants and also provides foreign litigants a forum with decorum appropriate for foreign parties.

An ongoing debate involves whether diversity jurisdiction (but not alienage jurisdiction) has outlived its usefulness, particularly in light of the complexities and burdens it engenders. The argument against diversity jurisdiction is that state-court bias against out-of-state litigants is marginal in most instances, that state courts are no longer so provincial, and that the burdens on federal dockets in hearing and deciding cases presenting only issues of state law is high. The counterargument is that bias and provinciality still exist in some courts, and that the need to provide an impartial federal forum outweighs the concomitant burdens on federal courts. A striking example of a recent *expansion* of federal diversity jurisdiction is the Class Action Fairness Act of 2005, which greatly expanded diversity jurisdiction for large interstate class actions based on the perceived bias of some state courts against out-of-state defendants.

HYPOTHETICAL

You are an associate at a small law firm. A partner asks you to attend a meeting regarding your firm's case, *Moore v. Dodge L.P.*, presently pending in the Western District of Texas. The partner tells you she is worried about jurisdiction. "When we filed in federal court on diversity jurisdiction grounds, I assumed we would have some basis for federal subject-matter jurisdiction, but now I am not sure. Are we out of luck? I'll need a memo with your analysis in an hour."

You review the file and ascertain the following facts. Sam Moore was born in Louisiana. When he turned 18, he enlisted in the U.S. Army, where he was stationed primarily at a U.S. military base in San Antonio, Texas. While Moore was stationed in San Antonio, he had vague intentions about what he would do after completing his Army stint. He intended to go to college after his four-year stint was complete, though he wasn't sure where he would get into school, and he never ruled out the possibility of making the Army a career. In his second year in the Army, he was injured and honorably discharged, whereupon he immediately enrolled in college at the University of New Mexico. He majored in computer science and hoped to get a job in New Mexico, though he realized that the job market might take him outside of New Mexico. At the time of the lawsuit, Moore was in his final year of college and had job offers from employers in New Mexico and Texas, and he was unsure which job he would take. He was living in on-campus student housing at the University of New Mexico. He held a New Mexico driver's license, car insurance, and car registration, but he voted in Texas and still had bank accounts based there.

Ana Lopez was born and raised in Mexico City, Mexico, where she met Javier Lopez (who had been born in Texas). Javier worked in San Antonio and owned a house there. After a few years of long-distance dating, they decided to get married. Ana was issued a green card and became a lawful permanent resident of the United States, though she maintained her Mexican citizenship. Because of Ana's traditionalist family, however, she was not allowed to live permanently with him before the marriage, and therefore she rented her own apartment in San Antonio while they dated, though she fully intended to live with him permanently after the wedding. Three months after getting engaged, Javier's job transferred him to New Orleans, Louisiana. As a result, both Javier and Ana decided to move permanently to New Orleans after the wedding. Javier went to New Orleans without her for two weeks to find housing and get settled before the wedding. During the week of the wedding, Javier asked Ana to tidy up some loose ends in Texas and then come to New Orleans to see the new house where they both would live. He asked Moore, whom he knew socially from Moore's Army days and who was on spring break visiting friends in San Antonio, to drive Ana to the airport for her first trip to Louisiana.

On the way to the airport, their car tire blew out and caused their car to collide with a tree. The experts hired by Moore and Lopez concluded that the blowout was caused by a faulty tire placed on the car by Dodge LP, a limited partnership organized under the laws of Texas that sells and installs tires. Dodge's headquarters is based in Texas and has significant operations in Texas, Louisiana, and New Mexico. Dodge has one general partner, Solid Tires, Inc., and four limited partners. Solid Tires is a Delaware corporation. Its headquarters is located in Delaware, but it does almost all of its business in Texas and Louisiana. It has shareholders in all 50 states. The four limited partners of Dodge are individual investors, all of whom are citizens and residents of New York.

Moore and Lopez are suing Dodge for claims under state tort law in the Western District of Texas. Moore seeks $25,000 in medical bills for his physical injuries, and Lopez seeks $30,000 in medical bills for her physical injuries. Each also claims $50,000 for pain and suffering. The evidence suggests that their physical injuries are severe and that they continue to experience significant psychological injuries. They both also assert a claim for punitive damages in the amount of $1 million.

Texas law caps claims for pain and suffering at an amount equal to the award of physical damages. It also restricts punitive damages to a showing of "willful and wanton conduct."

After the lawsuit was filed, Moore graduated, took the New Mexico job, bought a condo in downtown Santa Fe, and transferred his voter's registration and bank accounts to New Mexico. Lopez eventually made it to Louisiana, married Javier, and still lives in New Orleans.

SUGGESTED READINGS

U.S. CONST. art. III § 2
28 U.S.C. §§ 1332(a)–(c)
Carden v. Arkoma Assocs., 494 U.S. 185, 185–98 (1990)
Hertz Corp. v. Friend, 559 U.S. _ (2010)
Zahn v. Int'l Paper Co., 414 U.S. 291, 294, 294–95 (1973)
Mas v. Perry, 489 F.2d 1396, 1396–401 (5th Cir. 1974)
J. A. Olson Co. v. City of Winona, 818 F.2d 401, 401–04, 409–13 (5th Cir. 1987)

SAMPLE ESSAY

MEMORANDUM

To: Ms. Partner
From: Me
Re: Subject-Matter Jurisdiction in *Moore v. Dodge LP*

ISSUE

Does the federal court have subject-matter jurisdiction over the case?

SHORT ANSWER

The court likely has subject-matter jurisdiction, though only if the plaintiffs have, in good faith, alleged willful and wanton conduct.

DISCUSSION

For a federal court to have subject-matter jurisdiction over a case, the court must have constitutional authorization to hear it, such as federal-question "arising under" jurisdiction or diversity jurisdiction. Here, the complaint raises only state issues, rendering federal-question jurisdiction unavailable. Therefore, the only potential basis for subject-matter jurisdiction in this case is diversity (or alienage) jurisdiction.

A court must have both constitutional and statutory authorization to hear a diversity case. Although Article III requires only minimal diversity and has no amount-in-controversy requirement, 28 U.S.C. § 1332(a) generally requires complete diversity (as interpreted by *Strawbridge v. Curtiss*) and that the amount-in-controversy exceed $75,000, exclusive of interest and costs. Both requirements must be met for diversity jurisdiction to attach.

A. Complete Diversity

1. SAM MOORE

For diversity of citizenship purposes, a U.S. citizen is a citizen of a state if he is "domiciled" there. Domicile means being physically present there with a subjective intent to remain there indefinitely. *See Mas v. Perry*. Here, Moore is probably a citizen of Louisiana, his birth citizenship, because he never changed his domicile before the lawsuit was filed. While he was in Texas, he never formed an intent to permanently reside there. While he was in school in New Mexico, he never formed an intent to permanently reside in New Mexico, either. He did have a driver's license, car insurance, and car registration in New Mexico, but those are poor indices of a student's intentions. The fact that he kept his voter's registration and bank accounts in a different state suggests that he did not expect to be in New Mexico indefinitely. In addition, his residence in student housing undermines any intent of permanence. Coupled with his reasonable statement that he had to be prepared to go where the job was, these facts suggest that Moore was still a Louisiana citizen for purposes of diversity jurisdiction while he was in school.

By taking the job in New Mexico, buying a condo there, and transferring his voter's registration and bank accounts there, Moore probably did change his citizenship for diversity purposes from Louisiana to New Mexico. However, citizenship for diversity purposes is assessed as of the time the case is filed in federal court, and, at that time, he had not yet done those things. *See Mas v. Perry*. Thus, at the time of filing, his citizenship for diversity purposes was very likely Louisiana.

2. ANA LOPEZ

Lopez is an alien because she is a Mexican citizen. At the time of the lawsuit, however, she was a lawful permanent resident domiciled in Texas. While she and Javier were dating, she was physically living in Texas with the intent to permanently reside there. The evidence of her pending marriage to Javier, who had a permanent job and home in San Antonio, and the fact that she was renting an apartment in Texas, support that subjective intent. Thus, at that time, she became a citizen of Texas for diversity jurisdiction purposes. Her later change of intent to move to Louisiana did not change her domicile because she never was physically in Louisiana until after the lawsuit was filed. *See Mas v. Perry*. Thus, Lopez is an alien who was a lawful permanent resident and domiciliary of Texas for purposes of diversity jurisdiction.

3. DODGE LP

An unincorporated association is a citizen of each state of which its members are citizens. *See Carden v. Arkoma Assocs*. Under *Carden*, that rule applies to both general and limited partners in a limited partnership.

Thus, it is irrelevant for diversity jurisdiction purposes that Dodge is organized under the laws of Texas, that its headquarters is based there, or that it has significant operations in Texas, Louisiana, and New Mexico. What matters, for diversity jurisdiction purposes, is the citizenship of its partners. The individual partners are citizens of New York. Therefore, Dodge is at least a citizen of New York.

The general partner is a corporation. Under § 1332(c)(1), corporations are citizens of their state of incorporation and the state of their principal place of business. Solid Tires, the general partner, is incorporated in Delaware, and therefore it (and Dodge) is a citizen of Delaware.

Principal place of business is no longer determined by the "total activity" test of *J.A. Olson* but instead is determined by the place where the corporation's high-level officers direct, control, and coordinate the corporation's activities, usually the company's "headquarters." *Hertz.* As the Supreme Court indicated, the headquarters may not always be an easy determination. Here, the company's headquarters is in Delaware. Because the inquiry is fact dependent, more facts likely would be necessary to confirm that, in fact, Delaware is the place where the high-level officers of Solid Tires direct, control, and coordinate the corporation's activities. If, for example, Delaware is just the place where the directors hold their board meetings, it might not qualify as the company's principal place of business for diversity jurisdiction purposes. However, based on the facts given, the headquarters is likely Delaware.

4. SUMMARY

Moore is a citizen of Louisiana, Lopez is an alien who is a lawful permanent resident of the U.S. and a domiciliary of Texas, and Dodge L.P. is a citizen of both New York and Delaware. Section 1332(a) of the diversity statute extends diversity jurisdiction to actions between citizens of different states and in which aliens are additional parties. The parties here meet that statutory element of diversity jurisdiction.

B. Amount in Controversy

Even if the citizenship requirements are met, Section 1332(a) still requires satisfaction of the amount-in-controversy requirement. The requirement is that the amount in controversy must exceed $75,000, exclusive of interest and costs. The plaintiff's good-faith allegations control unless the defendant can show to a legal certainty that the threshold cannot be exceeded. *See Mas v. Perry.* Two plaintiffs suing a single defendant may aggregate their claims only if they are joint claims. *See Zahn v. International Paper.*

Here, Moore's and Lopez's compensatory damages claims relate to their own individualized injuries. They therefore are several and independent, not joint. Thus, they cannot be aggregated. The claims do appear to have been made in good faith, based on the facts given. Thus, Moore has alleged $75,000 in compensatory damages, and Lopez has alleged $80,000. However, it is a legal certainty that they cannot recover all that they have claimed. Because Texas law limits recovery of emotional damages to an amount equal to that of physical damages, Moore's compensatory damages are capped at $50,000, and Lopez's are capped at $60,000. Without additional damages, the amount-in-controversy requirement is not met.

Punitive damages can be added into the amount in controversy. However, Texas law restricts the availability of punitive damages to torts based on willful and wanton conduct. Therefore, if Moore and Lopez have alleged willful and wanton conduct in good faith, they likely each will exceed the amount-in-controversy threshold. If not, neither will exceed it, and diversity jurisdiction will be lacking.

CONCLUSION

For these reasons, it appears that the court may lack subject-matter jurisdiction over this case because of a failure to exceed the amount-in-controversy requirement. Additional facts should be taken to make this determination.

Even if diversity jurisdiction is lacking, however, the plaintiffs are not out of luck. State courts are generally open to hear the case, and so the plaintiffs may be able to refile the same claims in state court. If a federal forum is crucial, they may be able to obtain federal-question jurisdiction by adding a federal cause of action, if one exists.

TOOLS FOR SELF-CRITICISM

As is typical with diversity jurisdiction questions, this question requires a series of interrelated analyses of the diversity and alienage rules. The two major components were citizenship and the amount in controversy. Within each of these broad components were additional rules implicated by the facts. Did you successfully identify which rules were at issue and how they were to be organized?

This question was drafted to test your ability to recognize and apply fairly clear legal rules to fairly clear facts. That may be easy in some contexts, but the diversity rules implicated here are complicated enough so that the question, though it has right and wrong answers, is still challenging because it requires meticulous navigation of the rules. This is a different skill than the ability to distill nuanced doctrinal rules and apply them to complicated facts in a situation that does not have a clear answer, such as in personal jurisdiction. Both skills are important. Did you find one easier than the other? That is not to say that diversity and alienage jurisdiction do not have their uncertainties—some of those uncertainties are explored in the Variations subsection below.

Did you get tripped up by the red-herring reading of *J.A. Olson*? That is a Fifth Circuit precedent suggesting the "total activity" test for principal place of business. Although Fifth Circuit precedent usually would control here, the Supreme Court in *Hertz* recently directed that the "nerve center" test should control. Thus, *J.A. Olson* is no longer good law, and you should not have followed it.

On the flip side, one issue—the principal place of business of Solid Tires—was uncertain. To make the question manageable, the facts necessary to answer this question definitively or at least analyze it comprehensively were omitted. That is not unlike real-world situations, in which you may be asked to analyze an issue and only after analyzing it halfway realize that you need more facts. The ability to realize the need for more facts is also an important legal skill. Of course, if you conclude that more facts are needed in order to answer the question, be sure to identify the kinds of facts that you will need and how they would assist in making the determination. But be careful not to cross the line between identifying critical factual gaps and making factual assumptions that change the hypothetical. If you make factual assumptions, be sure to discuss how you would answer if your factual assumption is wrong.

The facts provide that Moore stated that he had prepared to go where he received a job. This is a critical fact because it goes to Moore's subjective intent to reside in a state indefinitely. As long as his statement is reasonable, a court likely will give great weight to Moore's statement as evidence of his subjective intent. And, so, as a result, Moore probably did not have the requisite subjective intent to change his citizenship while he was in school. Note, however, that not every statement of subjective intent will be conclusive, which is why courts often seek objective confirmations (such as driver's licenses, voter's registration, and homeownership).

Did you catch the time-of-filing determination for citizenship? Moore probably did not change his citizenship until after the case was filed. In most cases, that means that his change of citizenship was irrelevant for diversity purposes. (Why might that be?)

Pay special attention to the last paragraph in the sample answer. Pointing out that the case could be filed in state court demonstrates two things. First, it demonstrates that you are thinking creatively and strategically about litigation. If you can't win one way, try another! Second, it demonstrates that you grasp the underlying policy considerations of federal jurisdiction. It is okay that federal jurisdiction is limited because, generally, state courts are available (and perhaps better able) to hear the dispute.

VARIATIONS ON THE THEME

What if Dodge were a professional corporation or an LLC rather than a limited partnership? *Compare* Rolling Hills MHP, L.P. v. Comcast SCH Holdings, L.L.C., 374 F.3d 1020 (11th Cir. 2004) (holding an LLC to be treated like a partnership), *with* Hoagland v. Sandberg, 385 F.3d 737, 740 (7th Cir. 2004) (holding a professional corporation to be treated like a corporation), *and with* Carden v. Arkoma Assocs., 494 U.S. 185, 197 (1990) ("The 50 States have created, and will continue to create, a wide assortment of artificial entities possessing different powers and characteristics, and composed of various classes of members with varying degrees of interest and control. Which of them is entitled to be considered a 'citizen' for diversity purposes, and which of their members' citizenship is to be consulted, are questions more readily resolved by legislative prescription than by legal reasoning.... We have long since decided that having established special treatment for corporations, we will leave the rest to Congress..."). What would your answer be as a judge? As a Senator proposing legislation?

Consider what might change if one of Dodge's limited partners had been a citizen and resident of Mexico. Then the lineup would include aliens on both sides of the lawsuit, though one alien would be a lawful permanent resident of a diverse state, and a U.S. citizen would also be included. Would jurisdiction extend to this lawsuit?

Say the evidence showed that Solid Tires held its board meetings in Delaware in a small office that the company leases, but all of its directors and officers are citizens and residents of Texas or Louisiana and generally work from home. They often conduct business via e-mail, though they hold their formal board meetings in Delaware. How would you analyze the principal place of business inquiry under these facts?

What if Moore, though a U.S. citizen, took up permanent residence in Mexico, in effect becoming a "stateless citizen"? *Cf.* Mas v. Perry, 489 F.2d 1396, 1399–400 (5th Cir. 1974) (noting that a U.S. citizen who takes up domicile in a foreign country is neither an alien nor a domiciliary of any state and therefore destroys diversity and alienage jurisdiction).

Say that, in addition to damages, the plaintiffs sought injunctive relief by, for example, seeking an injunction against any and all sales of the defective tire. How would injunctive relief be calculated into the amount in controversy? *See generally* Brittain Shaw, *The $75,000 Question: What is the Value of Injunctive Relief?*, 6 Geo. Mason L. Rev. 1013 (1998).

OPTIONAL READINGS

For more on the controversy underlying diversity jurisdiction and whether it should be abolished, see Larry Kramer, *Diversity Jurisdiction*, 1990 B.Y.U. L. Rev. 97 (summarizing some of the arguments for and against diversity jurisdiction).

As mentioned in the introductory subsection, Congress has expanded diversity jurisdiction under the Class Action Fairness Act of 2005, or CAFA. Among other things, Congress granted subject-matter jurisdiction over certain class actions based on minimum, rather than complete, diversity and defined unincorporated associations to be citizens of the state under whose laws they are organized and the state where they have their principal place of business. For more, see 28 U.S.C. § 1332(d); *Fairness to Whom? Perspectives on the Class Action Fairness Act of 2005*, 156 U. Pa. L. Rev. Issue 6 (2008).

REMOVAL AND REMAND

6

OPENING REMARKS

So far, the problems have tested the propriety of a forum chosen by the plaintiff. Removal is a doctrine that gives the defendant a say in where the case is heard. Removal allows a defendant to move a case originally filed in state court to federal court.

Removal vindicates the purposes of federal subject-matter jurisdiction. Although most federal-question and diversity cases can be heard by state courts, removal allows either party to invoke the federal forum, thereby ensuring that those cases that really ought to be heard by federal courts are more likely to be so heard. This is particularly important for diversity cases in which an out-of-state defendant may be subject to some state bias. Without removal, a plaintiff could select a state-court forum for the purposes of capitalizing on that bias, while the hapless defendant could not move the case to a more neutral federal forum, even though diversity jurisdiction may exist.

Removal is entirely a creature of statute. The general removal statute allows defendants to remove a case that could have originally been filed in federal court. Thus, for most purposes, removed cases must meet one of the bases for federal subject-matter jurisdiction. The statutory gloss on federal subject-matter jurisdiction applies to removal; thus, for example, removal on the basis of federal-question jurisdiction must be based on the plaintiff's well-pleaded complaint.

There are important restrictions on removal. First, only defendants have the right to remove; plaintiffs, even if nominally defendants to a counterclaim, cannot remove. Second, all defendants must join in or consent to removal. This is commonly called the unanimity requirement. Third, removal can be made only to the federal district court that embraces the state court where the action is pending. Fourth, no removal is permitted on the basis of diversity jurisdiction if one of the defendants is a citizen of the state where the case is filed. The rationale for this limitation is that diversity jurisdiction presumes bias against an out-of-state defendant but not against an in-state defendant. Fifth, removal must be made within 30 days of the filing of the first complaint providing grounds for removal. Thus, if the original complaint initially asserts no ground for federal subject-matter jurisdiction but is later amended to include a federal question, then the 30-day deadline begins from the date of the amended complaint. If, however, the basis for removal is diversity jurisdiction, then removal is generally barred if made more than one year after the date of the original complaint.

Removal is automatic upon filing with the federal and state courts—no motion is required. A case that is removed improperly is subject to remand back to the state court. Cases removed without satisfying the federal subject-matter jurisdiction requirement must be remanded as soon as that jurisdictional defect is noticed. Cases removed without satisfying the nonjurisdictional procedural requirements, however, may only be remanded back to state court if one of the parties makes a motion to remand within 30 days of removal. A remand order for improper removal or for lack of subject-matter jurisdiction is not subject to appellate review.

As one can see, the removal rules are intricate and mechanical. The following problem will test your ability to navigate through them as well as to explore how they might be applied in unique circumstances.

HYPOTHETICAL

Tom Peterson is a New Jersey domiciliary. He applies for a bartending job at Eddie's Sports Bar in New York but is turned down. Tom believes that he was turned down because of his gender and that Eddie's intentionally hires female bartenders to attract its predominantly male clientele. Tom therefore sues Eddie's and the manager who rejected him, Dolores Caldones, for gender discrimination under New York state law. He does not allege any federal claim. He sues for no more than $75,000 in compensatory damages. He files his lawsuit in New York state court on January 1, 2009.

Dolores is a Connecticut domiciliary. Eddie's is a Delaware corporation with locations all over the Northeast. Between the time Tom was turned down and the time he files his lawsuit, Dolores has quit Eddie's and taken a different job in New York.

Tom properly serves Dolores on the same day that he files his complaint in New York state court, but he claims he is unable to serve Eddie's. Meanwhile, Dolores answers and admits in her answer that Eddie's told her never to hire a man. Tom continues to seek additional time to serve Eddie's, which the state court grants. Tom then amends his complaint to allege $1 million in punitive damages, which would be permitted by state law under these circumstances. He files and serves his amended complaint on Dolores. On January 1, 2010, Tom finally serves Eddie's with the amended complaint.

Eddie's, the day after being served, files a notice of removal on the basis of federal-question jurisdiction and diversity jurisdiction in federal court. Eddie's alleges in the removal notice that its principal place of business is in Massachusetts, where it has its flagship locations. Eddie's also alleges any punitive damages in excess of $100,000 would be unconstitutional under the Due Process Clause of the U.S. Constitution. Dolores consents to removal.

Tom does not file a motion to remand immediately. Instead, the case proceeds to discovery. Six months into discovery, Eddie's produces evidence that shows that its headquarters are in New York. Based on that evidence, the district judge finds that Eddie's is a citizen of New York, not Massachusetts.

Tom moves to remand the case back to state court. How should the judge rule?

SUGGESTED READINGS

28 U.S.C. § 1441
28 U.S.C. § 1446
28 U.S.C. § 1447
Shamrock Oil & Gas Corp. v. Sheets, 313 U.S. 100, 102–09 (1941)

As an initial matter, it appears that the district court would have had original jurisdiction over the amended complaint if it had been filed in federal court. The district court would not have had original federal question jurisdiction because no federal issue appears in Tom's well-pleaded complaint, and the federal defense raised by Eddie's would not give rise to federal question jurisdiction.

However, the district court would have had original diversity jurisdiction over the amended complaint. Tom is a New Jersey citizen. Dolores is a Connecticut citizen. Eddie's is a citizen of both Delaware and New York. Thus, the parties are completely diverse. In addition, Tom's good faith allegation of punitive damages exceeds the amount-in-controversy threshold. Accordingly, the federal court would have had diversity jurisdiction over the amended complaint if it had originally been filed in federal court.

However, there are several potential defects in removal here. First, removal violated the forum-defendant rule of § 1441(b), which states that a case based on diversity jurisdiction may be removed only if no defendant is a citizen of the state in which the case is filed. Here, Eddie's is a citizen of the New York, where the case was filed. Thus, § 1441(b) does not allow Eddie's to remove the case.

Second, removal violated the timing rules. It is worth noting that Dolores's refusal to remove during the 30 days after she was served did *not* prohibit Eddie's from removing the case. Section 1446(b)(2) of the removal statute specifically gives each defendant its own 30-day period to remove. Eddie's removed within 30 days of being served, and Dolores consented to that removal. The removal was therefore timely under § 1446(b)(2) and (b)(3).

However, removal was *not* timely under § 1446(c). That provision bars removal of a diversity case more than one year after the original filing. Eddie's removed the case more than one year after the date of the original complaint, and thus removal violated § 1446(c). An exception to the one-year bar does apply if the plaintiff acted in bad faith to prevent removal. That could be the case here. Perhaps Tom intentionally withheld his punitive-damages claim and delayed service on Eddie's until the one-year deadline was at hand. Section 1446(c)(3) specifically deems a plaintiff's intentional failure to disclose the actual amount in controversy as bad faith.

But the court need not decide the bad-faith issue here. Even assuming that Tom acted in good faith and that the one-year bar applies, Tom waived his right to seek a remand for a violation of the one-year bar. Section 1447(c) requires a remand motion for any ground other than lack of subject-matter jurisdiction to be made within 30 days of removal. The one-year bar is not a defect in subject-matter jurisdiction. Accordingly, Tom cannot obtain a remand order based on the defendants' violation of the one-year bar.

Violation of the forum-defendant rule is a tougher question. The forum-defendant rule could be construed as a limitation on diversity jurisdiction, and § 1447(c) allows a remand motion based on a lack of subject-matter jurisdiction to be made at any time. Thus, the question is whether a violation of the forum-defendant rule is a defect of subject-matter jurisdiction.

The forum-defendant rule could be a limitation on subject-matter jurisdiction. After all, the purpose of the rule is to ensure that defendants removing on the basis of diversity jurisdiction are doing so to avoid the presumed bias that a state court has against out-of-state defendants. By limiting removal to these situations, the forum-defendant rule vindicates the purposes of diversity jurisdiction. It is therefore tied to diversity jurisdiction in a way that the other potential defects, such as those involving the timing rules, are not.

In addition, there are good reasons why the forum-defendant rule ought not be subject to the 30-day remand time frame. If it were, it would place the burden of raising and proving the violation on the plaintiff, who is least likely to know the facts necessary to make that determination of a defendant's citizenship. And, the plaintiff would have to do so within 30 days of removal, usually without any discovery, and constrained by the requirements of Rule 11. By contrast, a jurisdictional characterization would require courts to raise the issue sua sponte and would enable the violation to be raised at any time, thereby deterring defendants from attempting to remove the case in violation of the forum-defendant rule in the hopes that the plaintiff will not suspect a violation until after the 30-day window has passed.

On the other hand, a jurisdictional characterization comes with significant costs. In this case, for example, six months' worth of discovery would be wasted. Indeed, there may be reason why the forum-defendant rule should not be jurisdictional. The forum-defendant rule benefits the plaintiff by immunizing her choice of forum in a diversity case, when that choice normally is subject to a defendant's ability to remove. Because it is a rule that inures to the plaintiff's benefit, it may be appropriate to allow the plaintiff to be able to waive the benefit or to require the plaintiff to assert it within a certain time period.

In sum, remand in this case will turn on whether the violation of the forum-defendant rule in this case is a defect of subject-matter jurisdiction or not. If so, then remand is required. If not, then Tom waived his ability to remand the case by failing to move within 30 days of removal.

TOOLS FOR SELF-CRITICISM

First, the organizational structure of this problem may have created a road-block for you. Did you try to write one long paragraph on the rules of removal jurisdiction and then another long one applying the rules to the facts in the hypothetical? If so, that approach may have caused unnecessary difficulty and wasted valuable time. This question provides an opportunity to apply a multileveled analysis to a similarly multileveled legal rule. Given the mechanical nature of the removal rules, using conventional issue-spotting methods to craft an answer may not be the best approach. Instead, try a tiered analysis in which the isolated removal rules should be explained and analyzed individually, as the sample answer demonstrates. The tiered method allows you to construct your analysis step by step, a useful methodology when applying the multifaceted removal rules.

How did you begin your answer? While you may have been tempted to frame your answer chronologically, beginning with the initial complaint, this structure does not isolate the ultimate question raised by the hypothetical: how should the judge rule on the plaintiff's motion to *remand*? You may find working backward more effective.

Next, did you know the removal rules well enough to write an effective essay answer? The fact that the answer alleged a question of federal law, for example, should have been an easy issue to spot and resolve quickly if you knew that the well-pleaded complaint rule of *Mottley* applies equally to removal. On the other hand, the multiplicative iterations of complaints and defendants might be confusing unless you have a firm grip on the removal rules and issues that they leave open. By the time you begin drafting an essay answer to the hypothetical, you should know the removal rules such that complicated facts do not shake the legal principles in your mind. If you had to look back at the rules to remind yourself of the requirements for original jurisdiction, for example, you were not ready to tackle the essay.

How did you organize the timing issues? With this type of hypothetical, you should consider mapping out a time line. That way, you can refer back to it as you write your answer and avoid wasting time re-reading the facts for dates.

The facts indicate that when Eddie's removed the lawsuit to federal court, it asserted that its principal place of business was Massachusetts. Later, a judge ruled that its principal place of business was actually New York. Did you recognize that, after the judge's ruling, the removal violates the forum-defendant rule? Do not let the timing of the judge's ruling (after the case had already been removed) distract you from its impact: the removal violated the forum-defendant rule, period.

Of course, it would not do to stop with that conclusion. Deeper and more complicated questions naturally follow from identifying a violation of the forum-defendant rule. Those questions are these: So what? Is there a remedy? If so, what analysis is required? If not, why not?

Contrast the "so what" line of reasoning in the forum-defendant rule issue with the same reasoning on the timing issue. Note how the sample answer asks the question for both issues, with different conclusions. The timing issue is likely irrelevant because it was a procedural defect that could be waived. (Nevertheless, the sample answer appropriately discusses the issue in some depth, even if it ultimately concludes that the resolution is irrelevant.) By contrast, the "so what" reasoning of the forum-defendant rule would have led to an important discussion of its jurisdictionality, a feature that was critical to a complete answer of the essay question.

Finally, did you reach a conclusion? The hypothetical required you to indicate how the judge should rule on the plaintiff's motion. Inevitably, there will be answers that turn on an ambiguous area of the law, and this was one of them. You should acknowledge the ambiguity, but answer the question. Remember that public policy may help you justify your conclusion by tipping the scales in favor of a particular outcome. Did you address or utilize the public policy of allowing the plaintiff to choose the forum without encouraging forum shopping? Of avoiding subjecting a defendant to state bias? If your answer omitted these policies, do you think mentioning them would have augmented your answer?

VARIATIONS ON THE THEME

Say Dolores had removed the case before Eddie's was served, but Eddie's did not want the case to be heard in federal court. What recourse might Eddie's have? Would its argument be stronger or different if Eddie's had been served at the same time as Dolores?

Say remand is denied, and Tom then tries to join a third defendant, its parent company, which is a citizen of New Jersey. Joinder would then destroy complete diversity. What should the court do? *See* 28 U.S.C. § 1447(e).

Note that Tom originally sued for "no more than $75,000," possibly to try to keep the case from being removed. Most courts hold that if the plaintiff agrees not to take more than the jurisdictional minimum, the defendants cannot remove on the basis of diversity. What if, however, Tom seeks an unspecified amount of damages? May defendants remove on the grounds that Tom *might* recover more than the jurisdictional minimum? Who has the burden of proof? What facts might both sides wish to explore to make their arguments? *See* 28 U.S.C. § 1446(c).

What if the district judge decides to remand the case for lack of subject-matter jurisdiction—can either party appeal? Section 1447(d) would suggest not. *See* Holstrom v. Peterson, 492 F.3d 833, 838–39 (7th Cir. 2007) (holding such a remand nonreviewable). *But see* Lively v. Wild Oats Markets, Inc., 456 F.3d 933, 937–38 (9th Cir. 2006) (reviewing a remand for lack of subject-matter jurisdiction).

OPTIONAL READINGS

Courts are split as to whether the forum-defendant rule is jurisdictional or not. *Compare, e.g.*, Lively v. Wild Oats Markets, Inc., 456 F.3d 933, 939–42 (9th Cir. 2006) (nonjurisdictional), *with* Hurt v. Dow Chem. Co., 963 F.2d 1142, 1146 n.1 (8th Cir. 1992) (jurisdictional). For a deeper discussion of the problem and potential solutions, see Scott Dodson, *In Search of Removal Jurisdiction*, 102 Nw. U. L. Rev. 55 (2008).

Although rarely covered in a first year civil procedure course, there are interesting (and complicated) issues relating to the timing of jurisdictional defects. The Supreme Court has allowed jurisdictional defects in removal to be "cured" before final judgment without necessitating remand. For more, see Caterpillar Inc. v. Lewis, 519 U.S. 61 (1996).

VENUE

7

OPENING REMARKS

Venue rounds out the third and final consideration in establishing a forum. Subject-matter jurisdiction determines whether the case is heard in the federal or state system, and personal jurisdiction determines in what states the case can be heard. Venue determines where, among those courts, it would be most convenient to hear the case.

Unlike subject-matter jurisdiction and personal jurisdiction, however, venue is not constitutional. States have their own venue laws, but, in federal court, federal venue statutes control. Those statutes determine what federal districts can hear the case.

Three venue statutory sections are of primary importance to most civil procedure courses. The first is 28 U.S.C. § 1391, which prescribes where venue is proper. Generally, venue is proper where any defendant resides, if all defendants are from the same state. Venue is also proper where a substantial part of the events or omissions giving rise to the claim occurred.

Note that venue hinges on *residence* rather than citizenship. For individuals, however, the test for residence is the same test for citizenship under diversity jurisdiction: domicile. Residence for corporations, however, is prescribed by the statute, which treats corporations as residents of districts where they would be subject to personal jurisdiction. Importantly, the test requires the personal jurisdiction analysis to be conducted by *district* rather than by state. If a corporation would not meet the personal jurisdiction test for any single district of a state in which it is subject to personal jurisdiction, then the corporation is a resident of the district with the most contacts.

Under § 1391, venue might be proper in multiple districts. If so, then the plaintiff gets to choose which of the proper venues she wishes to file suit. She need not pick the most convenient of them.

The other two venue statutes that are of most importance in a typical civil procedure course are § 1404 and § 1406. Section 1406 allows a court to dismiss a case that is filed in an improper venue or, in the interest of justice, to transfer it to a proper venue. Section 1404 allows a court to transfer a case from a proper venue to another proper venue for the convenience of the parties and witnesses and in the interest of justice. Under § 1404, the transferee court must have been a court in which the action could have been brought (both in terms of venue and also in terms of personal jurisdiction over the defendant) unless all parties consent to the transferee court. Interestingly, the transferor court need not have personal jurisdiction over the defendant in order to transfer venue.

Venue transfer overrides the plaintiff's choice of forum, which is entitled to some deference, and, as a result, transfer is the exception rather than the rule, and the party seeking transfer bears the burden of establishing that the transferee court meets the requirements of § 1404. Courts often consider where the "center of gravity" of the case is, relative docket loads, familiarity with applicable law, and the existence of any forum selection clause.

Venue transfer essentially allows a case to move within a single judicial system. (Contrast this with removal, which allows a case to move from a state court system to the federal system.) As a result, state courts cannot transfer a case from one state to another because each state has its own judicial system. Federal courts are not constrained by state court borders and thus can transfer venue in a federal court case across state lines.

When a case is filed in an inconvenient forum, and a convenient forum is in a different judicial system, venue transfer generally cannot be used. Instead, courts can use the doctrine of forum non conveniens. Forum non conveniens allows a court to dismiss a case with the anticipation that it will be refiled in the more convenient judicial system. Forum non conveniens is not a transfer power—the forum court can only dismiss the case. As a result, many courts will condition the dismissal for forum non conveniens on a waiver by the defendant to any statute of limitations or personal jurisdiction defense that it otherwise might have in the new forum. In considering whether to dismiss for forum non conveniens, courts use a combination of public and private factors similar to those used in considering whether to transfer venue under § 1404.

HYPOTHETICAL

You are a solo practitioner in Arkansas. One day, the general counsel of Oklahoma corporation AutomaticCarHorn Corp. (ACH) calls you and tells you the following:

> We need a local counsel in Arkansas to help us with a lawsuit and to give us some advice on venue. We've been sued by Sam Slyfox in federal court in Fayetteville in the Western District of Arkansas for a variety of state common law tort and contract causes of action. Apparently, Sam was injured in Oklahoma when he was driving a car installed with one of our patented automatic car horns.

> Let me tell you something about our automatic car horns. Genius. You know, most regular horns are just about the dumbest contraptions around. You are trying to avoid hitting someone, so...you take your hands **off** the wheel to honk? Ridiculous! We came up with a better system. Our automatic car horns are voice activated. You just say "honk" loudly and clearly, and the horn honks for you. You never have to take your hands off the wheel! It's a great feature. Plus, they are easy to install—any person with a screwdriver can do it.

> We sell everywhere but Arkansas, which may seem funny because that state is right next to our corporate headquarters in Tulsa, Oklahoma, in the Northern District of Oklahoma. But, in fact, we specifically do not sell into Arkansas because Arkansas has a law that makes it illegal to honk a horn at any place where cold drinks or sandwiches are served after 9:00 p.m. So, to avoid any implication that we might be inducing a violation of law, we don't sell into Arkansas deliberately.

> Our car horns occasionally break. Because we offer a 100% guarantee, we accept returns. We refund the money and keep the broken horns, and,

often, we are able to fix the broken horns. We usually sell these refurbished horns on eBay. We can't tell who is buying the horns until a purchase is made and we have to ship them. I have to admit that we have made a few sales to Arkansas residents that way. But whenever we make a sale via eBay, we include as a condition of the sale that any lawsuits based on the performance of the product shall be governed by the laws of Oklahoma. That's because Oklahoma tort law is particularly favorable to us, or at least it has been ever since we started making large political donations to the incumbent Oklahoma state legislators.

In any case, Sam Slyfox was one of those Arkansas eBay purchasers. He purchased his automatic car horn off eBay from Fayetteville, we shipped it to Fayetteville, and he alleges that he installed it into his car in Fayetteville.

Now, although we guarantee our fixed car horns as well, they also occasionally fail. This was one of those unfortunate times. Apparently, Sam lives in Fayetteville but works in Tulsa. One morning, during his commute, he was doing 90 mph down I-40 West and yelling "honk" to clear the road ahead of him. Just as he passed into the Eastern District of Oklahoma from the Western District of Arkansas, the horn gave out, and, as a result, he rear-ended a car in front of him in Oklahoma. Sam was injured pretty badly, and he has sued us under state tort causes of action for more than $1 million in damages.

We really want to avoid having this case to go to trial anywhere in Arkansas. Arkansas juries have a reputation of giving extraordinarily high punitive damage awards. Oklahoma juries are far more defendant-friendly. In fact, since we are one of the largest employers in Tulsa, a jury with a lot of Tulsa residents is likely to be extremely favorable to us. How likely is it that we get this case away from an Arkansas jury?

In answering the general counsel's question, please discuss only options implicating venue considerations.

SUGGESTED READINGS

28 U.S.C. § 1391
28 U.S.C. § 1404
28 U.S.C. § 1406
Carnival Cruise Lines, Inc. v. Shute, 499 U.S. 585, 587–95 (1991)
Stewart Org., Inc. v. Ricoh Corp., 487 U.S. 22, 24–33 (1988)
Hoffman v. Blaski, 363 U.S. 335, 335–44 (1960)
Piper Aircraft Co. v. Reyno, 454 U.S. 235, 238–61 (1981)

SAMPLE ESSAY

First, I would consider filing a Rule 12(b)(3) motion alleging improper venue under 28 U.S.C. § 1406, assuming that objection to venue has not been waived. Prevailing on that motion would require dismissal (or transfer, in the interests of justice) and thus take the case away from the Western District of Arkansas jury. Unfortunately, it is unlikely that such a motion would be successful.

Whether venue is proper or not is governed by 28 U.S.C. § 1391. Under that section, venue is appropriate (1) where any defendant resides, if all defendants are from the same state; (2) where a substantial part of the events or omissions giving rise to the claim occurred; or (3) if neither (1) nor (2) is available, where the defendant is subject to personal jurisdiction at the time the action was commenced.

The Western District of Arkansas is probably a proper venue under (1). Under § 1391, a corporate defendant is deemed to reside in any judicial district in which it is subject to personal jurisdiction. In some cases, this test may be different than the test for personal jurisdiction because, unlike the whole-state test for minimum contacts under personal jurisdiction, venue looks to the defendant's minimum contacts with a specific district within a state. Here, however, ACH's relevant contacts with the Western District of Arkansas are nearly identical to its contacts with the state of Arkansas. ACH sold the horn to Fayetteville and shipped it to Fayetteville to be installed in Fayetteville. It seems likely that ACH's contacts with the Western District of Arkansas would give rise to the minimum contacts necessary to establish personal jurisdiction over ACH there, meaning that ACH would then be deemed to reside in that judicial district.

In addition, the Western District of Arkansas is probably a proper venue under (2) as well because a substantial part of the acts or omissions giving rise to the cause of action occurred in the Western District of Arkansas. ACH shipped the horn to the Western District of Arkansas, and Slyfox installed it there. And, Slyfox was driving there around the time the horn gave out.

ACH may argue that other acts or omissions occurred outside of Arkansas. The horn gave out in Oklahoma, and the accident and injuries occurred in Oklahoma. And, the horn was not manufactured in Arkansas, and thus any defect in design or manufacture arose outside of Arkansas. But the fact that a substantial part of the acts or omissions giving rise to the cause of action occurred outside Arkansas does not mean that Arkansas is not a proper venue because more than one venue could be proper under (2). In short, venue may be proper in Oklahoma, but it may *also* be proper in Arkansas, and the fact that certain acts and omissions occurred in Oklahoma does not mean that venue is improper in the Western District of Arkansas, where a substantial part of the acts and omissions giving rise to the cause of action likely occurred.

In sum, then, a challenge to venue under Rule 12(b)(3) is unlikely to succeed because the Western District of Arkansas is likely a proper venue.

Second, I would consider filing a motion to transfer venue. Even if the Western District of Arkansas is a proper venue, ACH could still seek to transfer the case to a different venue under § 1404. That statutory provision allows a court to transfer the case for the convenience of the parties and witnesses, and in the interest of justice, to a venue where the case might have been brought.

Here, ACH has a strong argument that, even if the Western District of Arkansas is a proper venue, the case should be transferred to a venue in Oklahoma for the convenience of the parties and witnesses and in the interest of justice.

The first consideration is whether either the Eastern District of Oklahoma or the Northern District of Oklahoma is a district where the action might have been brought. Both appear to be. Slyfox could have brought the case in either district because ACH is subject to personal jurisdiction in Oklahoma by virtue of its incorporation there and because venue would have been appropriate in either district.

Venue is appropriate in the Northern District because ACH, which has its corporate headquarters there, is subject to personal jurisdiction there, meaning that ACH is deemed to reside there for venue purposes. In addition, a substantial part of the acts and omissions giving rise to the cause of action occurred in the Eastern District, where the accident occurred. Thus, venue is proper in either the Eastern District or the Northern District of Oklahoma.

The second consideration is whether the case should be transferred to one of those districts for the convenience of the parties and witnesses and in the interest of justice. ACH has a good argument for transfer of venue here. Because ACH's headquarters are located in the Northern District of Oklahoma, most of its records and witnesses presumably will be located there, whereas very few witnesses will be located in Arkansas. It would certainly be more convenient for ACH to litigate in the Eastern District of Oklahoma because it is based there, and it has no operations in Arkansas.

In addition, the choice-of-law provision makes Oklahoma law apply to the claim, and it would be somewhat more convenient for an Oklahoma court to apply familiar Oklahoma law than for an Arkansas court to try to apply a foreign state's law (though most states' tort laws are similar enough that it might not be too burdensome for an Arkansas court to apply Oklahoma law). In addition, because venue transfer does not change the choice-of-law inquiry, there would not be any injustice to Slyfox in terms of changing the applicable law. Finally, the interest of justice might favor a venue transfer because ACH deliberately avoided selling into Arkansas, with a few exceptions. Thus, justice would tend to dictate that ACH defend this case outside of Arkansas. For all these reasons, ACH has a strong argument that the convenience of the parties and witnesses, and the interest of justice support a transfer to Oklahoma.

Slyfox does have counterarguments. Slyfox's choice of forum is entitled to significant weight. However, it does not seem terribly inconvenient for Slyfox to litigate in the Northern District of Oklahoma because he works there and thus spends many of his waking hours there, not to mention the fact that his daily commute takes him next to the scene of the accident, in Oklahoma. Even if Slyfox did not work in Tulsa, the 90-mile distance between the two cities ameliorates any inconvenience for Slyfox to litigate in Oklahoma.

This is a close call, but, on balance, ACH probably will prevail in its transfer motion because the Northern District of Oklahoma is the most convenient forum. Slyfox's choice is entitled to significant deference, but it likely would not be too inconvenient for him to litigate in the Northern District of Oklahoma.

Finally, it is worth pointing out that forum non conveniens is not a likely option here. Forum non conveniens can be used by a federal court to dismiss a case with the anticipation that it be refiled in a different judicial system, such as a foreign country's courts. Absent statutory authority to the contrary, it is not a doctrine that enables a federal court to dismiss a case in anticipation of transfer to another federal court in the same system. Because there is no indication that a foreign country's courts would be more convenient to the parties and witnesses, dismissal based on forum non conveniens will not be a persuasive argument for ACH to make.

TOOLS FOR SELF-CRITICISM

As an initial consideration, did you analyze the hypothetical under the mistaken assumption that § 1391 requires the *most* convenient forum rather than just a proper venue? Remember that § 1391 does not require that the venue be the most convenient. Rather, venue may be proper in multiple districts. Therefore, the fact that the place of filing is not the most convenient forum is not particularly persuasive in a § 1406 improper-venue analysis, as it is for a § 1404 transfer analysis. This is a common confusion between § 1406 and § 1404.

That is not to say that you should not mention the most-convenient-venue argument in a § 1406 argument; you might still mention it if only to explain why it is not particularly persuasive. In a similar vein, you should certainly discuss the § 1406 issue even if it seems clear to you that the case was filed in a proper venue under § 1391. Note that the sample answer contemplates filing a motion to dismiss for improper venue and discusses those issues even though it ultimately concludes that such a motion would be very unlikely to succeed. Generally, even weak points are worth discussing to some degree.

Did you point out the relative strengths and weakness in the § 1404 arguments? Do not ignore arguments that do not support your conclusion. Instead, address them and call attention to their shortcomings. Specifically, if you concluded that transfer was appropriate, you should have discussed how the policy factors outweigh the deference that the plaintiff's choice of forum is entitled to. Conversely, if you concluded that transfer was inappropriate, perhaps in light of the deference accorded the plaintiff's choice of forum, you also should have reasoned how that deference outweighs the significant gains in convenience and economy that a transfer would produce.

Don't forget that § 1404 requires not only that the transferee court be a venue where the action could have been brought originally, but also that the transferee court would have had personal jurisdiction over the defendant originally (unless the defendant consented to the new venue). It is a minor issue on these facts because the defendant is subject to personal jurisdiction in the transferee court, but it is worth pointing out in your answer.

Did you spend time discussing the fact that Slyfox had been driving 90 miles per hour at the time of the accident? Seeing that figure might cause you to think about issues going to the merits of the case, such as contributory negligence, or of issues going to public policy considerations. If so, then you may have wasted valuable time. The question did not ask you to address any of those issues, and they are largely irrelevant to the venue question actually posed.

How did you treat the choice-of-law provision? Note, of course, that it was not a choice-of-forum provision (commonly called a forum-selection clause). Such a clause would have had a tremendous impact on the venue issues in the question. But the choice-of-law provision is not irrelevant. It affects the venue issue in subtle ways that require some purposive thinking. How did you address its impact?

Did you catch the possibility of forum non conveniens? Given that forum non conveniens does not enable a federal court to dismiss a case in anticipation of a transfer to another federal court in the same system, you might have been tempted to ignore the doctrine altogether. You probably recognized at least that it was an unlikely possibility, but that does not mean you should not address it. Raising it as a possibility and writing a short paragraph on why the doctrine does not apply records the valuable thought process that you actually went through. Anytime a question calls for a broad answer, use the flexibility to address all possible, not just the most probable, options. After all, the skill of identifying which issues are of limited utility is almost as important as the skill of identifying which issues are of the most utility. Note, though, that you should address the major issues first if time pressures prevent you from addressing all of them completely.

VARIATIONS ON THE THEME

How might your analysis change if Slyfox bought the product in Oklahoma, received it in Oklahoma, installed it in Oklahoma, and then unilaterally drove to Arkansas?

What if ACH was based in Maine instead of Oklahoma? Would venue transfer still be appropriate?

Say that Slyfox also sued the president of ACH, who is a resident of Mexico. Where would venue be proper then? *See* 28 U.S.C. § 1391(c)(3). What if the president of ACH were a citizen of Mexico but a lawful permanent resident of the United States domiciled in the Northern District of Oklahoma?

What if ACH were an unincorporated association rather than a corporation? *See* 28 U.S.C. § 1391(c)(2).

Change the existence of a choice-of-law provision in the contract between ACH and Slyfox to a forum selection clause, assigning the Eastern District of Oklahoma as a proper venue. Would this change your analysis under § 1391? Under § 1404? What if the forum selection clause mandated the Northern District of Oklahoma as the exclusive forum for lawsuits between the parties? What if the forum selection clause mandated the Eastern District of Arkansas?

OPTIONAL READINGS

Some commentators have criticized equating individual "residence" with "domicile," favoring instead a flexible approach that takes into consideration the convenience goals of venue. For more, see RICHARD D. FREER, INTRODUCTION TO CIVIL PROCEDURE 236 (2006) (urging such a flexible approach for individuals long residing in a particular state even though they have an intent to leave, such as a student or a member of the military).

8 ERIE

OPENING REMARKS

Ask any lawyer what two cases from civil procedure he dreaded the most, and it's a good bet that one of them will be *Erie* (and the other may very well be *Pennoyer*). The *Erie* doctrine is really a choice-of-law doctrine. What law should a federal court apply? For federal claims, the answer is pretty easy: federal law. But what about for state claims? For 95 percent of the time, the answer is fairly straightforward. A federal court applies state substantive law and federal procedural law. Thus, a federal court hearing a state negligence case applies the federal rules of procedure and state substantive law on negligence. But what happens when federal procedure affects state substance, or state substantive law is arguably procedural? In that 5 percent of the time, the answer can be exceedingly complicated.

It is important to understand the development of the *Erie* doctrine, for, in many ways, the doctrine is developing still. Part of the challenge is in integrating the many pronouncements from the Court into a coherent choice-of-law jurisprudence.

Erie presents primarily a vertical choice-of-law inquiry (i.e., whether to apply state or federal law). Once state law is chosen, the inquiry becomes horizontal (i.e., which state's law to apply). Usually, a federal court applies the horizontal choice-of-law principles of the state in which it sits. Thus, a New York federal court hearing a diversity case generally will apply New York state choice-of-law principles to determine which state law to apply to the dispute. If New York state courts would apply Pennsylvania law, for example, then the federal court should do the same.

But what happens when a diversity case is venue transferred from one state's federal courts to another state's federal courts under § 1404? In that case, the transferee state's federal court applies the law the transferor federal court would have applied had it kept the case. Accordingly, if the District of Massachusetts receives a venue transferred diversity case from the Southern District of New York, it will apply the law the Southern District of New York would have applied, which would be the state choice-of-law principles of New York, which could point to any number of state substantive laws (including, by the way, federal law!).

Erie stated that there is no federal general common law. That does not mean that there is no federal common law. Indeed, another case decided the same day as *Erie*, *Hinderleider*, recognized the existence of federal common law and the power of federal courts to create it in certain instances. Federal common law can arise in a variety of contexts, such as filling in gaps in federal statutory regimes and the development of federal procedural doctrines. Legitimate federal common law trumps countervailing state law under the Supremacy Clause, and thus controls in federal courts and state courts alike. Some federal common law, however, incorporates state law. In this *Erie*-that-is-not-*Erie*, the federal court will apply state law, not as a matter of formal *Erie* doctrine (though perhaps for some of the same policy reasons) but as a matter of federal common law.

The following problems will help guide you through the process of understanding and applying these difficult doctrines.

HYPOTHETICALS

1. Double Down

Double Down, Inc., a Delaware corporation with its principal place of business in Colorado, manufactures dice, card dispensers, and other equipment used in casinos. The Palacio Hotel, a hotel-casino in Las Vegas, is a Nevada corporation with its principal place of business in Nevada. Double Down and Palacio entered into a contract for the sale of casino equipment. A dispute arose regarding the quality of the equipment, and Palacio refused to pay. Double Down sued Palacio for breach of contract in Nevada federal court on diversity grounds. During discovery, the parties engaged in extensive settlement discussions. Those discussions ultimately proved fruitful, and the parties settled their dispute. At the parties' request, the district court entered a settlement order, accompanied by a confidentiality clause, and ordered the settlement sealed.

Double Down had contracts with two other hotel-casinos: Players Hotel and Hotel Paradise, both corporations with principal places of business in Nevada, though Players was incorporated in Nevada, while Paradise was incorporated in Delaware. Both Players and Paradise were aware that Palacio had settled a dispute with Double Down. Fearing that Double Down had something to hide, and suspecting that Double Down's products were of poor quality, they decided to sue in Nevada state court but in separate suits.

Double Down immediately removed Players' suit to federal court on diversity grounds, but Double Down could not remove Paradise's suit because they were both citizens of Delaware.

Discovery commenced in both suits. During discovery, both Players and Paradise sought discovery of communications and statements Double Down made during its settlement negotiations with Palacio in the settled lawsuit. Double Down objected and argued that settlement discussions were privileged from discovery.

The Nevada state court ordered the discovery. The state court, citing controlling Nevada Supreme Court precedent, held that Nevada state law does not recognize such a privilege from discovery involving settlement discussions in Nevada courts. The Nevada Supreme Court reasoned that the benefits of discovery outweigh the burdens of discovery, that other mechanisms existed to control disclosure of confidential information outside of the context of the lawsuit, and that other mechanisms exist to protect against the admission of unreliable evidence at trial. Relying on this precedent, the Nevada state court held that Nevada does not recognize a settlement privilege in Nevada state courts even when the settlement discussions took place in a federal court.

The Nevada federal court, however, refused to order the discovery. The Ninth Circuit recently recognized a "settlement privilege" of communications and statements made during confidential settlement discussions in a federal question case, based on the strong federal policy of encouraging settlement of cases in federal court. The Ninth Circuit reasoned that such policy would be hindered if parties' communications and statements could be divulged in subsequent lawsuits. Relying on this precedent, the Nevada federal court held that federal settlement privilege equally applicable to settlement communications made in a federal diversity case.

Both cases are appealed and affirmed. The Supreme Court grants certiorari review in both cases and consolidates them for argument. You are a law clerk for the Chief Justice, who has decided to write the opinion for the Court deciding both cases. Assume that Rule 501 of the Federal Rules of Evidence does not apply. Please draft a memo to the Chief Justice with your analysis of all of the vertical choice-of-law issues. Do not discuss facts or procedural history other than what is necessary to your analysis.

2. Dogs-R-Us

Dogs-R-Us is a pet store chain that does business in all 48 contiguous states. It is incorporated in Delaware with its principal place of business in Oregon. It has never done any business in Hawaii, however.

Purdy is a domiciliary of Hawaii. He purchased a pit bull from Dogs-R-Us in Oregon. Purdy then returned to Hawaii. Shortly after returning to Hawaii, the pit bull mauled Purdy. Purdy then sued Dogs-R-Us for breach of implied warranty in Hawaii state court. Based on applicable Hawaii choice-of-law principles, the Hawaii state court would apply Hawaii substantive law to the claim. Hawaii substantive law recognizes a cause of action for breach of implied warranty of living animals.

Dogs-R-Us removed the case and then moved to dismiss for lack of personal jurisdiction. The federal court deferred ruling on that defense. Dogs-R-Us then moved for a transfer of venue to Oregon under § 1404, asserting that the evidence and witnesses concerning the dog's fitness when sold to Purdy were all in Oregon. The court then issued a ruling on both motions, holding that it lacked personal jurisdiction over Dogs-R-Us in Hawaii and that a transfer under § 1404 to Oregon was warranted. Thus, the court transferred the case to the District of Oregon.

In Oregon, Dogs-R-Us moved to dismiss the case, asserting that Oregon choice-of-law principles would require the application of Oregon substantive law, and that Oregon substantive law does not recognize a cause of action for breach of implied warranty of living animals.

Meanwhile, Purdy files a motion to amend his complaint to add a tort claim of negligence against Dogs-R-Us. Both Oregon and Hawaii would recognize such a claim on these facts. However, the limitations period under an Oregon negligence claim expired between the time Purdy filed his original lawsuit and the time Purdy moved to amend his complaint. The limitations period under a Hawaii negligence claim had not expired by the time Purdy filed his motion to amend.

Federal Rule 15(c) allows a claim to relate back to the date of the original complaint if the new claim arises out of the same transaction or occurrence as the original claim. Both Hawaii and Oregon also have analogous rules governing amendments, but their rules specifically disallow relation back of claims. Under both states' laws, an amendment must be made within the time period for the statute of limitations.

Please discuss all choice-of-law issues presented by these facts.

SUGGESTED READINGS

U.S. Const. art. VI, cl. 2
28 U.S.C. § 1652

28 U.S.C. § 2072

Swift v. Tyson, 41 U.S. 1, 14–22 (1842)

Erie R.R. Co. v. Tompkins, 304 U.S. 64, 69–80 (1938)

Guaranty Trust Co. v. York, 326 U.S. 99, 99–112 (1945)

Byrd v. Blue Ridge Rural Elec. Coop., Inc., 356 U.S. 525, 526–40 (1958)

Hanna v. Plumer, 380 U.S. 460, 460–74 (1965)

Walker v. Armco Steel, 446 U.S. 740, 741–53 (1980)

Stewart Org., Inc. v. Ricoh Corp., 487 U.S. 22, 24–33 (1988)

Gasperini v. Ctr. for Humanities, Inc., 518 U.S. 415, 418–39 (1996)

Semtek Int'l Inc. v. Lockheed Martin Corp., 531 U.S. 497, 499–509 (2001)

Dice v. Akron, Canton & Youngstown R.R., 342 U.S. 359, 360–70 (1952)

Clearfield Trust Co. v. United States, 318 U.S. 363, 364–70 (1943)

Ferens v. John Deere Co., 494 U.S. 516, 518–33 (1990)

Shady Grove Orthopedic Assocs. PA v. Allstate Ins. Co., 559 U.S. _ (2010)

SAMPLE ESSAY

1. Double Down

The issue in both *Players v. Double Down* and *Paradise v. Double Down* is whether a settlement privilege attaches to settlement discussions in a previous federal diversity case. Federal common law as understood by the Ninth Circuit recognizes the privilege. Nevada state law does not. Although there are arguments to the contrary, my analysis suggests that the issue is one of federal common law that does not incorporate a state's refusal to recognize the privilege.

I

As an initial matter, neither the Full Faith and Credit Clause nor the Full Faith and Credit Act apply; they govern only the effect of state court judgments. No rules or statutes directly control. Thus, the only source of positive law is judge-made common law.

Erie held that there is no federal *general* common law. What *Erie* meant was that federal courts are not allowed to create, under the sole authority of the diversity statute, a general common law of torts or contracts or commercial paper.

The privilege that would attach to confidential settlement discussions made during federal diversity court proceedings is not the kind of *general* common law held to be unconstitutional in *Erie*. Privilege is not a remedial area of the law such as torts or contracts. It is a transsubstantive rule bound up with the process of settlement and discovery. *Erie* alone, therefore, does not remove federal court authority to develop the law of privilege.

II

If the federal court has constitutional power to create federal law governing the issue here, the next question is what law to apply. Before answering that question, however, there is an interstitial question involving what effect the choice of federal law will have. That interstitial question arises because this Court previously has viewed *Erie* questions in two ways.

In *York*, *Byrd*, *Hanna*, and *Gasperini*, this Court decided whether to apply federal common law or state law in the first instance. In other words, this Court, even though constitutionally able to apply federal common law, instead applied state law if applying federal law would raise the twin fears of *Erie* (forum shopping and inequitable administration of the laws) and no strong federal interest justifies applying federal law anyway.

In *Semtek*, however, this Court announced that federal common law controlled in the first instance but then focused on whether, in the second instance, that federal common law incorporated state law. Whether state law was incorporated depended upon the same kind of factors as mentioned above: whether the twin aims of *Erie* were implicated, and whether there was a strong federal interest that counseled against incorporating federal law.

Although at first glance the analysis under both views is the same, the effects can be very different. In *Erie*, *York*, *Byrd*, and *Gasperini*, the federal rule or standard that applied in federal court would not apply in state courts. State courts would apply their own different rules or standards. That dichotomy then resulted in a continuing conflict between the two judicial systems, giving rise to the twin aims of *Erie*.

In *Semtek*, however, the Supreme Court held that the preclusive effect of a federal judgment (even a federal diversity judgment) is governed by federal law, and that that federal rule applies in state courts as well. In *Semtek*, a plaintiff's diversity claims in California federal court were dismissed on state statute of limitations grounds. The plaintiff refiled in Maryland state court, where the Maryland statute of limitations had not yet run. The defendant moved to dismiss the Maryland case on grounds of claim preclusion. The question was whether federal claim preclusion law or state preclusion law applied. This Court held that federal law governs the claim preclusive effect of all federal judgments, even federal diversity judgments, and that that federal law applied in the Maryland state court. *Semtek* relied on the Supremacy Clause for this last proposition, though it did not go into much explanation of why the Supremacy Clause controlled the particular federal issue of preclusion. As a result, though, federal preclusion law would apply in both federal and state court, potentially creating a uniform federal standard (though *Semtek* ultimately opted for a standard dependent upon state law).

The difference between *Semtek* and *Erie* and its progeny is that the federal common law at issue in *Semtek* controlled in both federal and state court, potentially creating a uniform federal standard that would eliminate the fears of forum shopping and inequitable administration of the laws that concerned *Erie*. By contrast, the rules implicated in *Erie* and its progeny would apply in federal court but not state court, thus creating an intersystem conflict. Accordingly, the question of what state effect the federal rule will have is an antecedent step.

III

A

The usual rule is that the Supremacy Clause directs that substantive federal law controls in state court but that state procedural law governs. Nevertheless, the Supreme Court in *Dice* held that some federal procedural law may control in state court as well. *Dice* confronted procedural rules that were bound up with a federal substantive cause of action. The Court held that state courts hearing the federal cause of action had to apply the accompanying procedural rules as well; otherwise, the federal substantive law could be undermined.

The federal procedural rule here—that settlement discussions in federal court are privileged from discovery in subsequent proceedings—is of a different ilk than the procedural rules in *Dice*. The federal rule is not tied to a particular federal cause of action. Indeed, the rule applies to original diversity actions under state law causes of action.

Nevertheless, restriction of the federal rule to federal court would essentially eviscerate the purpose of the rule. The federal purpose of the rule is to encourage settlement and control the federal court docket by keeping settlement discussions of federal cases confidential. Allowing state law to dictate the privilege issues of confidential federal settlements would undermine their confidential nature and could reduce the number of federal settlements. State law would, in effect, substantially interfere with the exclusive federal interest in federal docket management.

Thus, there are strong policy reasons why the federal rule ought to apply in state court, though it is not clear what legal authority would allow or require such application. No congressional statute so provides. And, it is unclear whether the Supremacy Clause would stretch so far. *Semtek* does provide some support for the application of the federal rule in state court.

Given the strong policy reasons why the federal rule ought to apply and the analogous support of *Semtek*, it is my recommendation that the Supremacy Clause will require the federal rule, if it controls, to apply in state court as well, just as it did in *Semtek*.

B

Even if federal law applies here, the question is what that federal law should be. *Semtek* recognized that federal law can incorporate the state rule. There, although this Court held that federal law governs the preclusive effect of federal diversity judgments, that federal law incorporated state claim preclusion law of the state in which the federal diversity court sat. This Court reasoned that since state, not federal, limitations law was at issue in the underlying dispute, there is no need for federal uniformity. And, any other rule would give rise to the twin aims of Erie. Thus, *Semtek* teaches that if the application of a settlement privilege depends upon federal law, then incorporation of state law nevertheless may be warranted if *Erie* concerns are high and the need for uniformity is low.

As discussed above, the *Erie* concerns are low if the settlement privilege is entitled to preemptive force under the Supremacy Clause and thus will apply in state court as well. Because both state and federal courts are required to privilege settlement communications from a federal proceeding, then there will be no forum shopping or inequitable administration of the laws because all privileging courts will follow the same federal law.

There still might be *Erie* implications in the filing decision of the original settlement parties. In other words, a party might chose federal court over state court if the party wants the settlement privilege to attach to any settlement communications. But those *Erie* concerns are probably fairly low. As *Hanna* explained, the twin aims of *Erie* must be gauged from an ex ante perspective. Few litigants chose a forum based on that forum's rules regarding settlement; if settlement were the expected outcome, mediation would be preferred over litigation. Thus, the *Erie* concerns of the initial filing are low.

Thus, this case is different than *Semtek* because here the incorporation of state law as the federal rule is not justified by strong *Erie* concerns and, as discussed above, would undermine the purposes of the federal rule. As a result, the incorporation of state law into the federal common law is not appropriate.

IV

Although Part III concluded that the Supremacy Clause would require the federal rule to apply in state courts, it is worth discussing what the outcome would be if the federal rule did *not* control in state court. In such a case, this Court should look primarily to *Erie*, *York*, *Byrd*, and *Hanna* to determine whether federal or state law should control in federal court.

Assuming the federal settlement rule would not control in state court, application of the federal settlement privilege rule in federal court implicates the twin aims of *Erie*. Plaintiffs who have claims that will be furthered by discovery of information regarding a confidential settlement will sue in state court, where the privilege does not apply; prospective defendants might try to prevent a state court lawsuit by bringing a declaratory judgment action in federal court instead, or by removing a state case to federal court. The result is rampant forum shopping. Whether the existence of the federal settlement privilege rule would promote inequitable administration of the laws is less clear. The federal rule would tend to benefit out-of-state defendants in the usual case, for those out-of-state defendants could invoke federal jurisdiction and the more favorable federal rule. Inequitable administration would, however, result if the out-of-state party were the party seeking the confidential settlement communications, either as a primary claim or as a counterclaim or cross-claim. In addition, even if out-of-state defendants are primarily benefited by the federal rule, the federal rule still creates inequitable administration of the laws because an in-state defendant would not be able to take advantage of the privilege even if an out-of-state defendant could. For these reasons, the conflict between the federal rule and the state rule likely implicates the twin aims of *Erie*.

Byrd, however, directed the consideration of strong federal interests balanced against these twin aims. In *Byrd*, the federal preference for jury resolution of factual issues overrode the application of state law and *Erie*. Here, federal courts do have a strong interest in the efficient and effective management of their dockets. Encouraging settlement is a reasonable way to do so, and the settlement privilege may effectuate that encouragement. If so, then it is possible that that federal interest could overcome the twin aims of *Erie* and result in the application of federal law.

V

For these reasons, I believe that the privileged status of confidential settlement communications made during a federal court proceeding is governed by federal common law, that that federal common law controls in state court by virtue of the Supremacy Clause, and that that federal common law should not incorporate state law. Even if the federal common law does not have preemptive force of the Supremacy Clause, however, the federal settlement privilege might still apply at least in federal court if the federal interests are strong enough to overcome the twin aims of *Erie*. If not, then the federal court should defer to the state law on the settlement privilege.

2. Dogs-R-Us

ISSUE 1: WHAT SUBSTANTIVE LAW APPLIES TO THE WARRANTY CLAIM?

Under *Klaxon*, a federal district court sitting in diversity applies the choice-of-law principles of the state in which it sits. Under general principles of *Ferens*, if a case is transferred under § 1404, the transferee court applies the law that the transferor court would have applied. Thus, if *Ferens* applies, the District of Oregon should apply the law that the District of Hawaii would have applied, which would be Hawaii choice-of-law principles, which would point to Hawaii substantive law. Accordingly, Dogs-R-Us's motion to dismiss based on Oregon law should be denied.

But, there is a strong argument that *Ferens* should not apply when the transferor court lacked personal jurisdiction over the defendant. (Venue transfer under § 1404, however, was nevertheless lawful under *Goldlawr*.) In such an event, the defendant could never have been subject to the law of the transferor's forum court. Unlike in *Ferens*, in which the plaintiff always had the option of filing in Mississippi and having Mississippi limitations law apply to the claim, Purdy could not have pursued his claim in Hawaii courts because they lacked personal jurisdiction over Dogs-R-Us. Absent some consent to Hawaii personal jurisdiction or Hawaii substantive law by Dogs-R-Us, Hawaii law was never available to Purdy. As a result, Dogs-R-Us can argue that *Ferens* did not address this situation and that, in light of the lack of personal jurisdiction in Hawaii, Hawaii law ought not to apply. In addition, Dogs-R-Us could argue that applying *Ferens* here would result in far more rampant forum shopping than contemplated in *Ferens* because a plaintiff could chose *any* of the 50 states in which to file initially, capture that state's law, and then move to transfer venue to a more convenient location. If this argument is credited, then the transferee court's law (here, Oregon's law) should apply, and Dogs-R-Us's motion to dismiss should be granted.

ISSUE 2: WHAT LIMITATIONS LAW APPLIES TO THE NEGLIGENCE CLAIM?

As noted above, *Klaxon* instructs district courts to apply the state choice-of-law rules of the state in which they sit, but *Ferens* requires transferee courts to apply the law that the transferor court would have applied. This case implicates the issue of which rule controls when the plaintiff adds a new claim *after* a venue transfer. If Hawaii law could not apply because Hawaii could not exercise personal jurisdiction over Dogs-R-Us, then the answer is easy: Oregon law (and its limitations period) would apply. But, assuming Hawaii law is potentially applicable, the question is more difficult.

Hawaii law might apply for a couple of reasons. First, the lawsuit was filed there initially, and because the new claim arises from the same transaction or occurrence as the original claim, the parties would naturally have expected Hawaii law to apply to the new claim as well, had it been filed before transfer. The fact that it was asserted only *after* transfer should not negate the expected applicable law covering all claims related to the underlying transaction—as *Ferens* stated, venue transfer for convenience is not a choice-of-law mechanism. Otherwise, parties might move to transfer venue for purposes of getting access to more favorable law (as, perhaps, Dogs-R-Us attempted to do here). Relatedly, a narrow resolution on the facts of this case might be a rule that requires the transferee law to apply when the transferor's law would be adverse to the party seeking a transfer for convenience.

On the other hand, there are reasons to apply Oregon law (independent of the lack of personal jurisdiction of Hawaii). No Hawaii court ever had the negligence claim before it. Thus, even under *Ferens*, there was nothing that the transferor court could have applied. In addition, the fact pattern in *Ferens* could be read to support the application of the transferee law here. In *Ferens*, the plaintiff filed two lawsuits—one in Pennsylvania and one in Mississippi. The Mississippi lawsuit was transferred to Pennsylvania and joined with the Pennsylvania lawsuit, resulting in two claims in the same lawsuit being governed by two different states' laws. Here, the plaintiff could have easily filed a separate action for negligence in Oregon court and had the cases consolidated. In such as case, as in *Ferens*, the negligence action then would be governed by Oregon law. There is little distinction from a practical standpoint between the two-lawsuit scenario and the amended-lawsuit one. As a result, Oregon law ought to apply to the amended-lawsuit scenario as well. Finally, the narrow rule proposed in the previous paragraph might be unworkable in practice if there are difficulties determining whether a law is favorable or not to a particular party, or whether a party is seeking transfer. *Ferens* itself discussed some of these difficulties and concluded that a nuanced rule for venue choice-of-law was unworkable. Such might be the same case here.

ISSUE 3: WHAT RELATION-BACK LAW APPLIES TO THE NEGLIGENCE CLAIM?

Under *York*, limitations periods for state causes of action generally are governed by state law. The same is true for tolling rules, under *Ragan* and *Walker*. However, under *Hanna*, if a Federal Rule is directly on point, constitutional, and valid under the Rules Enabling Act, then the Federal Rule applies, notwithstanding *Erie*, *York*, or *Byrd*.

Here, Rule 15(c)'s relation-back rule has a direct collision with the state rules. Rule 15(c)(1) does allow relation back whenever state law would allow relation back. But Rule 15(c)(2) also allows relation back even where a state law would not if the new claim arises from the same conduct, transaction, or occurrence as the original claim. Thus, Rule 15(c)(2) applies in this case and specifically applies where the state law does not allow relation back. *Hanna* involved a similar comparison with Rule 4 and held Rule 4 to be on point. More recently, five Justices found in *Shady Grove* that Rule 23 directly collides with a state law prohibiting class actions for statutory penalties, even though the dissent in that case would have read Rule 23 with more sensitivity to state policies. In light of the way the Court has treated arguable collisions in the past, it is clear that Rule 15 directly conflicts with the state rules.

Rule 15(c) is also constitutional. It arguably regulates procedure, which renders it constitutional under Article III and the Necessary and Proper Clause.

It is likely that Rule 15(c) is valid under the Rules Enabling Act (REA), at least as applied here. The REA forbids rules from enlarging, modifying, or abridging any substantive right. Three Justices, following Justice Scalia's opinion in *Shady Grove*, would validate Federal Rules under the REA if they "really regulate procedure." That seems to fit Rule 15(c), which fosters the procedural value of allowing joinder of related claims. Rule 15(c) is not about imposing a federal limitations period; it is a transsubstantive rule that applies to claims whose underlying facts were pleaded timely and that were asserted against defendants who should have known of the new claim within the applicable limitations period. That it also affects the substantive right at stake does not vitiate its primarily procedural character.

But the "really regulates procedure" interpretation may not command the support of a majority of the Justices. If the REA test tracks the REA's language, as Justice Stevens's concurrence and Justice Ginsburg's dissent in *Shady Grove* would hold, then even a truly procedural Federal Rule could be invalid. In determining that question, Justice Stevens would look to the character of the state rule. If the Federal Rule would displace a state law that is procedural in the ordinary use of the term but is so intertwined with a state right or remedy that it functions to define the scope of the state-created right, then the Federal Rule would be invalid as applied to that specific state cause of action because it enlarges a substantive right by allowing a state right to be asserted at a time in which the state courts would bar it.

Applying Justice Stevens's approach is difficult because it is highly case specific. But it seems likely that the Hawaii and Oregon rules are not sufficiently tied to the substantive right at stake. The facts stated that the state rules are general joinder rules that disallow relation back of claims. If such rules could displace Federal Rules, then the state statute at issue in *Shady Grove* should also have limited the applicability of Rule 23, which was not the case for Justice Stevens. Now, if the Hawaii and Oregon rules specifically limited the relation back of amendments for the particular claims at issue, then they might be sufficiently intertwined with the substantive rights at stake under the state laws. But that does not appear to be the case here. As a result, it is likely that even Justice Stevens would find Rule 15(c) to be valid as applied to this case.

Because Rule 15(c) is valid, constitutional, and on point, it applies and controls over conflicting rules of state procedure.

TOOLS FOR SELF-CRITICISM

These hypotheticals may be the most difficult in the entire book. The answers to them are unclear, as are the proper analyses. The most important part of answering these *Erie* questions is how you discuss them. A solid grounding of *Erie* principles and a clear understanding of how the cases fit together will allow you to discuss them intelligently and comprehensively.

A caveat at the outset: Civil procedure course coverage of *Erie* varies widely, and because the hypothetical strives to provide an opportunity for everyone, there may be portions of the hypothetical that are either more detailed or broader in coverage than your particular course would expect. If more detailed, treat the answers as aspirational and do not be intimidated by them. That said, they should be useful in providing you with an opportunity to think deeply about these issues, which should itself help prepare you for even simpler *Erie* questions down the road. If of broader coverage (in particular, some courses may not cover the federal common law cases or *Semtek*), consider focusing on the second hypothetical, though the first hypothetical still may hold significant value for understanding some of the *Erie* basics.

In the first hypothetical, you should note first that there are no issues of federal substantive law at play. Thus, the *Erie* issues are strongly implicated. You then should notice that there are three different lawsuits at issue. Consider diagramming them to keep them straight and for easy reference as you answer the question.

This question also forces you to consider a two-pronged process involving both an initial lawsuit and the effects of that initial lawsuit in two subsequent lawsuits. That scenario ought to raise *Semtek* in your mind, and, as you can see from the sample answer, *Semtek* has much to say about these facts.

The sample answer begins the substantive analysis with a consideration of privilege. Privilege is one of those quasi-substantive, quasi-procedural matters that give diversity courts so much trouble. It is not general common law as *Erie* understood it. But it is the kind of matter that might yield to state law under *York*, for limitations periods are akin to privilege issues here. There is a difference between this and limitations issues, though: The limitations issues in *York* were matters of equity between the parties, whereas the settlement privilege at issue here goes to the important federal policy of maintaining efficient federal docket control. This should cause you to consider *Byrd* and its Seventh Amendment interest. Thus, you should take that federal policy into account when analyzing the *Erie* prong.

Federal common law, though, has other underpinnings, and here is where *Semtek* really comes into play. *Semtek* held that the preclusive effect of federal court judgments is a matter of federal law. Likewise, you should analogize, the protective effect of confidential settlement communications made in federal court should be determined by federal law. There are some differences, and you should explore those in your answer, but *Semtek* provides a nice grounding point for the discussion.

Do not forget, of course, whether the federal law ought to incorporate state law. The Court has indicated a preference for that result, in cases like *Semtek* and *Gasperini*, because of the sensitivity it shows to state law and the discouragement of forum shopping. Naturally, that entails an analysis of the twin aims of *Erie*.

The second hypothetical presents several difficult issues of *Erie* and venue transfers. The easy answer—which you of course should mention—is based on generalizations of *Ferens*—the transferee court applies the transferor court's law. But the lack of personal jurisdiction and the amendment after transfer should give you pause. Do they provide bases for more thoughtful responses? Most would say yes. Use these complications to test the limits of *Ferens* and explore your own application of the underlying *Erie* principles, especially the policy rationale behind the entire *Erie* doctrine.

The last issue presented—on Rule 15(c)—implicates *Hanna* and the recent decision by the Court of *Shady Grove*. Although the Supreme Court has never held a Federal Rule to be beyond the mandate of the REA, there are several rules that are close. Rule 15(c) is one (Rule 68 is another), and so this question forces you to avoid the normally easy REA answer (Federal Rules control) and confront a more difficult analysis. Indeed, the sample answer here concludes that the validity of Rule 15(c) under the REA, as applied to these facts, is only "likely." The true answer may very well be the opposite of how the sample answer concluded—did you so conclude? If so, did your conclusion depend upon how you read Justice Stevens's opinion in *Shady Grove*?

VARIATIONS ON THE THEME

Rule 501 of the Federal Rules of Evidence explains that evidentiary privileges in federal question cases are governed by federal common law, but that evidentiary privileges in diversity cases are governed by the applicable state law. Does Rule 501 change the analysis?

On a related point, what if Rule 26 of the Federal Rules of Civil Procedure specifically stated that confidential settlement communications were privileged from discovery?

How would you answer the questions in the second hypothetical if the venue transfer was based on § 1406 instead of § 1404?

The sample answer explained that, absent some consent to Hawaii personal jurisdiction or Hawaii substantive law by Dogs-R-Us, Hawaii law was never available to Purdy. What if the choice-of-law rules of a different state, perhaps the state of Washington, would have directed a Washington court to apply Hawaii substantive law? Would the mere fact that Hawaii substantive law was available in *some* court change the analysis?

OPTIONAL READINGS

For a thorough treatment of *Erie* and the resulting vertical and horizontal choice-of-law inquiries, see Michael Steven Green, *Horizontal* Erie *and the Presumption of Forum Law*, 109 MICH. L. REV. 1237 (2011).

For more on *Semtek*, particularly implicating some of the issues in the above fact pattern, see Stephen P. Burbank, Semtek, *Forum Shopping, and Federal Common Law*, 77 NOTRE DAME L. REV. 1027 (2002).

For lively debates about the Court's success in its development of the doctrine, compare Richard D. Freer, *Some Thoughts on the State of* Erie *After* Gasperini, 76 TEX. L. REV. 1637 (1998), with Thomas D. Rowe, Jr., *Not Bad for Government Work: Does Anyone Else Think the Supreme Court is Doing a Halfway Decent Job in its* Erie-Hanna *Jurisprudence?*, 73 NOTRE DAME L. REV. 963 (1998).

The background story of *Erie* and the personalities involved are compelling. For more, see Irving Younger, *What Happened in* Erie, 56 TEX. L. REV. 1011 (1978). For more background in a historical context, see EDWARD PURCELL, JR., LITIGATION AND INEQUALITY: FEDERAL DIVERSITY JURISDICTION IN INDUSTRIAL AMERICA, 1870–1958 (1992).

Although the Supreme Court has never so said, the circuit courts largely agree that *Ferens* is restricted to § 1404 transfers, and that § 1406 transferee courts should apply the law of the state in which they sit. *See, e.g.,* Eggleton v. Plasser & Theurer Export von Bahnbaumaschinen Gesellschaft, MBH, 495 F.3d 582 (8th Cir. 2007); Lafferty v. St. Riel, 495 F.3d 72 (3d Cir. 2007); Adam v. J.B. Hunt Transport, Inc., 130 F.3d 219 (6th Cir. 1997); Tel-Phonic Servs., Inc. v. TBS Intern., Inc., 975 F.2d 1134 (5th Cir. 1992).

Some of the issues in the first hypothetical were adapted from Goodyear Tire & Rubber Co. v. Chiles Power Supply, Inc., 332 F.3d 976 (6th Cir. 2003) (recognizing a federal settlement privilege in a diversity case); and Ohio Consumers' Counsel v. Public Utilities Commission, 856 N.E.2d 213 (Ohio 2006) (refusing to recognize a settlement privilege under Ohio law).

The *Ferens* issue in the second hypothetical was resolved in favor of the transferee court in McTyre v. Broward General Medical Center, 749 F. Supp. 102, 108 (D.N.J. 1990).

For a survey of courts struggling with Rule 15(c) and *Hanna*, see Mary Kay Kane, *The Golden Wedding Year:* Erie Railroad Company v. Tomkins *and the Federal Rules*, 63 NOTRE DAME L. REV. 671, 684–90 (1986). For the view that Rule 15(c) exceeds the mandate of the REA, see Stephen D. Easton, Note, *Doe Defendants and Other State Relation Back Doctrines in Federal Diversity Cases*, 35 STAN. L. REV. 297 (1983).

9

THE COMPLAINT, THE ANSWER, AND RULE 12

OPENING REMARKS

Pleadings are documents filed with the court that set out the factual allegations and legal claims of the parties. In federal court, they comprise, primarily, the plaintiff's complaint (and any amendments) and the defendant's answer (and any amendments). Other pleadings generally are not allowed and are rarely seen. A primary purpose of pleadings is to provide notice to the parties and the court of their respective claims and positions.

The plaintiff's complaint initiates the case. It usually sets forth the plaintiff's legal causes of action, factual allegations supporting them, and relief sought. Many complaints also contain a demand for a jury trial. Although the Rules generally require only a "short and plain statement" (though the standard is more rigorous for those allegations specifically identified in Rule 9), most complaints are long and detailed.

When the defendant is served with the plaintiff's complaint, the defendant must serve and file an answer. The answer must respond to each allegation in the plaintiff's complaint by admitting it, denying it, or explaining why it cannot be admitted or denied. The idea is to isolate the areas that require further litigation from the areas that do not. The defendant may also assert affirmative defenses in her answer.

The defendant may also assert her own causes of action in the answer. They may comprise counterclaims against the plaintiff, cross-claims against another defendant, or third-party claims. If the defendant asserts additional claims in her answer, the sufficiency of those claims will be evaluated as if they were a complaint. Similarly, the party defending against those claims will be required to serve and file an answer to them.

Instead of filing an answer, the defendant may attack the complaint by filing a pre-answer motion (which is not a pleading) under Rule 12. Typical motions include a motion to dismiss under Rule 12(b), a motion for a more definite statement under Rule 12(e), and a motion to strike under Rule 12(f). Perhaps the most important of these is the motion to dismiss for failure to state a claim upon which relief can be granted. That motion, governed by Rule 12(b)(6), tests the legal sufficiency of the complaint's allegations and has been the subject of recent turmoil after the Supreme Court's decisions in *Bell Atlantic Corp. v. Twombly* and *Ashcroft v. Iqbal*. If a motion to dismiss for failure to state a claim is granted, the claim usually is dismissed without prejudice, meaning that the plaintiff usually will be allowed to replead to correct the defects.

Pleadings are not verified or made under oath. However, the allegations made in the pleadings (and pre-answer motions) are policed by Rule 11, which requires, under penalty of court sanctions, that they be made in good faith.

Pleadings procedure in the United States has a long and storied history. It was adopted from the English common law, changed dramatically under the Field

Code, and changed again under the Federal Rules. Your professor may provide you with some background on the development of pleadings practice in the United States, or perhaps with a comparison of pleadings practice of other nations, but, for your purposes here, the Federal Rules will be your benchmark.

HYPOTHETICAL

You represent Dan Dastardly regularly. Dastardly is an insurance salesman, and he is very good at it...sometimes too good. He often gets sued for misrepresenting the terms of the insurance and threatening customers if they haven't paid their premiums on time.

On May 1, Dastardly walks into your office and slaps a federal complaint down on your desk. "Got another crazy person suing me in federal court," he says. "He owes me money for a policy I sold him on January 1, 2007. I explained all of the terms and conditions just as they are written in the policy that he agreed to and signed. Well, he never paid a single monthly premium. So, on April 1, I knocked on his door. No one answered, yet I knew he was home because a light was on. But I am a peace-loving guy. So, rather than break down the door, I simply pressed the doorbell...and kept pressing it. I had nothing better to do, and, hey, the guy was avoiding me. Well, after about four hours, the guy finally poked his head out of the second-floor window and yelled that I was trespassing and ordered me to leave. I said okay, but that that was his choice and that if he happened to have an unfortunate accident sometime soon, that wasn't going to be my fault. Then I left."

You review the complaint, which contains 50 numbered allegations and asserts claims for trespass, assault, and fraud. Paragraphs 10–13 of the complaint state the following:

10. On January 1, 2007, Defendant misrepresented the terms and conditions of the insurance policy. For example, Defendant said that premiums would be due every six months when, in fact, the premiums were due every month.
11. On April 2, Plaintiff arrived home through the back door. As he walked upstairs, he heard his doorbell ringing constantly, like it was broken. He poked his head out of the upstairs window and saw Defendant pressing the doorbell so that it rang continuously.
12. Plaintiff politely asked Defendant to leave and explained that he had to make some urgent telephone calls. Defendant then threatened him with bodily harm like some mercenary.
13. Later, Plaintiff heard from neighbors that Defendant had been ringing his doorbell constantly for about four hours prior to Plaintiff's arrival home.

You see that the complaint was filed and served on April 15, and you are immediately worried that you do not have much time left. Assume that subject-matter jurisdiction, personal jurisdiction, venue, service, and joinder are not at issue. Please do all of the following:

A. Discuss what you might do to buy yourself some additional time to file your answer and the likely outcome of your efforts. Do not discuss waiver of service.

B. Discuss what pre-answer motions you might file, what legal and strategic considerations will inform your choices, and what the likely outcomes of those motions would be.

C. Draft answers to the four paragraphs in the complaint and explain what legal and strategic factors caused you to draft them they way you did.

SUGGESTED READINGS

FED. R. CIV. P. 8
FED. R. CIV. P. 9
FED. R. CIV. P. 10
FED. R. CIV. P. 11
FED. R. CIV. P. 12
FED. R. CIV. P. 41
FED. R. CIV. P. Form 11
Bell Atl. Corp. v. Twombly, 550 U.S. 544 (2007)
Ashcroft v. Iqbal, 556 U.S. 662 (2009)
Dioguardi v. Durning, 139 F.2d 774 (2d Cir. 1944)

SAMPLE ESSAY

A. Buying More Time

The easiest way to buy more time to answer the complaint is to request an extension of time from the opposing counsel. Most attorneys are amenable to reasonable extensions, and my explanation that I just received the complaint is sympathetic. I might also offer to be liberal with reasonable extensions that opposing counsel requests in the future. Finally, I might hint that if opposing counsel is not agreeable to an extension, I will consider filing one or more of the motions listed below, which would put more work on him. Reasonable requests for extensions are routinely agreed to by opposing counsel, so my chance of getting an extension seems likely. If I get an agreement to extend my time to answer, I should get opposing counsel to sign a stipulation for an extension of time that must be "so ordered" by the Court.

I also could ask the plaintiff's attorney to voluntarily dismiss the complaint under Rule 41. That obviously would provide me more time because an answer would be unnecessary unless and until he filed a new complaint. However, without some reason to do so in the plaintiff's own interests, it seems unlikely that the plaintiff would choose to voluntarily dismiss because the plaintiff only gets one voluntary dismissal as of right, and he may wish to save that. If, however, I could point to something in the complaint that might be sanctionable under Rule 11, he might be interested in dismissing the complaint. In addition, I might suggest that he voluntarily dismiss the complaint in exchange for Dastardly's agreement to engage in good faith alternative dispute resolution (ADR), such as mediation. I would have to get Dastardly's commitment to do so before agreeing to mediation, and, it is likely that I would also have to agree to waive any statute of limitations defense if the mediation runs beyond the statute of limitations and no new lawsuit is filed within it. In sum, this option might be worth exploring, but, on balance, there are probably too many moving parts for it to be effective.

If there are defects in the complaint, I could point them out to the plaintiff's attorney and suggest that he might wish to file an amended complaint under Rule 15(a) correcting the defects (because if he does not, I will consider filing motions attacking the complaint anyway). If he does elect to amend his complaint (which he may do as of right) and file and serve the complaint within the next few days, I will have a new 14 days from the date of service of the amended complaint to file an answer.

If opposing counsel refuses these options, I have two options for getting more time. First, I could file with the Court a motion for extension of time—before the deadline expires—even without the plaintiff's consent. Extensions of time are routinely granted under Rule 6(b)(1) for good cause, and the time to answer is not subject to the exceptions in Rule 6(b)(2). I likely would argue that it would be just to allow the extension (perhaps because I could not file an answer that complies with Rule 11 in that time) and nonprejudicial to the plaintiff. Second, I could file a motion under Rule 12(b)(6) or Rule 12(e). Under Rule 12(a), such a motion will delay the need to answer until the motion has been decided. The motion must be made in good faith, however, or I may be subject to sanctions under Rule 11, so I should be careful to ensure that there is a colorable basis for so moving. I discuss these in more detail in Part B below.

If none of these options work, I have two remaining options. First, I could file a timely answer and, even if defective, seek to amend the answer, which I can do as of right within 21 days. Of course, filing an answer that lacks a good faith basis might subject me to sanctions, but the safe harbor provision of Rule 11 would allow me to correct my answer by amendment without fear of sanctions. Second, I could not answer at all, suffer default, and attempt to set aside the default. This is, of course, extremely risky.

B. Pre-Answer Motions

I could file a Rule 12(b)(6) motion to dismiss for failure to state a claim on which relief could be granted. The trespass and assault claims would be evaluated under the pleading standard of Rule 8, which sets a relatively low bar. *See Dioguardi v. Durning.* The Rule 8 requirement, however, has been complicated recently by *Bell Atlantic v. Twombly* and *Ashcroft v. Iqbal*, which may provide more opportunity to argue my motion. Those cases require "plausibility" of the complaint's allegations before a claim is stated. Thus, I could argue that the allegations do not rise to the level of plausibility. On the other hand, even the allegations provided are suggestive enough of the claim that they probably meet the plausibility standard. Indeed, Form 11, as a model complaint for what would be required of the kind of garden-variety tort alleged here, suggests as much. Nevertheless, *Twombly* and *Iqbal* probably should be read as inviting more Rule 12(b)(6) filings and more dismissal grants, and arguing that the complaint fails the plausibility test here likely satisfies the good faith strictures of Rule 11, so I would probably file the motion even were I unlikely to win.

The fraud claim, however, must meet the heightened pleading standard of Rule 9. Rule 9(b) requires the circumstances constituting fraud to be stated with particularity (i.e., the who, what, when, where, and why). Paragraph 10 does provide a concrete example of premium due dates, and that allegation probably is sufficient to allege fraud in that instance. I might seek confirmation from a documentary source for the allegation that the premiums were due every month, but the court probably would respond that such evidence is for discovery, not pleading (even under Rule 9). I might be more successful in moving to dismiss any other fraud or misrepresentation claims outside of the specific example provided in the second sentence of Paragraph 10, and such a motion might be successful because the bare allegation of misrepresentation in the first sentence of Paragraph 10 likely is stated too generally to satisfy Rule 9's particularity requirement.

Even were I to succeed on a Rule 12(b)(6) motion, the plaintiff likely would be given leave to amend the complaint to cure the defects and replead the claim. Nevertheless, as long as it complies with Rule 11, the motion is a good strategic move because it will cause the plaintiff to expend resources opposing the motion and allow me time to get my own facts straight.

Although I have been careful to suggest a Rule 12(b)(6) motion only if it complies with Rule 11, it nonetheless may strike me as an odious act if I am using it primarily to gain time or to increase the cost pressures on my opponent. As a result, I should talk this option over carefully with my client and ask myself whether this is really an option I wish to pursue.

I also could file a Rule 12(e) motion for a more definite statement. This motion is unlikely to be granted unless the complaint is "so vague or ambiguous that a party cannot reasonably prepare a response." Here, I might attack Paragraph 10, which states neither whether the due date of the premiums is the only misrepresentation alleged nor, if it is not, what the other misrepresentations alleged are. I might also attack Paragraph 11, which appears to have an incorrect date. However, these defects probably are not so vague or ambiguous that I could not prepare a response. It would not be difficult to structure an answer that appropriately addressed them. In addition, filing the motion would obligate me to point to defects in the complaint, essentially doing the plaintiff's attorney's homework for him. And, any defect could be cured even if my motion is granted. Accordingly, unless some other portions of the complaint are vague or ambiguous, I probably would not file this motion.

I also could file a Rule 12(f) motion to strike the simile "like a mercenary." Rule 12(f) allows motions to strike any "redundant, immaterial, impertinent, or scandalous matter." As a non-litigation strategic matter, this may be important to protect Dastardly's business reputation. This motion also may be granted if the court believes that the simile is unnecessary and pejorative.

C. Draft Answers

In crafting these answers, I kept in mind (1) the legal obligation to respond to each and every allegation without vague or evasive answers (under penalty of having the allegation be deemed to be admitted), (2) the need to avoid negative pregnant answers and conjunctive denials, and (3) the general goal to admit only those facts that are necessary to admit and deny the rest, paragraph by paragraph. These answers also are based on the assumption that I have fulfilled my obligation under Rule 11 to make a good faith assessment of the truth of Dastardly's version of the facts.

10. Defendant admits that he explained the terms and conditions of the insurance policy to Plaintiff on January 1, 2007, and that the premiums were due every month, but denies the remaining allegations in this paragraph.

11. Defendant admits that Plaintiff poked his head out of the upstairs window and that, at the time, Defendant was pressing the doorbell so that it rang continuously, but Defendant denies that these events happened on April 2. Defendant is without sufficient information to admit or deny the remaining allegations in this paragraph.
12. Defendant admits that Plaintiff ordered him to leave but denies the remaining allegations in this paragraph.
13. Defendant lacks sufficient information to admit or deny the allegations in this paragraph.

TOOLS FOR SELF-CRITICISM

This hypothetical provides an opportunity to apply some practical and creative strategies to achieve a particular result. Litigation is often about more than just what is allowed under the rules; it often is about which lawful options are the best strategically. Thus, this question calls for you not only to define the legal parameters of litigation conduct but also to think creatively and strategically about what options are available within those confines.

Thus, the first part of the question asks you to discuss how you can extend the time you have to file your answer. Did you ignore the practical option of dealing directly with the plaintiff's attorney? You might have been tempted to focus on the motions you could file with the court. You certainly should discuss the motion for extension of time and the Rule 12(b)(6) or Rule 12(e) motions, as the sample essay does, but do not forget the potentially easier, practical solutions. One methodology for answering this kind of question to ensure that you cover it fully might be to brainstorm all the ways to get more time first, and then go back to discuss how viable they are.

Did you mention other practical considerations, like filing a 12(f) motion to strike the simile "like a mercenary?" As the sample answer points out, this statement could harm Dastardly's business reputation. Did you recognize this potential harm as something you should attempt to prevent as his lawyer? Consider what your strategic, legal, and ethical obligations might be if you actually believed that the simile was an accurate representation of what happened.

Ideally, you remembered to comply with Rule 11 throughout your answer. You should not have decided to file bad-faith motions for strategic reasons. Regardless of the benefits to your client, you cannot file a motion if you are fully aware that it has no merit. Relatedly, even motions that comply with Rule 11 might give either you or your client ethical pause. What might you do in such a situation? (This is not necessarily something you will want to discuss in any depth on an exam, but it is something you may confront in practice!)

Did you mention *Bell Atlantic v. Twombly* or *Ashcroft v. Iqbal* in your answer? If not, why not? Because the question calls for a discussion of the likely outcomes of the pre-answer motions, you should have discussed *Twombly* and *Iqbal* objectively. However, if the question had elicited a persuasive answer, you could have argued that their plausibility standard either does or does not apply to tort claims. Do not omit important precedent based on an ambiguity. Instead, use the ambiguity to show both sides of the issue or, in this case, consider its potential effects on the outcome of your motion.

Your client told you that he knocked on the plaintiff's door on April 1. The plaintiff's complaint, however, states that this occurred on April 2. Did you catch this error? While it may seem insignificant, you never know what repercussions this particular discrepancy could have. If you fail to deny an allegation in the plaintiff's complaint, you are deemed to have admitted the allegation. Given this rule, it is not in your client's best interest for you to ignore anything in the plaintiff's complaint with which Dastardly disagrees. Make sure you do not ignore any factual errors—even if they seem insignificant—when drafting your answer.

On the flip side, do not make too much of the error. It almost certainly is an error that will be corrected immediately and leave no residual effect. It would be too cute by half to deny Paragraph 11 in its entirety simply because the allegation began with an incorrect date. The safer and more productive course is to admit or deny the substance of the allegations and then point out the incorrect date.

Note the difference between a stipulation for an extension of time and a motion for extension of time. Both are permitted (as long as they are so ordered by the court). Stipulations are routinely granted by opposing counsel in a tit-for-tat spirit and are routinely ordered by the court unless there is some persuasive reason not to so order them. Motions will be made if the opposing counsel refuses to stipulate and just contain additional justifications for the court to order. Importantly, they are two different options that you should have discussed separately.

VARIATIONS ON THE THEME

Assume that the events surrounding Dastardly's sale of the insurance policy happened on January 1, 2000, and that is what the complaint alleges. The statute of limitations on the claims has therefore expired. Would that change your Rule 12 analysis? What if the events happened on January 1, 2000, but the complaint does not mention that date? What might you put in your answer?

Suppose that Question A had not stated "Do not discuss waiver of service." How might you discuss waiver of service?

In drafting motions or your answer, what would your obligations be under Rule 11 if you knew, as Dastardly's regular attorney, that Dastardly was prone to misrepresenting the facts of his case?

Say that Paragraph 12 stated "Defendant then threatened him with Abu-Ghraib-style torture." Would that alter the viability of your motion to strike? *See* Alvarado-Morales v. Digital Equip. Corp., 843 F.2d 613, 618 (1st Cit. 1988) (striking similar allegations).

Consider what additional information you might voluntarily assert in your answer if Dastardly's business were likely to be affected by one-sided allegations made public by the complaint.

If you filed a Rule 12(f) motion before any other motion or answer, have you waived any defenses? *See* Fed. R. Civ. P. 12(h).

Change the allegation in Paragraph 13 to the following: "Upon information and belief, Defendant had been ringing Plaintiff's doorbell for about four hours prior to Plaintiff's arrival home." How would you answer?

OPTIONAL READINGS

The Supreme Court's decision in *Bell Atlantic v. Twombly* was the first significant pronouncement on pleading standards in 50 years. As a result, the scholarly commentary on the case and the future of pleading is particularly voluminous, even for such a recent case. *See* Scott Dodson, *The Mystery of* Twombly *Continues*, PRAWFSBLAWG (Feb. 5, 2008) (collecting sources as of early 2008). *Ashcroft v. Iqbal* answered many of the questions that *Twombly* raised, and some commentators have argued that *Iqbal* and *Twombly* represent a sea change in pleading standards from a liberal notice regime to a factual-sufficiency focus. *See, e.g.,* Scott Dodson, *Beyond* Twombly, CIVIL PROCEDURE PROF BLOG (May 18, 2009).

The U.S. pleading system is the most lax pleading system in the world. Nearly all other countries require more factual allegations than the Federal Rules do. For more on a comparative perspective, see Scott Dodson, *Comparative Convergences in Pleading Standards*, 158 U. PA. L. REV. 441 (2010); OSCAR G. CHASE ET AL., CIVIL LITIGATION IN COMPARATIVE CONTEXT 166–73 (West 2007).

Different statutes can impose different pleading standards for their substantive causes of action. For example, the Private Securities Litigation Reform Act of 1995 imposes pleading standards that are even more restrictive than Rule 9. *See* 15 U.S.C. § 78u-4(b). For a good overview of the PSLRA's pleading standards, see Hilary A. Sale, *Heightened Pleading and Discovery Stays: An Analysis of the Effect of the PSLRA's Internal-Information Standard on '33 and '34 Act Claims*, 76 WASH. U. L.Q. 537 (1998).

For an intriguing argument that *Twombly*'s standard makes Rule 12(b)(6) dismissals unconstitutional under the Seventh Amendment, see Suja A. Thomas, *Why the Motion to Dismiss is Now Unconstitutional*, 92 MINN. L. REV. 1851 (2008).

Although this question did not test knowledge of Rule 11 much, the history of it is fascinating. For more, see Carl Tobias, *The 1993 Revision to Federal Rule 11*, 70 IND. L.J. 171 (1994).

10

SERVICE

OPENING REMARKS

So, you have drafted the complaint, paying close attention to Rule 8 and with an eye toward surviving a motion to dismiss under Rule 12. But how do you actually start the lawsuit? You first must "commence" the action under Rule 3 by filing a complaint with a federal court. Then, you need to "serve" a copy of the as-filed complaint and a copy of the official court summons on all defending parties.

Service of process ("process" is the summons and complaint) thus begins the court's power over the lawsuit and parties. That power may be properly exercised under the doctrines of subject-matter jurisdiction and personal jurisdiction, but service of process is the procedural initiation of that power to a specific case. Although service is related to personal jurisdiction, service and personal jurisdiction are separate and often independent requirements. Thus, the mere fact that a defendant is properly served usually does not automatically extend personal jurisdiction over that defendant. Rule 4(k) is akin to a federal court long-arm statute, and service is tied to the exercise of personal jurisdiction under that rule. Satisfaction of Rule 4(k) is *necessary* but not *sufficient* to establish personal jurisdiction over the defendant.

Service of process rules are set out in great detail in Rule 4, but a general summary is appropriate here. Service may be made by a number of different persons—except, somewhat oddly, by a party, including the plaintiff himself. Service is usually made by a professional process server for a fee. Service also may be made in a number of different ways, such as via personal service or leaving process with someone of suitable age and discretion at the defendant's residence. Once service is accomplished, the process server normally files a "proof of service" in court, usually by affidavit under penalty of perjury, which explains how she served the defendant. The proof of service is presumptive evidence of effective service.

Process servers have broad leeway in accomplishing service, but some courts have held service ineffective when the process server uses trickery or deceit to effect service. In addition, the common law has recognized immunity from service when the defendant is in the state to participate in a different case.

The defendant can waive service. In fact, the Federal Rules encourage waiver. The justification is that, although service is an important component of notice and a formal component of the court's jurisdiction, the costs of effecting formal service can be high. Thus, the defendant has a duty to avoid causing unnecessary expenses of service. If the plaintiff formally notifies the defendant of the lawsuit in compliance with Rule 4(d)(1), and the defendant fails to waive service without good cause, then the defendant will be liable for expenses later incurred in formally effecting service. If, however, the defendant waives service, then the defendant receives a reward—60 days to answer the complaint, instead of the 21 days normally imposed by Rule 12. Consistent with the view that service and jurisdiction are separate, Rule 4 specifies that waiver of service does not waive personal jurisdiction or venue.

Service defects in either the documents or the method can be raised via a motion to dismiss under Rule 12(b).

Service of other papers besides the summons is governed by Rule 5, which provides more liberal methods of service after the defendants have been properly summoned by the court.

HYPOTHETICAL

On January 1, 2007, Paulie Pavarotti is fired from the Bearcat Bar in New York City by Dina Diva, the bar's night manager. Paulie wishes to sue both Dina and Bearcat, Inc. for gender discrimination under Title VII, a federal statute. On June 1, 2008, after complying with any pre-suit statutory requirements, Paulie files his complaint in the Southern District of New York based on federal-question jurisdiction.

Paulie mails, using first class mail, return receipt requested, a copy of the summons and complaint that is addressed to each defendant. He mails Dina's to her home in Samford, Connecticut. He mails Bearcat's to Dina at the Bearcat Bar in Manhattan. In each, he includes a copy of the waiver form and a self-addressed stamped envelope for return of waiver. He also includes a copy of Form 5. Finally, Paulie states the date the request was sent, names the court where the complaint was filed, and gives each defendant 45 days to return the waiver.

Paulie receives return receipts from the post office, confirming delivery of both requests. Nevertheless, 45 days pass without either defendant returning the waiver. Accordingly, Paulie turns to other methods of service.

Paulie gives his mother, who lives in Ft. Lauderdale, Florida, a copy of the summons and asks her to serve Dina at her winter home in Boca Raton, Florida. On September 10, 2008, she knocks on the door of Dina's Boca Raton home. A 30-something woman named Cheryl Green answers, and Paulie's mother gives her a copy of the summons. Paulie's mother then files a proof of service with the court.

Paulie also hires Bobby Brown, a 17-year-old paper delivery boy, to give a copy of the summons and complaint to Dina. Bobby delivers the Sunday *New York Times* to Dina at Dina's summer home in Samford, Connecticut. On August 10, 2008, Bobby hides the copy of the summons and complaint in Dina's paper and throws the paper to Dina's door. While Bobby watches, Dina opens the door and picks up the paper. Bobby then shouts, "Consider yourself served!" and pedals away. Bobby does not file a proof of service with the court.

Finally, Paulie discovers that Dina receives a daily digest from a community e-mail listserv on Samford happenings. The digest typically includes four or five e-mail posts a day. New York state law requires service of the summons and complaint to be made by (1) personal service or (2) e-mail, if the defendant acknowledges receipt by similar means. Accordingly, Paulie asks his friend, Ryan Redford, who happens to be the moderator of the Samford listserv, to post a message about the case and include a copy of the summons and complaint. Ryan does so on September 20, 2008. The listserv includes an acknowledgment function that, unless disabled by the individual user, automatically generates a receipt acknowledgment to the listserv moderator for each listserv e-mail that is opened. Ryan files a proof of service affidavit with the court, averring that he received an e-mail acknowledgment from Dina.

Paulie hires a process serving company to serve Bearcat. The process server who carries Paulie's papers, Trixie, is a 25-year-old door-to-door salesperson who moonlights as a process server during off hours. On September 15, 2008, she walks a copy of the summons and complaint to Bearcat's headquarters offices in Manhattan. A receptionist greets her and asks where she is headed. Trixie responds that she would like to see the CEO. The receptionist refuses to let Trixie in without an appointment. Trixie then states that she has a summons and complaint that needs to be served. The receptionist responds that she would be happy to take the papers from Trixie and deliver them to the CEO for her. Trixie obliges. Later, Trixie files a proof of service affidavit with the court.

The Southern District of New York requires electronic case filing (ECF) for all new cases filed after January 1, 2005. The terms of ECF require all parties to file pleadings and motions with the court and on each other via an uploading system on the court website that then distributes the filing to all parties via e-mail. By filing suit and not requesting an exemption from ECF filing, plaintiffs give written consent to receive service of papers filed in the case via the ECF system. On September 30, 2008, both defendants enter appearances in the case via ECF, consent to ECF service of papers, and immediately receive copies of the summonses and complaint.

In addition, on September 30, 2008, Dina files, via ECF, a motion to dismiss for insufficient service of process. In support of her motion, Dina states that it is her regular habit to spend exactly six months in Samford, from March 15 through September 15 every year, and the balance of her time in Boca Raton. She states that she arrived in Boca Raton on September 15, 2008. She rents the basement suite of her Boca Raton home to Cheryl Green, who has rented it for the last six years. As part of the rental arrangement, Cheryl agrees to maintain the home while Dina is in Connecticut and send Dina any mail or other important papers that arrive. Cheryl and Dina, however, had some disputes about damages to the home in early 2008 and, as a result, have not been on good terms since. In particular, Cheryl has refused to give Dina her mail or messages delivered to the Boca Raton home while Dina is in Connecticut. In addition, Cheryl has withheld rent since June. In response, in late August, Dina told Cheryl that she was terminating their rental agreement, effective immediately, and that she expected Cheryl to move out by October 1, 2008, which Cheryl did. Before leaving, Cheryl apparently burned all of Dina's mail, including the summons delivered by Paulie's mother. She did, however, mention to Dina when she arrived on September 15, that some woman had brought her a summons of a lawsuit involving Paulie.

Dina admits that she received a copy of the summons and complaint from Bobby's Sunday *Times* on August 10, 2008. She also admits that, on September 20, 2008, she received and read the e-mail listserv digest that contained a copy of Paulie's summons and complaint and that she downloaded both documents on that day. However, Dina states that she disabled the listserv receipt acknowledgment function in April 2008 and never re-enabled it.

On September 30, 2008, Bearcat also files, via ECF, a motion to dismiss for insufficient service of process. In its motion, the company states that it is a bar-owning business incorporated in Delaware with its principal place of business in Manhattan. Bearcat owns more than a dozen bars in New York and more than 50 in the United States. Bearcat has appointed Larry Lawless, Bearcat's CEO, as its agent authorized to receive and accept service of process. Lawless offices are located in Bearcat's Manhattan headquarters. Bearcat states that the receptionist that took process from Trixie is not specifically authorized to receive process. However, Bearcat admits that the receptionist is authorized to receive and accept other mail deliveries. She is a long-time employee of the company who routinely takes important communications directly to high-level managers of the company, including the CEO. Bearcat also admits that, on June 15, 2008, Dina transmitted to Bearcat's general counsel the waiver request papers that were sent to her at the Bearcat Bar.

Paulie now hires you to represent her in this matter. Please provide Paulie with an objective analysis of the legal and factual issues involved in the motions.

SUGGESTED READINGS

FED. R. CIV. P. 3
FED. R. CIV. P. 4
FED. R. CIV. P. 5
FED. R. CIV. P. 12
FED. R. CIV. P. Form 5
Nat'l Equip. Rental, Ltd. v. Szukhent, 375 U.S. 311, 312–18 (1964).
Nat'l Dev. Co. v. Triad Holding Corp., 930 F.2d 253, 254–58 (2d Cir. 1991)
Direct Mail Specialists, Inc. v. Eclat Computerized Techs., Inc., 840 F.2d 685, 686–89 (9th Cir. 1988)

SAMPLE ESSAY

ISSUE 1: Was the waiver request proper?

Perhaps, as to Dina. Rule 4(d) requires a waiver request to be in writing and addressed to the individual defendant; name the court where the complaint was filed; be accompanied by a copy of the complaint, two copies of the waiver form, and a prepaid means for returning the form; inform the defendant of the text in Form 5; state the date when the request was sent; give the defendant a reasonable time of at least 30 days to return the waiver; and be sent by first class mail. Paulie did all of these things for Dina except include two copies of the waiver form. Paulie should argue that he substantially complied with the waiver requirements and that a failure to include an extra copy of the waiver form should not defeat his waiver request, particularly when the policy underlying the waiver provision is an encouragement to both parties to avoid the costs of formal service. Dina, however, may argue that the waiver requirements are set forth in specific detail, and therefore compliance with the letter of the law is critical. It is unclear what a court would do.

The waiver request probably was not proper, as to Bearcat. Paulie failed to meet two of the requirements for requesting waiver from Bearcat. First, Paulie failed to include two copies of the waiver form. As discussed above, this failure itself may be fatal to Paulie's waiver request. But Paulie also failed to properly address the request. Rule 4(d)(1)(A) requires the request to be addressed "to an officer, a managing or general agent, or any other agent authorized by appointment or by law to receive service of process." Here, Paulie addressed the waiver request to Dina at the Bearcat Bar, just one of several bars owned by Bearcat, Inc. Dina is a location manager, probably not the kind of officer or managing agent contemplated by Rule 4(d) who would transmit the waiver request to those within the company with decision-making authority on such matters. Had Paulie addressed his waiver form to the CEO or to some other high-level manager or officer at Bearcat's headquarters offices, Paulie might have met that requirement. But addressing it to Dina, one of a number of low-level managers without express or implied authority to receive such papers, is unlikely to validate the waiver request. Accordingly, Bearcat probably did not receive effective service of the waiver request.

ISSUE 2: If the waiver request was proper, what are the repercussions?

If a court holds that either defendant was properly sent a waiver request, then such defendant will be liable for Paulie's expenses in effecting formal service and Paulie's reasonable expenses in bringing a motion to collect those expenses. Rule 4(d)(2) requires the court to cost shift if the defendant received a proper waiver request and failed to return the waiver without good cause. Here, there does not appear to be good cause for either defendant's failure to return the waiver. It appears that both defendants actually received the waiver request, and the facts provide no legal reason why formal service should be implemented. Accordingly, if a court finds that a waiver request was proper, then the court likely will also find that defendant liable for Paulie's expenses under Rule 4(d)(2).

ISSUE 3: Assuming the request was improper, was service on Dina effective?

Maybe. Rule 4(e) allows service on an individual via four methods: (1) in accordance with state law, (2) by delivering a copy of the summons and complaint to the defendant personally, (3) by leaving a copy of process at the individual's dwelling or usual place of abode with someone of suitable age and discretion who resides there, and (4) by delivering a copy of process to an agent authorized by appointment or law to receive it. In all cases, Rule 4(c) requires service of the summons to be made with a copy of the complaint and by a person who is at least 18 years old. Paulie attempted to serve Dina by each of these authorized means.

Rule 4(l) ultimately requires proof of service, but Bobby's failure to file an affidavit proving service does not affect the *validity* of the service that was made (it just means that proof will be needed later). Nevertheless, Bobby's attempt at personal service still was ineffective because it was made by a 17-year-old and thus fails Rule 4(c)'s majority-age requirement. Otherwise, personal service by Bobby may well have been proper.

Paulie filed to include a copy of the complaint with the summons left at Dina's Boca Raton home, and thus that service attempt also fails Rule 4(c). In addition, service was made on September 10, when Dina's usual place of abode likely was Samford, not Boca Raton. Although in *National Development Co.*, service was held effective when made at 1 of 12 residences that the defendant owned and frequented, the court held it meaningful that the defendant was physically residing in that residence at the time of service. Here, Dina had yet to arrive at her Boca Raton home when service was made there. As such, it is likely that the Boca Raton home was not Dina's usual place of abode at the time of service. Finally, it is not clear whether Cheryl Green was a person of "suitable...discretion" because she and Dina had a somewhat adversarial business relationship that ceased to be contractual in late August and had deteriorated into open hostility by the time of attempted service. The Rule's requirement is designed to ensure that person can be trusted to pass service along to the defendant. Here, given the relationship between Dina and Cheryl, such a trust would be misplaced.

Paulie might argue that Cheryl Green also was Dina's agent to receive process while Dina was in Samford. Under the Supreme Court's interpretation of Rule 4, the agent must be specifically authorized to receive process. *Szukhent*. Here, it appears that Dina's rental agreement with Cheryl obligated Cheryl to receive and transmit Dina's mail until September 15 each year. But a rental agreement to receive and transmit mail does not necessarily transform the obligor into an agent, authorized by appointment or law, to receive process. Unlike in *Szukhent*, the rental agreement did not specifically designate Cheryl as an agent authorized to receive process. Even if so, the rental agreement was terminated by Dina in late August, thereby likely retracting any agency authorization Cheryl had. Accordingly, it is unlikely that service on Cheryl was service on an authorized agent under Rule 4(e)(2)(C).

However, Paulie's attempt to use methods prescribed under state law may have been effective. Rule 4(e)(1) allows a plaintiff to follow state law for service, even if jurisdiction is founded upon a federal question. State law allows service via electronic means if the defendant acknowledges receipt by similar means. "Electronic means" is not defined in the fact pattern, but that term is broad and would seem to encompass listserv e-mails. If so, then the only question is whether receipt was acknowledged "by similar means," also an undefined term. It may be that Dina's admission in her motion that she received the listserv e-mail is an acknowledgment of receipt by similar means because the motion was made via electronic filing. If so, then service may have been effective, even if the receipt was not acknowledged until many weeks after service was attempted. If, however, "by similar means" is construed narrowly to exclude electronic court filings in this circumstance, then Dina's admission of receipt was effective only if her listserv acknowledgment function was enabled. On this point, there is a contradiction between Ryan Redford's proof of service and Dina's assertion of fact in her motion. Usually, the facts alleged in a filed proof of service presumptively control, and therefore Dina has a high burden to rebut them. It is unlikely that Dina's allegations in her motion suffice at this point in time. However, because the factual issue is discrete and should be readily ascertainable, the court may wish to allow some limited discovery to resolve it. If Dina cannot meet her burden to rebut Ryan's proof of service, then service will be effective.

ISSUE 4: Assuming the request was improper, was service on Bearcat effective?

Unclear. Paulie's attempt to serve Bearcat has problems. Rule 4(h) requires service on a corporation by any means authorized under state law for service on an individual or by delivering a copy of the summons and complaint to an officer, managing or general agent, or any other agent authorized by appointment or law to receive service of process. The hypothetical does not suggest any opportunities for service under state law, and it was already concluded above that service on Dina at Bearcat likely was not service upon an officer or managing or general agent. Thus, the question becomes whether Trixie's service upon the receptionist qualifies.

In determining who is an appropriate level officer or managing agent for receipt of service, courts look to the level of responsibility and authority that person has. In other words, most courts ask whether equating service on an employee to service on the employer would be fair, reasonable, and just. In *Direct Mail Specialists*, the Ninth Circuit concluded that a receptionist could in fact be served with process where the company was relatively small, the receptionist's role was relatively large (indeed, she was the only one in the office at the time), and where the receptionist actually transmitted the service of process promptly.

Some facts here are akin to those in *Direct Mail Specialists*. Bearcat has authorized the receptionist to receive and accept mail and courier deliveries, including important communications to high-level managers of the company, including the CEO. These facts suggest that Bearcat has entrusted the receptionist with a high level of responsibility for accepting and transmitting important papers that could include process papers.

On the other hand, Bearcat seems to be a much larger company than the defendant in *Direct Mail Specialists*. In addition, Bearcat has officially authorized someone else in the organization as a designated agent to receive process and has not specifically authorized the receptionist to receive it. Finally, it is unclear whether or not the receptionist actually transmitted the process papers to the CEO or some other corporate officer.

Because the facts are not identical to those of *Direct Mail Specialists*, it is unclear how a court might hold on this issue. If the receptionist provided proper transmission of the process papers to the CEO, then a court would be more likely to hold service effective. If not, then a court would be less likely. In addition, the court may wish to hear additional evidence on the level of authority the receptionist has within the corporation.

ISSUE 5: Did actual receipt of process cure any defects in service?

No. The fact that Dina and Bearcat actually received timely notice of the lawsuit and copies of the summons and complaint will not cure defects in service. Just as the Due Process Clause in the Constitution does not require actual notice, nothing in Rule 4 requires actual service. The touchstone is the method, not the result. Actual receipt of process may be relevant in determining whether service was effective (such as in the discussion above in Issue 4), but actual service will not cure any defects.

ISSUE 6: If service and waiver were ineffective, what are the repercussions?

If the court finds that service was ineffective and not waived by one or both defendants, then the court likely will grant the motions to dismiss the complaint. (The motions were properly served on Paulie under Rule 5(b), which authorizes service by electronic means, including ECF, if the opposing party consents in writing.) In addition, more than 120 days have expired since Paulie filed his complaint with the court. Rule 4(m) requires service of process to be made on a defendant within 120 days of the commencement of the action. However, Rule 4(m) also requires a court to extend the time for service for an appropriate period if the plaintiff can show good cause for the failure. Here, Paulie has been diligent in attempting service in a variety of ways, at least on Dina. However, Paulie has made some obvious errors in his service attempts. The facts do not indicate that Dina has intentionally avoided service or made proper service difficult. There is some indication that Bearcat's receptionist may have done so by misleading (perhaps unintentionally) the process server into believing that such service would be effective, but it is unlikely that these actions amount to good cause. Still, defendants are under a duty to avoid unnecessary expenses of serving the summons under Rule 4(d)(1). There seems to be no question that both defendants have received actual notice of the lawsuit and even actual copies of the summons and complaint. Assuming there are no outstanding bars to suit, there would be little benefit to dismissing the complaint just to require Paulie to attempt service yet again. A court might simply hold that the service attempts to date were insufficient and allow the plaintiff time to try again. If, however, a court does dismiss for insufficient service of process, the dismissal will be without prejudice to Paulie refiling his action.

TOOLS FOR SELF-CRITICISM

It would be very easy to get lost or distracted in this hypothetical because there are lots of facts, several key issues, and a question that asked you to discuss the issues without identifying them for you. Thus, not only must you analyze the key issues, you also must identify them yourself. Some find it easiest to bifurcate the answering process by identifying all of the issues first and then going back to analyze each one thoroughly. Others identify an issue then answer it before moving on to identifying a different issue. Figure out which way works best for you. If you find that you are not identifying all of the key issues, try the former. If you find that you are identifying the issues but not addressing them in sufficient depth, consider trying the latter.

When confronted with this type of problem, pay close attention to the facts, no matter how small, in determining whether a fact is pertinent to an issue or irrelevant. For example, the hypothetical provides both Bobby's and Cheryl's ages. Although easily overlooked, their ages matter because the service rules contain age requirements. Bobby did not meet Rule 4(c)'s majority-age requirement, and as such, Bobby's personal service was ineffective. On the other hand, Cheryl, at age 32, did meet Rule 4(e)'s requirement that process be left at the individual's dwelling with someone of suitable age. Consequently, it is important to know and review the applicable rules before dismissing particular facts as irrelevant.

The first issue, whether the waiver request was proper, calls upon you to know with some detail the requirements for waiver of service. It also calls upon you to evaluate what defects in the waiver request might be fatal. Did you go beyond the technical requirements to analyze whether a defect might be excusable or not?

Did you catch that the failure of a process server to file a proof of service does not affect the validity of service? It may, as a practical matter, make it more difficult to prove that service was made, but the failure to file a proof of service does not render service ineffective.

Note that Rule 4(e)(1) is an inverse-*Erie* provision—even though the claim in the hypothetical is one arising under federal law, Rule 4(e) allows service as authorized by state law. Knowledge of this rule was particularly important here, because Paulie's attempt to serve Dina under methods prescribed by state law is the most likely to have been effective.

How did you analogize the facts in this hypothetical to *National Development Co.*? Note that the facts are different here, and so it would be important for your answer to distinguish that case and show why the distinction is meaningful.

Were you distracted by the fact that Bobby "hid" the copy of the summons and complaint in the Sunday *New York Times*? Perhaps you were tempted to discuss Dina's possible immunity from service because you thought Bobby might have engaged in trickery or deceit to effect service. But this level of trickery is very unlikely to have caused any court to reject service. Most courts have looked to trickery or deceit that causes the defendant to cross state lines. You certainly could have engaged in this analysis, but you should choose to address the key issues first before analyzing in-depth tangential issues like this one.

Did you recognize initially that the only way Paulie's attempt to serve Bearcat was proper was contingent upon the validity of Trixie's service upon the receptionist? Determining whether service on the receptionist was valid required analyzing applicable case law—did you make sure to acknowledge both the positive and negative facts with respect to the Bearcat receptionist and the *Direct Mail Specialists* receptionist?

Finally, did you address what the repercussions might be of failure to waive service if the waiver of service were effective, or of the failure to achieve effective service at all? Although the call of the question is not clear as to whether such analysis is required, the posture of the question—a lawyer presenting an objective analysis to a client about the service issues in a motion to dismiss—reasonably requires an analysis of the repercussions by implication. If you had been Paulie, wouldn't you have wanted to know that information? When in doubt, include such an analysis.

VARIATIONS ON THE THEME

What if Paulie had sent his waiver of service via FedEx or UPS instead of first class mail, as required by Rule 4(d)? *See* Magnuson v. Video Yesteryear, 85 F.3d 1424 (9th Cir. 1996); Audio Enterps. v. B&W Loudspeakers, 957 F.2d 406 (7th Cir. 1992). What textual and policy arguments might you make for or against your position?

Note that Dina is not a citizen of New York. If she ultimately is served properly in either Connecticut or Florida, can the New York federal court exercise personal jurisdiction over her? How? *See* Fed. R. Civ. P. 4(k).

Say that Paulie signed a severance agreement when he was terminated, in which Paulie and Bearcat each agreed to waive objections to ineffective service if actual service was provided. Could Bearcat then still challenge service? *See, e.g.,* D.H. Overmyer Co. v. Frick Co., 405 U.S. 174 (1972); Batya Goodman, *Honey, I Shrink-Wrapped the Consumer: The Shrink-Wrap Agreement as an Adhesion Contract,* 21 Cardozo L. Rev. 319 (1999).

Say a legally appropriate process server calls Dina, pretends to be an employee of Bearcat, and tells her, untruthfully, that she needs to report to the Bearcat Bar immediately or be fired. When Dina shows up, the process server personally serves her in New York. Would service be proper? Would the court have personal jurisdiction over her? *See, e.g.,* Tickle v. Barton, 95 S.E.2d 427 (W. Va. 1956); Wyman v. Newhouse, 93 F.2d 313 (2d Cir. 1937). What if Dina is served in New

York while she is there testifying under subpoena in an unrelated criminal case? *See, e.g.,* Pointer v. Ghavam, 107 F.R.D. 262 (D. Ark. 1985).

Change the fact that Cheryl was a full-time renter. What if Cheryl and Dina were co-owners of a timeshare for which they split the time that they stayed in the Boca Raton residence? Would Cheryl then still be a person of suitable discretion who resides there? What if Cheryl sublet her timeshare for the month of September to an unrelated renter who was only there for that month and who did not know Dina?

What if the Bearcat receptionist is not the general receptionist at the entrance to Bearcat's offices but instead is the CEO's designated secretary? Would that change your answer?

Would it matter to any of the service issues if Bearcat were a partnership organized under the laws of Delaware instead of a corporation?

Would it matter to any of the service issues if Paulie sues only under New York state antidiscrimination laws and establishes federal jurisdiction based on diversity?

OPTIONAL READINGS

Process servers inevitably must come up with creative ways to effect service. For some of the more colorful exploits of Depression-era process server Harry Grossman, see St. Claire McKelway, *Profiles—Place and Leave With I*, NEW YORKER 23, 23–26 (Aug. 24, 1935); St. Claire McKelway, *Profiles—Place and Leave With II*, NEW YORKER 21, 21–24 (Aug. 31, 1935).

Transnational litigation is booming. Rule 4(f) deals expressly and specifically with international service. For more on the nettlesome issues that arise during international service, see Samuel P. Baumgartner, *Is Transnational Litigation Different?*, 25 U. PA. J. INT'L ECON. L. 1297 (2004). The Hague Convention on International Service can be found at Convention on the Service Abroad of Judicial and Extrajudicial Documents in Civil or Commercial Matters, The Hague, 1965, 20 U.S.T. 361, T.I.A.S. No. 6638, 658 U.N.T.S. 163.

Electronic service may soon become the normal and accepted way to effect service of both court filings and of process. Rule 5(b)(2)(E) specifically allows service of non-process filings via e-mail if certain conditions are met, and many courts now require ECF, or ECF. For more, see John M. Murphy III, Note, *From Snail Mail to E-Mail: The Steady Evolution of Service of Process*, 19 ST. JOHN'S J. LEGAL COMMENT. 73 (2004); Jeremy A. Colby, *You've Got Mail: The Modern Trend toward Universal Electronic Service of Process*, 51 BUFF. L. REV. 337 (2003). Recently, it has been reported that Australian and New Zealand courts have upheld service via Facebook. *See Legal papers served via Facebook*, BBC NEWS (Dec. 16, 2008), *available at* http://news.bbc.co.uk/2/hi/asia-pacific/7785004.stm; Ian Llewellyn, *NZ court papers can be served via Facebook, judge rules*, NEW ZEALAND HERALD (Mar. 16, 2009), *available at* http://www.nzherald.co.nz/world/news/article.cfm?c_id=2&objectid=10561970.

11

AMENDING THE COMPLAINT

OPENING REMARKS

The liberal nature of pleading (even after *Iqbal*) mirrors the liberal nature of amendments to pleadings. If parties are allowed to plead without the extensive factual knowledge obtained through discovery, they ought to be allowed to modify the pleadings as the factual development of the case progresses. Liberal amendment also furthers efficiency values—as claims, allegations, responses, and defenses are winnowed out or discovered, amendment allows those changes to take place in the existing lawsuit rather than through a new and separate litigation. Amendments can change legal or factual allegations.

Rule 15 governs amendments to pleadings. Rule 15(a) allows a party to amend his pleading once as a matter of course if the amendment is made in a timely fashion. It allows other amendments with the opposing party's consent or with leave of court, which is "freely give[n] . . . when justice so requires." This directive favors amendment, though the court will balance a number of factors, including prejudice to the nonmoving party, the good faith conduct of the moving party, and the viability of the proposed amendment.

Rule 15(b) permits amendments during trial if relevant evidence is presented beyond the scope of the current pleadings. If the non-presenting party does not object, then Rule 15(b) considers the pleadings to have been amended by consent to conform to the evidence. If the non-presenting party objects, then, upon motion by the presenting party, the court may allow the evidence and amend the presenting party's pleadings to conform to the evidence. The idea is that the trial on those new issues should be allowed if the parties are ready to present evidence on them. Like Rule 15(a) amendments, Rule 15(b) amendments are freely allowed under the rule.

Rule 15(c) addresses when amendments "relate back" to the time of the original pleading. Thus, Rule 15(c) does not address *whether* amendment is allowed but rather *when* the amendment is deemed to be effective. Rule 15(c) issues emerge most regularly with claims asserted by amendment after the statute of limitations has expired or when parties are substituted.

HYPOTHETICAL

On January 2, 2004, Paul falls off his tractor and injures his right arm. On January 1, 2007, he sues Delaware Tractor Company for products liability in federal court. He files the Complaint and serves Delaware Tractor on that day. On January 3, Paul files and serves an Amended Complaint alleging an additional claim for breach of implied warranty arising out of the same alleged defect in the tractor. On January 5, upon Delaware Tractor's written consent, Paul files and serves a Second Amended Complaint that repeats the other claims and also alleges a new claim for breach of warranty related to a different piece of machinery, a combine.

Delaware Tractor files and serves an Answer on January 20, denying liability and damages. Delaware Tractor does not assert any affirmative defenses.

Discovery ensues. Approximately six months into discovery, Delaware Tractor learns that the combine broke down on January 4, 2004. Accordingly, Delaware Tractor moves to file an Amended Answer to assert a defense to the combine warranty claim based upon the three-year statute of limitations that governs contract claims in the state.

At the same time, Paul realizes that Delaware Tractor is merely the holding company of the entity that should have been named as the defendant, Denver Tractors Inc., which manufactured and sold the machinery. He therefore moves to file a Fourth Amended Complaint that substitutes Denver Tractors for Delaware Tractor. Delaware Tractor opposes the motion on the ground of futility and argues that the three-year statute of limitations would bar the amended claims.

A. Did Paul's first and second amendments to his complaint require a motion?
B. Assuming that they did not, how should the court rule on Delaware Tractor's motion to amend its answer?
C. How should the court rule on Paul's motion to amend the parties?
D. Assume that the tractor claims go to trial against Delaware Tractor. At trial, Paul presents evidence that Delaware Tractor knew or should have known of its subsidiary's shoddy manufacturing. Delaware Tractor objects to this evidence as beyond the scope of the active complaint, whereupon Paul moves to amend the complaint to assert a cause of action for negligence against Delaware Tractor. How should the court rule?

SUGGESTED READINGS

Fed. R. Civ. P. 15
Krupski v. Costa Crociere S.p.A (09-337) (U.S. 2010)
Beeck v. Aquaslide "N" Dive Corp., 562 F.2d 537, 537–42 (8th Cir. 1977)
Foman v. Davis, 371 U.S. 178, 178–82 (1962)Moore v. Baker, 989 F.2d 1129, 1130–32 (11th Cir. 1993)
Bonerb v. Richard J. Caron Found., 159 F.R.D. 16, 17–20 (W.D.N.Y. 1994)

SAMPLE ESSAY

A. No.

Rule 15(a)(1) permits a party to amend a complaint once as a matter of course, without leave of court or permission of the opposing party, if the amendment is filed within 21 days of the original pleading. Thus, Paul's first amendment, made 2 days after he filed his complaint, was permitted as a matter of course.

Paul's second amendment of January 5, however, because it was a second amendment, is not entitled to amendment as a matter of course under Rule 15(a)(1). Instead, the amendment falls under Rule 15(a)(2), which requires either permission of the opposing party or leave of court. Here, however, Paul obtained Delaware Tractor's written consent for this second amendment. Assuming that the consent was validly obtained, then Paul's amendment was proper under Rule

15(a)(2), even without leave of court, and so there was no need for him to file a motion with the court to obtain that leave.

B. The court should grant Delaware Tractor's motion to amend.

A defendant can amend its answer under Rule 15(a). Although Delaware Tractor is not entitled to amend as a matter of course under Rule 15(a)(1) because more than 21 days have elapsed since it filed its answer, Delaware Tractor is entitled to amend with leave of court under Rule 15(a)(2). The rule states that leave should be freely given when justice so requires.

In determining whether leave should be given under Rule 15(a)(2), courts consider the following factors: (1) prejudice to the opponent in relying on the unamended pleading, (2) prejudice to the movant if not permitted to amend, (3) any fault of the movant in not asserting the amended claim or defense originally, and (4) any public interest considerations. The decision is committed to the discretion of the district court, but the burden is on the party opposing the amendment.

Here, there is little prejudice to Paul in allowing the amendment. Notably, Paul's prejudice is not based on any harm to his case (otherwise, every amendment would likely prejudice the opposing party). Rather, prejudice is measured by a reduction of the ability to litigate the new defense, such as if witnesses have become unavailable or evidence destroyed. The facts do not suggest any such effects on Paul's ability to contest the applicability of the statute of limitations to his claim.

On the other hand, not allowing the defense will prejudice the movant, which may have a viable defense to the relief sought. Accordingly, Delaware Tractor's prejudice is relatively high. In addition, there is no evidence that Delaware Tractor's failure to include the defense initially was the result of bad faith or negligent omission. Rather, the facts suggest that Delaware Tractor had no knowledge of the date the cause of action accrued, and had no way of knowing that date, until discovery. Finally, the public interest in having the claims defended fully and fairly support amendment. As a result, it is likely that the factors weigh in favor of allowing Delaware Tractor's amendment.

Paul may argue that the amendment is futile for the following reason: The statute of limitations defense is inapplicable because his amendment on January 5, 2007, relates back to the date of the original complaint, which was filed within the three-year limitations period. Paul would argue that the amendment relates back under Rule 15(c)(1).

If the law that provides the applicable statute of limitations would allow relation back in this case, then Paul would be correct. Rule 15 (c)(1)(A) would allow the relation back and would then render Paul's claim timely under the statute of limitations. Paul then would have a very good argument that Delaware Tractor's amendment would be futile.

If, however, the law that provides the applicable statute of limitations would not allow relation back, then Paul would have to argue that Rule 15(c)(1)(B) allows relation back because his combine claim arises out of the same conduct, transaction, or occurrence set out in the original pleading. These facts do not suggest that the claims arose out of the same conduct, transaction, or occurrence. The claims deal with different products, and the causes of action arose at different times, presumably for different reasons. Nothing appears to connect the combine or its defect to the tractor or its defect except the identity of the parties. If Paul could allege that both defects arose from a common defective manufacturing process, or if Paul could allege that they were part of the same contract and sale, then Paul might be able to show a close enough relationship between the claims. But, without more, Paul's ability to prove entitlement to relation back under Rule 15(c)(1)(B) is unlikely.

C. The court probably should grant Paul's motion to amend the parties.

Because Paul's fourth amendment requires leave of court under Rule 15(a)(2), he must overcome Delaware Tractor's futility argument. Unless the fourth amended complaint relates back to an earlier date, Delaware Tractor's futility argument based on the statute of limitations is likely to convince a court to deny Paul's motion to amend.

Rule 15(c)(1)(C) allows an amendment to change parties to relate back to the date of the original pleading for statute of limitations purposes when (1) Rule 15(c)(1)(B) is satisfied, (2) within the period provided by Rule 4(m) the new party received such notice of the action that it will not be prejudiced in defending on the merits, and (3) within the period provided by Rule 4(m) the new party knew or should have known that the action would have been brought against it, but for a mistake concerning the proper party's identity. The Supreme Court has made clear in *Krupski* that a "mistake" can exist even if the plaintiff knew that the correct party existed but instead sued the incorrect party.

Here, Rule 15(c)(1)(B) is satisfied because the amendment asserts claims that are identical—save for the change in party—to the claims set out in the original and amendment complaints.

It is unclear whether Denver Tractors received sufficient notice of the action within 120 days of its filing so as not to be prejudiced in its defense. Some discovery may need to be ordered or allowed before that fact could be determined. However, it is likely that Denver Tractors, as the subsidiary of the named defendant, did in fact receive such notice of the lawsuit. Having received such notice, it would not be prejudicial at this stage to substitute the parties, particularly when the parties are so closely related and when court has the power to delay the trial and discovery proceedings to allow the new defendant a fair opportunity to obtain the information it needs to defend against the claims.

It is also unclear whether (though also likely that) Denver Tractors knew or should have known, within 120 days of the filing of the complaint, that it was the proper party in Paul's lawsuit. Again, more facts may need to be discovered and presented to the court, but, as the named defendant's subsidiary, it is likely that Denver Tractors knew that Delaware Tractor was the incorrect party, that Denver Tractors was the proper party, and that the plaintiff would have sued Denver Tractors had the plaintiff not made a mistake about the identity of the proper party.

D. The court should grant Paul's motion.

Rule 15(b)(1) states that the court may, upon a trial objection that evidence is beyond the scope of the pleadings, permit the pleadings to be amended, and that the court should freely permit the amendment when doing so will aid in presenting the merits and when the opposing party fails to satisfy the court that the evidence would prejudice its defense.

Here, the public interest in having the claim litigated while both parties are already before the court supports amendment, but more facts are needed to make a conclusive determination. Unlike amendment during discovery, in which prejudice is likely to be low, amendment during trial may be highly prejudicial to the nonmovant, who has structured his or her defense in reliance on the unamended claims. It is possible that Delaware Tractor may be prejudiced by Paul's trial amendment of a new tort claim. On the other hand, it is not clear how much reliance was justifiable after Paul identified the party error during discovery. It may be that the court determines that Delaware Tractor should have expected Paul to amend his complaint to add a tort claim based on supervisory liability after it became apparent that Delaware Tractor was not the manufacturer. In addition, the court may be able to lessen any prejudice to Delaware Tractor by granting a continuance to allow Delaware Tractor the time and discovery to mount a defense.

If the statute of limitations for tort claims has expired, then Paul's prejudice might also be high if he cannot recover any other way. On the other hand, if the statute of limitations has not expired, then Paul could file a new complaint without amendment.

Paul will have to explain why he is amending his complaint only now, at trial, rather than before trial when it became clear that Delaware Tractor was not the proper party. If Paul has a reasonable excuse—perhaps Paul did not obtain the evidence until during trial—then Paul's fault may be low. If, on the other hand, Paul's late amendment efforts manifest bad faith or an attempt to hamstring Delaware Tractor's litigation defense, then Paul's conduct may undermine his amendment efforts.

In addition, prejudice is lessened by the ability of the court under Rule 15(b)(1) to grant a continuance to Delaware Tractor to enable it to meet the new evidence. Although a continuance would create a delay, that delay is for the benefit of Delaware Tractor, and Paul cannot complain about the delay because he will receive the benefit of the amendment.

TOOLS FOR SELF-CRITICISM

Note that Rule 15 addresses several different types of amendments and their requirements. Anticipate that an exam question will test the whole rule as a result. Such is the case in this hypothetical. Question A, for example, asks whether Paul's first and second amendments to his complaint require a motion. As Rule 15(a) provides, amendments before trial can be made a number of ways—by right, by consent, and by motion. The first amendment can be made by right because Rule 15(a)(1) is met. The second amendment can be made by consent because the defendant stipulated to it. Do not be lulled into an analysis of prejudices and equities! Tempting though it may be, amendments by right and by consent do not require such an analysis. Instead, Question A calls merely for a routine analysis of a few straightforward facts and rules of law.

Question B does call for more analysis of facts. Here, though, you should explain why an amendment by right is not available, for, if it were, the court would not need to undertake the factual analysis. Once engaged in the motion inquiry, you should consider both the balancing of the prejudice and futility factors and the presumption in favor of amendment. Here, of course, both weigh in favor of amendment.

Note that the balancing factors implicit in Rule 15(a) may require a consideration of the relation-back doctrine of Rule 15(c). Did you forget to address Rule 15(c) in part of your answer? Or, in the alternative, did you *only* address Rule 15(c)? Questions B and C test how you are able to explain how and when the two work together. Remember that Rules 15(a) and (b) govern *whether* amendment is proper, whereas Rule 15(c) governs *when* the amendment will be deemed effective. They are two separate inquiries (though they may affect each other), as Questions B and C demonstrate.

How did you treat the ambiguity surrounding whether Denver Tractors received sufficient notice of the action? It is important to acknowledge any ambiguities in your answer, explain how the ambiguity could be resolved, and examine each potential result. For example, the sample essay acknowledges that it is unclear whether Denver Tractors received sufficient notice of the action, explains that more discovery could be ordered to determine whether notice was received, and then examines the relevant outcomes.

Question D deals with Rule 15(b) amendments at trial. Note that Rule 15(b) merely confirms that Rule 15(a)(2) amendments are available during trial, but also note that the balance of prejudices and equities have special solicitude by the time the parties have reached trial. Although amendments at trial are still freely given, the burdens on the parties are higher at trial. Be sure to take those into consideration in your analysis.

With Rule 15 analyses, which often have detailed dates and events, it may be a useful tool to write out a time line of events. The time line can then be referred back to during the analysis. This can save you from having to re-read the hypothetical multiple times. Writing the dates down can also prevent careless errors, particularly when analyzing a rule in which exact dates play a major role in the relevant outcome.

VARIATIONS ON THE THEME

Would your answer to Question A change if Delaware Tractor only gave oral consent to the amendment? What practical effect might there be if Delaware Tractor continued to represent that it willfully and intentionally consented (but only orally) to the amendment and refused to make any kind of motion?

Why do you suppose Delaware Tractor consented to Paul's second amendment if the amendment was filed more than three years after the cause of action arose?

Say Delaware Tractor had not objected to the evidence identified in Question D. How should the court treat the pleadings? *See* Fed. R. Civ. P. 15(b)(2).

If Paul's original complaint had been filed on December 16, 2006, and thus his second amended complaint filed 21 days later, would Delaware Tractor's answer have been timely, assuming Delaware Tractor never waived service? If not, when would Delaware Tractor have had to answer or otherwise respond? *See* Fed. R. Civ. P. 15(a)(3).

Say Delaware Tractor had moved to dismiss the complaint on January 2, 2007. Would that change your answer to Question A regarding whether Paul's first amendment required a motion? *See* Adams v. Quattlebaum, 219 F.R.D. 195 (D.D.C. 2004).

OPTIONAL READINGS

If a plaintiff does not know the identity of a "John Doe" defendant when she files a lawsuit within the statute of limitations but then, after the statute of limitations has run, she amends her complaint to insert the actual name of the defendant based upon discovery, does the amendment relate back under Rule 15(c)? Some courts say yes. Others say that the original styling was not a "mistake" and therefore is not entitled to the relation-back provision of Rule 15(c). For more on this issue, including a discussion of the circuit split and an argument in favor of relation back, see Rebecca S. Engrav, Comment, *Relation Back of Amendments Naming Previously Unnamed Defendants under Federal Rule of Civil Procedure 15(c)*, 89 CAL. L. REV. 1549 (2001).

JOINDER AND SUPPLEMENTAL JURISDICTION

12

OPENING REMARKS

Before the adoption of the Federal Rules, the ability under the common law to join parties and claims in a single lawsuit was limited. Cases brought in equity, however, used joinder more liberally in an attempt to resolve an entire controversy.

The Federal Rules favor the equity practice and, in line with liberal pleading and amendment, offer liberal joinder rules as well. As just a few examples, plaintiffs may join different claims together and may sue multiple defendants. Defendants may counterclaim against plaintiffs and cross-claim among one another. Defendants may also implead third parties who may be responsible for any adverse judgment. Third parties may intervene into the lawsuit. The basic idea is that it is generally efficient to resolve at one time all related claims or all claims among existing parties. A secondary gain is consistency of judgment if all the claims are resolved by the same court.

Of course, there are downsides. Liberal joinder increases the complexity of a given case and, thus, its expense, both for the parties and for the court. Liberal joinder also undermines party control of the lawsuit. One way the rules attempt to resolve tension with party control is by making some joinder "permissive" rather than "mandatory" or "compulsory." Mandatory and compulsory joinder rules do exist, but they ordinarily exist only when the efficiency gains are overriding or when nonjoinder would be prejudicial to a party's interests. Another way the rules mitigate complexity is through the power of the court to sever or order separate trials under Rule 42.

Joinder of claims generally falls under Rules 13 and 18. Rule 13 governs counterclaims (claims by an original defendant against a plaintiff) and cross-claims (claims by an original defendant against another defendant). Generally, these claims may or must be joined if they arise from the same transaction or occurrence as the original claim. Rule 18 governs joinder of claims among existing parties to a claim. As long as a party properly asserts one claim against another, that party can join all of the claims—even the unrelated claims that she has against the other party.

Joinder of parties implicates primarily Rules 19, 20, and 21. Rule 20 allows parties to be joined as plaintiffs or defendants permissively, if the claims arise from the same transaction or occurrence and if they share at least one common question of law or fact. Rule 19, however, requires certain parties be joined if the prejudice of nonjoinder is prohibitively high. Rule 21 states that parties can be added or dropped by the court.

Joinder of parties also implicates impleader under Rule 14—in which a defendant sues a third party for contribution or indemnification of any judgment that may be entered against it—and intervention under Rule 24. Intervention takes two forms: intervention as of right and permissive intervention.

It is critical to remember that compliance with the rules is only half of any joinder issue. The other half is compliance with subject-matter jurisdiction doctrines. The Rules do not supply automatic jurisdiction. Thus, even if a claim satisfies the requirements of a Federal Rule, you must make a separate determination of whether the court has jurisdiction to hear the claim.

Joinder rules therefore implicate a form of subject-matter jurisdiction that was not addressed in earlier chapters—supplemental jurisdiction. Constitutional subject-matter jurisdiction applies to a "case" or "controversy," but we often think in terms of claims. Thus, if a plaintiff asserts two claims— one federal and one state—against a nondiverse defendant, is there jurisdiction over the state claim? There is no original statutory federal subject-matter jurisdiction over it under § 1331 or § 1332. If, however, the claims are so related to each other that they form one "constitutional case," then there is Article III jurisdiction over both claims together. On a claim-by-claim basis, there is § 1331 jurisdiction over the federal claim and "supplemental" Article III jurisdiction over the state claim.

Supplemental jurisdiction is granted by statute in 28 U.S.C. § 1367, which both authorizes and restricts its scope. Supplemental jurisdiction issues require close parsing of the statute's text, as well as proper understanding of the joinder rules.

Of course, a third feature of joinder is not dictated by either the Rules or jurisdiction. Once compliance with the Rules and jurisdictional principles is expected, litigation strategy becomes the overriding factor for joinder. Strategic considerations can be powerful. A plaintiff might, for example, want to join multiple defendants together so that, if they point fingers at each other, a jury is still likely to compensate the plaintiff. A plaintiff might oppose a defendant impleading its insurance company, which will create both extra costs for the litigation (because now there are two defendants) and may result in a sophisticated and well-counseled litigant driving the defense. A plaintiff might likewise oppose a cross-claim among codefendants out of fear that that ancillary dispute will overshadow the plaintiff's claim. Intervenors may consider carefully whether the cost is worth the effort of interjecting themselves into a litigation.

A fourth feature of joinder—the "join it or lose it" principle—is decreed by principles of issue and claim preclusion, which a later chapter will discussed more fully.

HYPOTHETICAL

Harry Homeowner buys a lot and wants to build his dream house on it. He contracts with General Home Builders to build his home in exchange for $450,000. General contracts with several subcontractors, including Fred's Foundations. After the house is fully constructed, General discovers that the foundation laid by Fred's is defective. The defective foundation renders the house uninhabitable, with, Harry claims, a fair market value of only $100,000 (General disputes this valuation). Fred's, meanwhile, has gone out of business and is being liquidated. Its residual value is expected to be between $70,000 and $80,000, which would limit the amount in controversy for any claim against it. General estimates that the cost of repairing the foundation will be $300,000.

General has a general liability insurance policy with Independence Insurance, a large, multinational insurance company. The policy covers all liability against General in the course of its general contracting work.

Harry is a citizen of Texas. General is incorporated in Delaware with its principal place of business in Florida. Fred's Foundations is incorporated in Georgia with its principal place of business in Georgia. Independence Insurance is incorporated in Delaware with its principal place of business in Texas.

With $50,000 left to pay General under the contract, Harry refuses to pay any additional money for the house until General repairs the foundation at its own expense. General refuses and demands the remaining $50,000. Harry then sues General in federal court under state contract law for specific performance or, in the alternative, for $300,000. Assume for each of the following questions that venue is proper and that personal jurisdiction extends to all parties.

A. Can Harry sue Fred's for negligence in the same lawsuit? Must he do so?

B. Assume the claim in Question A is filed. General would like, in this lawsuit, to:

   1. sue Harry for breach of contract for the remaining $50,000 due under the contract,

   2. sue Fred's for indemnification on Harry's claim and for a breach of contract action stemming from an unrelated job, and

   3. ensure that Independence will cover any liability.

   Can General do all this? How? Must General assert any of these claims?

C. Assume all the claims in Questions A and B are filed. Harry wants to be sure that he sues deep pockets and thus seeks to sue Independence for essentially the same claim he has against General for $300,000. Assuming the claim against Independence is cognizable under state law, may Harry do so?

D. Assume all the claims in Questions A and B are filed, but the claim in Question C is not filed. Independence suspects that Harry and General may be colluding to commit insurance fraud. Accordingly, Independence wishes to sue both Harry and General for fraud. Assuming this is a proper cause of action under state law, may Independence assert these claims in Harry's lawsuit? Must Independence do so?

E. Assume that only Harry's original claim against General and his claim in Question A are filed. It comes to the attention of the court that Fred's had subcontracted with Celenie's Concrete for the materials to build the foundation but never paid Celenie's. Celenie's therefore has a state breach of contract action against Fred's. Celenie's is incorporated in Delaware with its principal place of business in Georgia. Must Celenie's be joined?

F. Assume that only Harry's claims against General are filed. The property owners association (POA) in the neighborhood wishes to join in the lawsuit to sue General for the nuisance of building a house of significantly low fair market value to the detriment of the neighboring property values. The POA is organized under the laws of Texas, and all of its members are citizens of Texas. Assuming the cause of action is cognizable under state law, can the POA join? If so, should the court allow it?

SUGGESTED READINGS

U.S. CONST. art. III, § 2
28 U.S.C. § 1367

FED. R. CIV. P. 13

FED. R. CIV. P. 14

FED. R. CIV. P. 18

FED. R. CIV. P. 19

FED. R. CIV. P. 20

FED. R. CIV. P. 21

FED. R. CIV. P. 24

FED. R. CIV. P. 42

Moore v. N.Y. Cotton Exch., 270 U.S. 593, 601–03, 609–10 (1926)

United Mine Workers v. Gibbs, 383 U.S. 715, 717–29 (1966)

Owen Equip. & Erection Co. v. Kroger, 437 U.S. 365, 367–77 (1977)

Exxon Mobile Corp. v. Allapattah Servs., Inc., 545 U.S. 546, 549–72 (2005)

W. Md. R. Co. v. Harbor Ins. Co., 910 F.2d 960, 961–64 (D.C. Cir. 1990)

Temple v. Synthes Corp., 498 U.S. 5, 5–8 (1990)

Provident Tradesmens Bank & Trust Co. v. Patterson, 390 U.S. 102, 104–28 (1968)

SAMPLE ESSAY

A. Harry can join his claims against Fred's only if the residual value of Fred's exceeds $75,000.

Rule 20(a) allows joinder of defendants if the claims arise out of the same transaction, occurrence, or series of transaction or occurrences, and at least one common question of law or fact will arise. Here, the claims arise out of the same defective foundation, and the circumstances surrounding the defective foundation involve factual issues that likely will arise in both claims. Accordingly, Harry can join his claims against the two defendants under Rule 20(a). Rule 20(a) is permissive; thus, under the Rules, Harry may join them if he wishes, but he is not required to do so.

However, the court must also have subject-matter jurisdiction over the claims. All parties are diverse. Harry's claim against General exceeds the amount-in-controversy requirement and therefore has original diversity jurisdiction over it. Harry's claim against Fred's, however, may not exceed the amount-in-controversy requirement because the residual value of Fred's limits the amount in controversy on Harry's claim against it. If the residual value exceeds $75,000, then Harry's claim against Fred's meets the test for original diversity jurisdiction, and Harry can choose to assert the claim if Harry wishes. If, however, the residual value does not exceed $75,000, then Harry's claim against Fred's lacks original federal jurisdiction. Additionally, the supplemental jurisdiction statute does not extend subject-matter jurisdiction to it. True, Harry's two claims are so related as to form one constitutional case under § 1367(a) because they arise from the "same nucleus of operative fact," *Gibbs*, in that they both arise from the circumstances surrounding the defective foundation. But Harry's claim against Fred's is excepted by § 1367(b) because it is a claim by a plaintiff against a person made a party under Rule 20, the joinder of which is inconsistent with § 1332 because it does not satisfy the amount-in-controversy requirement. The Supreme Court in *Exxon Mobile* held that claims by different plaintiffs joined under Rule 23 did not all need to meet the amount-in-controversy requirement, but *Exxon Mobile* does not change the applicability of § 1367(b) to claims against defendants joined under Rule 20. Accordingly, although Rule 20 would permit the joinder of Harry's claim against Fred's, jurisdictional principles would not authorize a court to hear it if the amount-in-controversy requirement is not met.

B. General can file each claim except the unrelated claim against Fred's.

General can counterclaim against Harry under Rule 13. Harry's original claim made them "opposing parties." The claim likely will be a compulsory counterclaim under Rule 13(a). A compulsory counterclaim "arises out of the transaction or occurrence that is the subject matter of the opposing party's claim." Here, General and Harry both dispute what is owed to each under the contract between them. Harry's claim is based on the contract and arises out of the problems stemming from the foundation. General's claim also is based on the contract and arises out of the same problems. Assuming the counterclaim does not require adding another party over whom the court cannot acquire jurisdiction, General's claim against Harry is a compulsory counterclaim under Rule 13(a).

General also can sue Fred's for indemnification. Although indemnification claims are specifically addressed in Rule 14's impleader rule, Rule 14 cannot be used against an existing party. Consequently, General must file a Rule 13 cross-claim against Fred's. This is appropriate, however, because Rule 13(g) allows cross-claims for indemnification claims against existing parties. The cross-claim also is appropriate because it arises out of the same transaction or occurrence as Harry's original claim against General. The cross-claim is purely permissive, however. General may assert it if it wishes but need not do so.

The court has jurisdiction to hear both the counterclaim against Harry and the cross-claim against Fred's. The court lacks original jurisdiction over them because they are state claims that do not exceed the amount in controversy requirement ($50,000 for the counterclaim and at most $10,000 for the cross-claim). However, supplemental jurisdiction extends to them under § 1367(a). As a compulsory counterclaim and a proper cross-claim, they are so related to Harry's original claim that the three claims form one constitutional case. The claims are made by a defendant under Rule 13 and therefore are not excepted from supplemental jurisdiction by § 1367(b). Although the court may decline to exercise supplemental jurisdiction over them under § 1367(c)—an unlikely result at this point given the interrelatedness of the three claims and the commonness of the state claims—the court at least has jurisdiction to hear them. In addition, the court may order separate trials under Rules 13(i) and 42(b).

General also can sue Independence for indemnification under Rule 14, assuming the claim is made in a timely fashion under Rule 14(a)(1), and assuming the claim is cognizable under state law. The court has jurisdiction to hear this claim. Although the court lacks original jurisdiction over such a state claim between nondiverse parties, supplemental jurisdiction under § 1367(a) extends to it. As an indemnification claim, it is so related to Harry's original claim that the two claims form one constitutional case. The claim is made by a defendant and therefore is not excepted from supplemental jurisdiction under § 1367(b). Although the court may decline to hear it under § 1367(c)—an unlikely result at this point given the interrelatedness of it and Harry's original claim—the court at least has jurisdiction to hear it. In addition, the court may, upon a motion by any party, strike the claim, sever it, or try it separately under Rule 14(a)(4).

General probably cannot sue Fred's for breach of contract on the unrelated job in this lawsuit. General cannot sue Fred's under Rule 13(g) because its claim likely does not arise from the same transaction or occurrence as Harry's original claim. "Transaction" has a broad and "flexible meaning" under cases like *Moore*, but it likely cannot be extended this far. Thus, Rule 13(g) would not authorize such an unrelated cross-claim. However, if General decides to assert its indemnification cross-claim against Fred's—a claim that *is* sufficiently related to be authorized under Rule 13(g), as discussed above—then Rule 18(a) allows General to join any other claim it has against Fred's, even if unrelated. Accordingly, General can join its unrelated breach of contract cross-claim against Fred's under Rule 18(a) if General asserts its indemnification cross-claim against Fred's under Rule 13(g). However, although Rule 18(a) would allow such a joinder of the unrelated breach of contract claim, the court would lack jurisdiction over it. The court would lack original jurisdiction over the state claim because it does not exceed the amount-in-controversy threshold; even if this Rule 18 claim's amount in controversy of $10,000 is aggregated with the other cross-claim General has asserted against Fred's (also $10,000), the amount-in-controversy threshold has not been exceeded. In addition, the breach of contract claim is unrelated to the original claim and thus would not be entitled to supplemental jurisdiction under § 1367(a). As a result, although Rule 18(a) might allow General to assert its unrelated breach of contract claim against Fred's, jurisdictional principles would prevent the joinder.

C. Not in Harry's original action.

Rule 14(a)(3) does allow a plaintiff to assert against the third-party defendant any claim arising out of the transaction or occurrence that is the subject matter of the plaintiff's claim against the third-party plaintiff. Here, Harry's claim is the same claim as his original claim, and thus it arises out of the same transaction or occurrence. It therefore is allowed by Rule 14(a).

However, the court will lack jurisdiction to hear the claim. The court lacks original subject-matter jurisdiction over this state claim between nondiverse parties. Although § 1367(a) would extend supplemental jurisdiction to it because Harry's claims are so related that they form one constitutional case, the claim is excepted under § 1367(b) because it is a claim by a plaintiff against a nondiverse person joined under Rule 14.

Of course, assuming that the claim is cognizable under state law, nothing in the facts or applicable law would prevent Harry from asserting the claim in a different available forum, such as a state court.

D. Independence must assert its claim against General and may assert its claim against Harry.

As a third-party defendant, Independence's claims are governed by Rule 14(a)(2). That rule requires a third-party defendant to assert any counterclaim against the third-party plaintiff that arises out of the same transaction or occurrence. Here, Independence's claim against General arises out of the same transaction or occurrence as General's indemnification claim. Both claims arise from the same basic circumstances surrounding the defective construction overseen by General. Accordingly, Rule 14(a)(2) makes Independence's counterclaim against General compulsory.

Similarly, Rule 14(a)(2) allows a third-party defendant to assert against the original plaintiff any claim arising out of the same transaction or occurrence as the plaintiff's original claim. Here, Independence's claim against Harry for fraud arises out of the same basic circumstances surrounding the defective construction of Harry's home and overseen by General. Accordingly, Rule 14(a)(2) allows Independence to assert its fraud claim against Harry. Rule 14(a)(2) makes the claim permissive, however; thus, whether to assert the claim or not is Independence's option (at least under the joinder rules).

Both claims fall under federal jurisdiction. Neither qualifies for original jurisdiction because the opposing parties are nondiverse. However, supplemental jurisdiction extends to them under § 1367(a) because the claims are so related to Harry's original claim that they form one constitutional case. And, the claims are not excepted by § 1367(b) because they are brought by a defendant. Although the court may decline to hear them under § 1367(c), the court at least has jurisdiction to hear them. In addition, the court may, upon a motion by any party, strike, sever, or separately try them under Rule 14(a)(4).

E. No, because Celenie's is a necessary but not an indispensable party, and the court would lack subject-matter jurisdiction if Celenie's were joined.

Rule 19 requires a person to be joined if (a) the court cannot afford complete relief in its absence or (b) the person claims an interest relating to the subject of the action and is so situated that disposing of the action may, as a practical matter, impair or impede the person's ability to protect that interest or may leave an existing party subject to a substantial risk of incurring multiple liability or inconsistent judgments.

Here, Rule 19(a)(1)(A) likely does not apply because the court can afford complete relief to the existing parties in the absence of Celenie's. Celenie's was not a party to the general contract and has no bearing on what rights and obligations exist between Harry and General or Harry and Fred's. Nor does Rule 19(a)(1)(B)(ii) likely apply because neither Harry nor General nor Fred's are at risk of multiple or inconsistent obligations. It is true that Fred's might be sued by multiple persons, including both Harry and Celenie's, but those lawsuits are separable and would not be considered "multiple" or "inconsistent."

However, Rule 19(a)(1)(B)(i) may apply. Celenie's has an interest in recovering from Fred's on its unpaid contract. That interest is likely to be substantially impaired if the existing lawsuit is resolved to a conclusion before Celenie's can assert its claim because Fred's residual value of $10,000 likely will be exhausted by Harry's claim, leaving Celenie's with a judgment-proof defendant. Accordingly, Celenie's is a necessary party under Rule 19(a) because its interest will be impaired by the disposition of Harry's claim.

Whether the court has subject-matter jurisdiction to hear Celenie's' claim against Fred's depends upon how Celenie's is aligned among the parties. Celenie's' claim is against Fred's alone. No other party is affected by Celenie's' conduct, and Celenie's does not appear to have any claim against any other party. Because Fred's is aligned as a defendant, Celenie's likely will be aligned as a plaintiff.

If so, the court will lack subject-matter jurisdiction over Celenie's' claim. Celenie's' claim lacks original federal jurisdiction because it is a state claim against nondiverse parties (both Celenie's and Fred's are citizens of Georgia).

Supplemental jurisdiction likely extends to Celenie's' claim under § 1367(a) because it arises from a common nucleus of operative facts that also covers Harry's original claim. But, Celenie's' claim is a claim by a person proposed to be joined as a nondiverse plaintiff under Rule 19 and, thus, is excepted from supplemental jurisdiction by § 1367(b). (Note, however, that if the court deems Celenie's not to be a mandatory party under Rule 19 but nevertheless permissively joins Celenie's as a plaintiff under Rule 20, then the supplemental jurisdiction statute would permit the court to exercise jurisdiction over Celenie's' claim because § 1367(b) does not except Rule 20 plaintiffs.)

Because the court would lack jurisdiction to hear Celenie's' claim, the court must determine whether, under Rule 19(b), it should proceed without it or dismiss the entire action. Rule 19(b) requires the decision to be made "in equity and good conscience" under the consideration of a number of factors, including (1) the extent to which a judgment rendered in the person's absence might prejudice that person or existing parties, (2) the extent to which any prejudice could be lessened or avoided by protections in the judgment or relief awarded, (3) whether a judgment rendered in the person's absence would be adequate, and (4) whether the plaintiff would have an adequate remedy if the action were dismissed. As *Provident Tradesmens* explained, these factors delineate four interests to be considered: the plaintiff's interest in a forum; the defendant's wish to avoid multiple litigation; the outsider's interest in joining; and the court's interest and public interest in an efficient, complete, and consistent resolution of controversies.

Here, a judgment rendered in Celenie's' absence could prejudice Celenie's if the judgment is for Harry against Fred's for money damages because the amount of money left to satisfy any obligation owed to Celenie's would be lessened. A judgment rendered against Harry, however, would not prejudice Celenie's at all. Moreover, the prejudice to Celenie's could be lessened by the power of the court to delay execution of any judgment against Fred's until the separate lawsuit had concluded. The Supreme Court, in *Provident Tradesmens*, encouraged district courts to use their power to do so in Rule 19(b) cases. Further, a judgment between Harry and Fred's would be adequate without Celenie's because Celenie's' claim is independent of Harry's claim. The hypothetical does not provide sufficient detail of the applicable law and remedies to determine whether Harry would be prejudiced by having his claim dismissed at this point. If, for example, state law would not allow his claims to be heard in state court for some reason, then that prejudice to Harry would weigh in favor of the federal court's retention of Harry's claim. Nevertheless, the other Rule 19(b) factors tend to suggest that the district court should retain the case, refuse to join Celenie's, and carefully structure any judgment for Harry in a way that will avoid or mitigate any prejudice to Celenie's. As a result, the court probably should retain Harry's claims and refuse to join Celenie's.

F. The POA can intervene permissively, though it is unclear if the court will allow it.

Rule 24(a) requires the court to allow intervention if the POA has an unconditional right to intervene under a statute or if the POA claims an interest relating to the property or transaction and is so situated that disposing of the action may impair or impede the movant's ability to protect its interest, unless existing parties adequately represent that interest. Here, no statute appears to give the POA an unconditional (or even a conditional) right to intervene, so intervention of right under Rule 24(a) will only be allowed if the POA's interests justify it. Here, the POA's interests can be prosecuted in a separate lawsuit for the POA's own injuries; nothing in Harry's lawsuit will prevent the POA's interests from being fully vindicated in a separate lawsuit. Because the disposition of Harry's claim likely will not impair or impede the POA's ability to protect its interest in maintaining high property values in the neighborhood, the POA probably cannot intervene as of right under Rule 24(a).

Rule 24(b) permits, upon court approval, a nonparty to intervene if the nonparty's claim or defense shares a common question of law or fact with the main action. The POA's claim shares common questions of fact with Harry's claim, including whether the foundation is defective, whether General is responsible for the defect, and what the resulting value of the home is. Accordingly, the POA has a conditional right to intervene under Rule 24(b)(1)(B).

Additionally, the court will have subject-matter jurisdiction over the POA's claim. The POA's claim is a state claim between diverse parties. It is unclear whether the amount in controversy exceeds the jurisdictional threshold. If so, then the court will have original diversity jurisdiction over this claim. If not, then the court will have supplemental jurisdiction over the claim because it is so related to Harry's original claim as to form one constitutional case under § 1367(a). Section 1367(b) does not except the claim from supplemental jurisdiction here. Although the POA likely will intervene as a plaintiff because its claim is against General, section 1367(b) excepts claims by persons seeking to intervene as plaintiffs only if complete diversity would be destroyed. Here, the POA's intervention does not destroy complete diversity and, thus, is allowed.

Conditional intervention is subject to the discretion of the court, however, and therefore although intervention is permitted under Rule 24(b), the court must still consider whether the intervention will unduly delay or prejudice the adjudication of the original parties' rights, as mandated by Rule 24(b)(3). Here, the facts do not suggest any undue delay or prejudice because the POA's interests are closely aligned with Harry's. If, however, the POA moves for intervention at a late stage in the litigation such that discovery would have to be extended or the trial postponed, such delay would weigh against intervention. But, barring any undue delay or prejudice, intervention probably should be allowed under Rule 24(b).

In addition, if the claim lacks original jurisdiction, then the court may decline to exercise supplemental jurisdiction over the intervened claim under § 1367(c) if (1) the claim raises a novel or complex issue of state law, (2) the claim substantially predominates over the claim over which the court has original jurisdiction, (3) the district court has dismissed all original jurisdiction claims, or (4) other exceptional circumstances compel the declining of jurisdiction. Here, more facts are needed to make a conclusive determination, and, in any case, the court's decision will be within its sound discretion. Based on the limited facts provided, the court probably would be justified in retaining the claim because the facts suggest neither that the POA's claim is novel or would predominate over Harry's diversity claim nor that other exceptional circumstances counseling dismissal exist. If facts are uncovered that suggest that the POA's claim is novel or would predominate, or if the court dismisses Harry's diversity claim, then the court should revisit the question of whether to retain the POA's claim under § 1367(c).

TOOLS FOR SELF-CRITICISM

The federal joinder rules are extremely complicated and difficult to navigate. Attempting to draft an answer to the hypothetical without a firm understanding of the concepts involved in joinder can only lead to confusion and frustration. You should begin only after a thorough examination of the suggested readings and remember that merely reading the rules once will not suffice. This problem, however, breaks down discrete joinder issues into separate questions, each of which is answerable independently. Accordingly, this problem hopefully will give you a severable assessment of your proficiency with the various joinder issues. In addition, if you find the problem too long, you can break the problem out into its various questions and answer each separately.

As an initial consideration, what method did you use to identify and consider each fact relevant to this multifaceted joinder problem? First, the parties must be aligned in terms of their relationship to one another. Next, the claims must be identified in terms of their relationship to the parties. Then, the applicable rule should be selected. Finally, the question of jurisdiction must be addressed. It would be difficult to determine the applicable rule or analyze jurisdiction before identifying the parties and claims at issue. Tackling each part of the question in this manner serves organizational purposes and also prevents you from skipping a portion of the analysis. For example, even if you realize the court will not have jurisdiction, you should still analyze the relevant joinder rule before disposing of the desired claim on jurisdictional grounds. Similarly, if you conclude the joinder rules would not allow the relevant claim, the jurisdictional issue should still be addressed.

In drafting your answer, did you draw a factual map to guide your analysis? Diagramming the facts is an effective way to keep the facts organized and answer these questions, given the complexity of the joinder rules and the way that the facts build on one another. Consider, for example, that most of the questions direct you to "assume" that a certain fact has occurred. Mapping out those assumptions will aid you in determining the status of each party based on their relationship to other parties, in pinpointing the applicable rule based on which party attempts to bring a particular claim against which other party, and in addressing the associated jurisdictional concerns. This problem likely requires several mini-diagrams, perhaps a small diagram for each lettered question. Question A, for example, might be diagrammed in the following way:

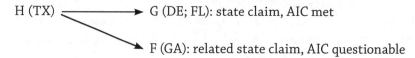

Notice how the diagram identifies the question (Harry wants to sue Fred's in the same lawsuit as Harry's suit against General), the status of each party and the parties' relationship to one another (Harry is the plaintiff; General and Fred's are codefendants), the types of claims (state claims that are related but only one meets the AIC requirement), and the residence of each party (Texas, Delaware, Florida, and Georgia). From here, you should think to look at Rules 19 and 20 and the supplemental jurisdiction statute, and this diagram should provide a useful reference tool as you do so.

Question B builds on Question A, adding three new claims:

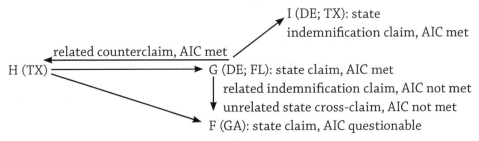

The diagram serves as a useful reference point and provides a visual reminder of how the claims are grouped. As to the latter, the diagram shows that G's indemnification claim against F must be a cross-claim under Rule 13(g) rather than an impleader claim under Rule 14. The diagram contrasts G's indemnification claim against F with G's indemnification (properly asserted under Rule 14) against I. Similarly, the diagram shows that G and F are opposing parties once G asserts its related indemnification claim against F, making G's unrelated state cross-claim against F available to be asserted under Rule 18(a). The diagram simplifies the analytical process and serves as a reminder of the established facts.

How did you organize your answer? This is a complicated hypothetical with many nooks and crannies into which the substance of your answer could easily disappear. Note how the sample essay provides a pointed conclusion in the first sentence of each respective answer, identifies the relevant rule based on the alignment of the parties and the nature of the desired claim, and then applies the facts to the rule in reaching a conclusion. IRAC may not be a required format for answering exam questions (although it may be—check with your professor!), but it has the virtue of being a clear, logical, or organized way to provide an answer, which may ensure that your analysis is identified and understood.

Be sure you do not forget about jurisdiction! The Rules are only half of the story. A claim must satisfy both the Rules and jurisdictional principles. One way to ensure that you do not forget is to create a chart for each claim on a piece of scratch paper or on the question itself with two boxes, perhaps like this:

Claim	Details	Rule	Jurisdiction
H v. G	Original state claim, diversity/AIC met	N/A	Original diversity jxn
G v. H	Related counterclaim, diversity/AIC met	13(a)	Original diversity jxn
G v. I	Related indemnity claim, no diversity	14(a)	Supplemental jxn met
H v. F	State claim, AIC questionable	20(a)	Original jxn if AIC met; if AIC not met, no jxn

Be sure to pay close attention to the "must" and the "may" of the joinder rules. Does your answer reflect a thorough understanding of what claims are compulsory or permissive and why? What about the court's discretion under the supplemental jurisdiction rules? Distinguishing between when a party is required to do something as opposed to when a party may do something is crucial in analyzing a problem relating to joinder. Similarly, you should always point out when the court may entertain a claim but has the discretion not to—then discuss why and how the court would use its discretion based on the provided facts or public policy.

Did your answer reflect your consideration of each alternative? For example, notice how the sample essay approaches the conclusion in Question C that Harry cannot sue Independence in the original action. The essay does not merely explain that the court would not have jurisdiction over the claim because of the parties' nondiversity. Instead, it follows the set organizational structure by identifying the relevant parties and their relationship to one another, the nature of the claim, and the relevant joinder rule. Then, it explains why the court would not be able to exercise jurisdiction over the claim even though it could be validly made under the joinder rules. Importantly, the sample essay also offers an alternative solution for Harry—sue in state court, rather than in federal court. This alternative is, indeed, directly responsive to the question of whether Harry may sue Independence. The simple answer to that question is, "Yes, but not in Harry's existing lawsuit."

Similarly, did you recognize the potential ramifications of alternative outcomes? In Question E, for example, if the court did not deem Celenie's a mandatory party under Rule 19 but joined Celenie's as a plaintiff under Rule 20, then the jurisdictional analysis changes. While the sample essay determined that Celenie's would be a mandatory party under Rule 19(a), it nevertheless noted the implications of an alternative conclusion. Given the unpredictable nature of courts and the law in general, proficient lawyering also mandates identification of and preparation for every possible outcome.

How, if at all, did the fact that the hypothetical involves contract issues affect your analysis? The joinder rules often require you to consider whether a particular claim arises out of the same transaction or occurrence as another claim. This requires limited inquiry into the contract claim. It does not, for example, require you to consider in detail the merits of the suit. You should not spend any significant time analyzing substantive questions outside the subject matter at hand. If a tangential issue of consequence catches your attention immediately, however, feel free to write a sentence or two for good measure.

Did you spend any time discussing *Kroger*? If so, you probably could have better used your time elsewhere. Section 1367(b) largely displaced *Kroger*. Thus, focusing your discussion on § 1367 probably would have been more useful. Discussing *Gibbs*, however, would have been proper because although § 1367(a) largely codifies *Gibbs*, the exposition in *Gibbs* of the constitutional standard—such as the "common nucleus of operative fact" language—is useful in interpreting § 1367(a)'s reach.

Notice that Subpart F is couched in terms of the POA "joining" the lawsuit. That may have induced you to discuss joinder of parties under Rules 19 or 20. Remember that those joinder rules are used when a nonparty is added by the existing parties or by the court. If a nonparty wishes to join on its own, the proper vehicle is intervention under Rule 24. Accordingly, you should have discussed Rule 24, rather than Rules 19 or 20, in Subpart F.

VARIATIONS ON THE THEME

Assume, for purposes of Question A, that Fred's is incorporated in Texas. Would the court be able to hear Harry's claims?

What if General and Fred's had a multicontract relationship, with each contract intertwined with the others, such that a breach of one would trigger obligations in the others, payments on one could offset payments on the others, the same insurance policy covered all of their jobs, etc. Might this closer connection change your answer to Question B(2)? How would you argue that it would? *See* United States v. Heyward-Robinson Co., 430 F.2d 1077 (2d Cir. 1970).

Assume, after the claims in Question B are filed, that Harry has his own liability insurance against General's counterclaim for breach of contract. May he implead his insurer under Rule 14 even though he is a plaintiff? For jurisdictional purposes, would it matter what state citizenship Harry's insurer has?

What if, after the claims in Question B are filed, Independence has claims to assert against General and Harry? What rules would govern those? *See* FED. R. CIV. P. 14.

Assume that Harry sues only Independence because the state in which Harry files the action cannot assert personal jurisdiction over General. If Independence has a counterclaim against General that arises out of the same transaction or occurrence, is it compulsory? *See* FED. R. CIV. P. 13(a) (stating that an otherwise compulsory counterclaim is not compulsory if the court cannot obtain personal jurisdiction over the defending party).

If, under Question E, Celenie's is deemed to be a necessary party but is aligned as a defendant, will the court have jurisdiction to hear its claim? If so, why do you think § 1367(b) would be written to exempt from supplemental jurisdiction Celenie's' claim as an aligned-plaintiff's claim but not as an aligned-defendant's claim?

Say that the POA's claim in Question F is against Harry for unpaid POA dues that are unrelated to the defective foundation but instead are owed based simply on property ownership. Can the POA intervene under Rule 24(b)? If so, would the court have jurisdiction?

What if Harry's original claim against General had given rise to federal-question jurisdiction? How would that change your analysis for any of the questions?

OPTIONAL READINGS

Joinder implicates the tension between efficiency and a plaintiff's autonomy to structure the litigation. For more on which value the joinder rules should favor, compare, e.g., Roger Transgrud, *Joinder Alternatives in Mass Tort Litigation*, 70 CORNELL L. REV. 779 (1985) (arguing for greater plaintiff autonomy in mass tort cases), with, e.g., Richard D. Freer, *Avoiding Duplicative Litigation: Rethinking Plaintiff Autonomy and the Court's Role in Defining the Litigative Unit*, 50 U. PITT. L. REV. 809 (1989) (arguing that plaintiff autonomy should bow to efficiency gains). For a recent analysis of Rule 19, see Katherine Florey, *Making Sovereigns Indispensable:* Pimentel *and the Evolution of Rule 19*, 58 UCLA L. REV. 667 (2011).

Most claims that meet the "same transaction or occurrence" test in the Rules should also form the "same case or controversy" in the supplemental jurisdiction statute. But Congress did not use the same phrase as the rule makers, and so some questions linger. If the joinder test is looser than the supplemental jurisdiction statute, then some claims might meet the "same transaction or occurrence test" but fail the jurisdictional test. On the flip side, if a claim does NOT meet the "same transaction or occurrence" test, then it probably will not meet the supplemental jurisdiction test. There are some rare exceptions in the case law. *See, e.g.*, Jones v. Ford Motor Credit Co., 358 F.3d 205 (2d Cir. 2004) (exercising supplemental jurisdiction over a permissive counterclaim).

Similarly, Congress, in enacting the supplemental jurisdiction statute, did not use the same language as the Supreme Court did in *Gibbs*. Might, then, some claims satisfy the *Gibbs* constitutional test but not the statutory test? *See* William A. Fletcher, *"Common Nucleus of Operative Fact" and Defensive Set-Off: Beyond the* Gibbs *Test*, 74 IND. L.J. 171 (1998).

Courts disagree about what theory justifies barring a claim in a second lawsuit that would have been compulsory in a previous lawsuit. *Compare, e.g.*, Dragor Shipping Corp. v. Union Tank Car Co., 378 F.2d 241 (9th Cir. 1967) (res judicata), *with* Martino v. McDonald's Sys., Inc., 598 F.2d 1079 (7th Cir. 1979) (waiver), *with* Dindo v. Whitney, 451 F.2d 1 (1st Cir. 1971) (estoppel).

The supplemental jurisdiction statute has generated spirited debate. *See, e.g.*, Richard D. Freer, *Compounding Confusion and Hampering Diversity: Life after* Finley *and the Supplemental Jurisdiction Statute*, 40 EMORY L.J. 445 (1991); Thomas D. Rowe, Jr. et al., 40 EMORY L.J. 943 (1991); Symposium, 74 IND. L.J. 1, 1–250 (1998); John B. Oakley, Kroger *Redux*, 51 DUKE L.J. 663 (2001).

CLASS ACTIONS

13

OPENING REMARKS

A class action is an action brought by one or more representatives on behalf of a group of similarly situated persons. In theory, it allows for cost and efficiency gains for both parties: for defendants, all claims are resolved at one time in one proceeding; for plaintiffs, the class as a whole shares the cost of the lawsuit, resulting in each plaintiff paying only a fraction of what it would cost to litigate individually. (Although a class action can be a class of *defendants*, the usual course is that the class is a class of plaintiffs. For simplicity, the usual course is assumed.) A corollary of the latter gain is that some actions that would be too expensive to litigate at all individually might be economically feasible in a class setting. Thus, class actions may even open the courthouse doors to allow in meritorious claims that otherwise would not be brought.

Class actions, however, are representative litigation, contrary to the usual rule that each party is master of his or her claim. Because unnamed class members are not parties to the litigation for most purposes, and because their claims are resolved for them by the representatives, class actions implicate important due process rights and notions of fairness.

Thus, the two overriding themes in class actions are efficiency and representation; the goal is to maximize efficiency while keeping the quality of the representation high.

Rule 23 governs class actions in federal court. Rule 23(a) sets out the "prerequisites" of a class action, which are colloquially termed numerosity, commonality, typicality, and adequacy. Numerosity ensures that the class is too large to use the preferred method of joinder (thereby preserving individual representation), and commonality ensures that there is something worth litigating as a group. Typicality and adequacy help ensure that the class representative and her counsel have interests that are aligned with the class's and that they are up to the task of representation.

Rule 23(b) then sets out the types of cases eligible for class treatment. Rule 23(b)(1) cases are so-called necessary classes, in which class treatment is needed to alleviate prejudice to either class members or to the defendant. Rule 23(b)(2) classes are those in which the defendant's conduct was directed to the class as a whole, and the class seeks injunctive or declaratory relief. Think discrimination cases here. Rule 23(c)(3) classes are "catchall" cases that do not by definition lend themselves to class treatment but may present circumstances in which the efficiency gains and representational quality are high enough to justify them. Rule 23(b)(3) imposes additional requirements beyond those of Rule 23(a).

Several additional features distinguish class litigation from individual litigation. Before a lawsuit becomes a class action, the district court must certify it as such under Rule 23(c)(1), which requires certification to be made at an early practicable time and obliges the district court to continually reevaluate the propriety of certification. To ensure that class members are adequately apprised of their rights, Rule 23(c)(2) requires notice to be given to (b)(3) class members and allows notice to be give for all other classes. Resolution of claims by settlement or voluntary dismissal, while normally up to the parties in individual litigation, must be approved by the court in class actions. Finally, Rules 23(g) and (h) impose additional court-approval requirements for class counsel and fees.

There is no doubt that class actions have had a successful impact in the United States in a number of ways. In addition to the benefits for the litigants at stake, class actions in the United States have become important tools for norm enforcement. The size and scope of many class actions have induced governments and private corporations to reform prison systems, eradicate unlawful discrimination, improve corporate governance, ferret out widespread charging errors in telecommunications service, combat antitrust violations, and improve consumer safety, just to name a few.

On the other hand, class actions are routinely criticized for their *in terrorem* effect of coercing defendants to quickly settle even weak class claims out of fear of huge liability exposure, massive pretrial cost, and negative public relations impact. Class actions also are criticized for the potential to enrich class counsel to the tune of millions of dollars in a settlement that garners only pennies for each class member.

Partly as a response to these criticisms, Congress enacted the Class Action Fairness Act of 2005, or CAFA. CAFA's primary impact has been to broaden statutory diversity jurisdiction for large, multistate class actions, which has resulted in more large class actions being heard in federal court.

HYPOTHETICAL

In 1990, General Hair Products, Inc., a Delaware company with its manufacturing facility in New Jersey and its corporate headquarters in New York, developed an over-the-counter remedy for hair loss called FollicAll, which invigorated dying hair follicles and slowed hair loss. General Hair Products distributed FollicAll in massive quantities to all 50 states. FollicAll's packaging instructed users to rub the product into the scalp on a daily basis. The warnings on the packaging stated that some side effects included mild irritation of the skin and recommended discontinuance if irritation continued for more than two weeks.

George Gladwell was a windsurfing instructor in San Diego, California. In 1992, when George was 37, he began to suffer from male pattern baldness. He began to use FollicAll on a daily basis. After approximately one month, he began to notice flakiness on his scalp. His scalp did not irritate him or itch, however, and so he thought nothing of it. Instead, he began to use an antidandruff shampoo. After three years, however, the flakiness became too unattractive for George to bear, and the antidandruff shampoo did not appear to work, so George discontinued use of FollicAll.

In 2001, George went into his physician's office for a routine checkup. While there, his doctor discovered unusual skin patches on his scalp. Suspecting something more serious, the doctor ran some tests. The tests confirmed that George had skin cancer.

The skin cancer was not at an advanced stage. An oncologist was able to remove the cancerous cells with minor surgery. Successful chemotherapy treatment followed, and, in 2005, George was declared cancer free.

At about that time, General Hair Products issued a recall of FollicAll based on a study performed by an independent research group that concluded that extended use of FollicAll caused skin cancer in laboratory rats. Immediately after the disclosure, one of General Hair Products' former employees disclosed that the company had performed a similar study internally in 1993 that produced similar results but had never disclosed the study or the results and had never issued any warnings.

George wondered whether his cancer might have been caused by FollicAll. No one in his family had ever had cancer. He was not a smoker, he was in good shape, and he led a healthy lifestyle. While doing some Internet research, George stumbled upon a website that began, "Have you ever used FollicAll? Have you ever had problems with your scalp? If so, call Stepfoot & Stepfoot, L.L.P. right away to discuss your legal rights!" George put in a call to Stepfoot and was asked to come to Stepfoot's Southern California office the next day.

The next day, George met with Sean Stepfoot, who told him that there was a good chance that FollicAll caused his cancer and that he should consider joining a group of other men who had experienced similar problems. George proved himself to be a sympathetic and credible person, and so Stepfoot suggested that he bring a lawsuit as a representative of a class of similar plaintiffs against General Hair Products. George agreed.

Stepfoot, through its advertising, had discovered over 1,000 others, from all 50 states, with heath problems potentially resulting from their use of FollicAll. The length and intensity of usage varied widely, as did the symptoms. Some had permanent scars where the skin had sloughed off. Some experienced a worsening of the baldness as the FollicAll appeared to accelerate the deterioration of their hair follicles. Some experienced painful burning and itching that lasted for several days after just one application of FollicAll. Others, like George, experienced more severe symptoms, including skin cancer. The users varied in terms of age, physical condition, and medical history. However, they were all men who used FollicAll for at least one week between 1990 and 2005. An expert retained by Stepfoot concluded that use of FollicAll for at least one week was likely to have caused or accelerated the injuries that each person complained of.

Based on this information, George, through his attorney Stepfoot, filed a class action lawsuit against General Hair Products in federal court in the Southern District of California on the basis of diversity jurisdiction alleging various state tort claims. He alleged that FollicAll caused a number of heath problems and that the warning on the packaging was insufficient. He sought to represent a class of FollicAll users in these tort claims. The class was defined as all men who had used FollicAll for at least one week between 1990 and 2005. He sought class compensatory damages for past and future medical bills, pain, and suffering. He also sought punitive damages of $500 million. Along with the complaint, George filed a motion for class certification under Rule 23(b)(3).

General Hair Products immediately answered and opposed the motion for class and subclass certification. General Hair Products argued that the putative class could not meet the requirements of Rule 23 because the different circumstances of each class member made causation, reliance, and damages—essential elements of the class claims—too individualized. General Hair Products also stated that the 50 states have different nuances of tort law, and different state law will apply to various claims of the class members. General Hair Products pointed out that the size of the class is simply too unwieldy—postage alone for individually mailed notices would be more than $20 million. General Hair Products challenged George's representation, suggesting that his claims were not typical of class claims and that his particular job, which caused him to be out in the sun all day, might have caused his skin cancer.

The district court granted the motion for class certification and certified the class. Immediately, General Hair Products and George entered into settlement negotiations. They reached a settlement and filed it with the court for approval. The settlement provided for a one-time lump-sum payment by General Hair Products to the FollicAll Fund of $25 million, to be administered by Stepfoot. In exchange, General Hair Products was to be released from all past, present, or future liability stemming from FollicAll usage. Under the terms, the class was divided into two groups. Those members who had already experienced injuries (approximately 150,000 persons) could seek compensation from the fund immediately. Those class members who had yet to experience any symptoms (approximately 50 million) could seek compensation from the fund only after they manifested some physical symptoms. Using a complicated metric, the administrator would distribute funds to class member claimants who properly supported their claims.

The district court issued a notice to all class members and then held a hearing on the proposed settlement. At the hearing, unnamed class members objected to the fairness of the settlement on various grounds. Nevertheless, after hearing the objections, the court approved the settlement.

1. Was the district court correct to certify the class?
2. Was the district court correct to approve the settlement?
3. If not, are all class members still bound by the judgment?

SUGGESTED READINGS

28 U.S.C. § 1332(d)
FED. R. CIV. P. 23
Hansberry v. Lee, 311 U.S. 32, 37–46 (1940)
Gen. Tel. Co. of the S.W. v. Falcon, 457 U.S. 147, 149–63 (1982)
Phillips Petroleum Co. v. Shutts, 472 U.S. 797, 799–814 (1985)
Amchem Prods., Inc. v. Windsor, 521 U.S. 591, 597–630 (1997)
Ortiz v. Fibreboard Corp., 527 U.S. 815, 821–65 (1999)
Supreme Tribe of Ben-Hur v. Cauble, 255 U.S. 356, 357–67 (1921)
Exxon Mobile Corp. v. Allapattah Servs., Inc., 545 U.S. 546, 549–72 (2005)
Wal-Mart Stores, Inc. v. Dukes, 564 U.S. _ (2011)
Castano v. Am. Tobacco Co., 84 F.3d 734, 737–52 (5th Cir. 1996)

SAMPLE ESSAY

1. The District Court Should Not Have Certified the Class.

Rule 23(c)(1) requires certification to be made at an early practicable time. The district court certified the class quickly but perhaps too quickly. Careful attention to Rule 23 is required in class certification determinations.

Rule 23(a) requires a class to meet the prerequisites of numerosity, commonality, typicality, and adequacy. Here, numerosity does not seem to be a problem at this point. It is possible that if the class definition is narrowed, numerosity may become a problem later, but because more than 50 generally satisfies numerosity requirements, and because joinder of more than 100,000 persons would be impractical, numerosity is met.

Commonality faces a more significant challenge. In *Wal-Mart Stores*, the Court interpreted commonality to require the class to demonstrate that each class member's claim depends upon a common contention whose resolution is central to the validity of each claim. There, the Court held that whether Wal-Mart allows excessively subjective decision making, though potentially supportive of a Title VII claim, was not a common question supporting class certification because it did not bridge the gap between generalized conduct of the defendant and the specific circumstances of every class member. The Court reasoned that such generalized decision making could have affected individual class members in a variety of ways, and perhaps some class members not at all. Here, although the question whether FollicAll causes severe adverse health effects not covered by the warning could be common, this level of generality distances the question from specific claims. In other words, showing that FollicAll causes *some* unwarned health effects does not mean that it causes *all* of the health effects suffered by the class. The problem for the class is as the level of generality of the common questions rises in the attempt to unite all class members, the questions become less connected to each individual class member. The same problem inheres in other potentially common questions: whether the warning was defective, whether General Hair Products's conduct rises to a sufficient level to warrant punitive damages, and what the proper assessment of punitive damages is. It is possible that a common question exists, but *Wal-Mart Stores* presents substantial obstacles to showing class commonality here.

Typicality and adequacy are perhaps even more problematic. These two factors "tend to merge," according to *Falcon*. They ensure that the class representative and class counsel are adequate representatives of the class. Here, George has several potential divergences to overcome. First, his claims are not typical of the claims of members of the class who have yet to experience symptoms. His claims are ripe and seek compensation primarily for past injuries. Their claims for future injuries are not yet ripe, and their present claims seeking, perhaps, medical monitoring or compensation for fear of future injury, are different relief. As a result, George should not be allowed to represent class members who have yet to manifest any symptoms.

In addition, George may not be able to represent even some present-injury class members. His cancer is a harm that stands on very different footing than class members who experienced only accelerated baldness or even painful burning and itching without long-term effects. The danger is that George may attempt to press hardest the claims that he personally has at stake, at the expense of the claims that he does not.

Finally, George may not even be able to represent some members of the class with skin cancer. If there is a substantial possibility that George's cancer was caused by his own excessive sun exposure, as opposed to the use of FollicAll, then George may not be the best representative.

For these reasons, it is likely that the putative class, as proposed, fails Rule 23(a). Of course, typicality problems may be able to be cured by substituting more suitable or multiple class representatives, or perhaps by creating subclasses, but, as presently defined, the class probably does not meet the Rule 23(a) requirements.

Class certification has an additional hurdle: Rule 23(b). A class need only meet one of the 23(b) types, but this is clearly a 23(b)(3) class. Rule 23(b)(3) classes for mass torts are generally disfavored because of the manageability and representation problems that they usually encounter. Rule 23(b)(3) requires common questions to predominate over individual questions, and it requires the class mechanism to be the superior method of resolving the case. This case likely fails both requirements.

Predominance is not necessarily a quantitative analysis but rather a qualitative one. Thus, fewer but more significant common questions may still predominate over many less significant individualized questions. Here, the common questions are important: causation, the defective nature of the warning, and punitive damages. On the other hand, the individual questions are significant as well and are likely to take up an overwhelming portion of the litigation: individualized issues affecting causation, individualized issues affecting reliance on the warning label, and individualized issues affecting damages. On balance, the common questions probably predominate. They are the critical questions in the case. They are diluted by the individualized questions, but it is not clear at this point that the individualized questions will become so prevalent that they predominate over the common ones. The district court always has the power—indeed, the obligation—to monitor class certification status under Rule 23. If the district court determines that the individualized issues are predominating, it can decertify or restructure the class at that time.

Superiority tests whether the class vehicle is the most appropriate one in light of alternatives, such as joinder, individual litigation, other forms of aggregate litigation, test cases, or alternative class structures. The factors the court considers include class members' interest in individualized litigation, the extent of any preexisting lawsuits, the desirability of concentrating the litigation in the particular forum, and the likely difficulties in manageability.

Here, the class members' interest in individualized litigation varies. Some may wish to have individualized litigation. They, of course, may opt out. But others who have low dollar-value claims, such as those claiming minor skin injuries, may need the class mechanism to make it economically feasible to have their claims adjudicated. As a result, the class members' interest probably does not tip the scales.

There is no mention of any other litigation; accordingly, that factor is irrelevant. There appears to be no concrete benefit to having the litigation concentrated in the Southern District of California, either. Were most users from California, or were General Hair Products from California, there might be good reason to have the case heard there. But the facts suggest that the products were used all over the country. Thus, this factor does not appear to tip the scales.

The most important factor, then, is manageability. Manageability may indeed be a problem for this class. The fact that 50 different state tort laws will apply is a significant manageability problem because it will require the court to determine whether, when, and what different state laws apply to whom. Different state standards may create conflicts among class members, depending upon the law and evidence. In addition, the sheer size of the class creates difficulties in cost and efficacy. The size problems are magnified by the substantial individualized issues that will likely come into play in this class. Thus, the manageability problems are impressive.

On the other hand, there may be opportunities to ameliorate these manageability problems. If, for example, the state tort laws are roughly equivalent, or perhaps the variations that do exist are not implicated, and thus they do not conflict, then the level of variation is much lower. It may even be that state laws can be grouped into two or three similar groups. In addition, the size of the class, while daunting, may not lead to the obstacles that General Hair Products fears. The Internet may provide opportunities for low-cost class management, notice, and opt-out recordings.

The alternative structures are costly as well. Individualized litigation would flood the dockets (while still precluding some low-value claims). Additional subclasses are possible, perhaps based on groups of state law, but they may not alleviate the cost considerations.

Thus, it may be that the class mechanism is the best method to resolve these claims. The district court, however, should have explored some of the suggestions made above before making a certification decision. If state law is substantially uniform, and if cost savings can be had via the Internet, then the manageability issues might be ameliorated.

In sum, the district court was wrong to certify this class. However, had it considered whether the adequacy and typicality defects could be rectified via subclasses or class representative changes, and had it considered whether manageability problems could be alleviated, then the class might have been certifiable.

As a final consideration, district courts always have an obligation to consider whether subject-matter jurisdiction is proper. Here, subject-matter jurisdiction was proper. For class actions not governed by CAFA, diversity of citizenship is determined by resort to the class representative, not by resort to individual class members. *Supreme Tribe of Ben-Hur.* Here, complete diversity exists because George is a citizen of California, and General Hair Products is not. The amount-in-controversy requirement, however, is determined with respect to each individual class member. As long as one class member meets the amount-in-controversy requirement, though, then the others can join under supplemental jurisdiction. *Exxon Mobile.* Here, George's individual claim likely exceeds $75,000. Accordingly, he meets the criteria for original diversity jurisdiction, and the class members who do not can join under supplemental jurisdiction. Hence, the district court has subject-matter jurisdiction over this case.

2. The District Court Should Not Have Approved the Settlement.

Under *Amchem*, settlement is relevant to class certification in some ways. For example, manageability problems may not have as much force in a settlement class because pretrial and trial procedures are not contemplated. Thus, the superiority and manageability issues that were discussed above were of only modest concern at the time of settlement.

But the Court also said that close—even heightened—attention to the representational requirements of Rule 23 is paramount in settlement classes because of the risk of collusion or misrepresentation. Here, settlement did not cure or ameliorate the typicality and adequate problems discussed above; indeed, it appears to have accentuated them. George now has a $25 million fund from which he may submit his claim and have it be resolved by a very friendly adjudicator—his own counsel.

This is to the detriment of other claimants, particularly those who have no symptoms yet. Those individuals likely will see the fund gobbled up by those who already have experienced symptoms. In the meantime, their claims for present fear of future injury, for medical monitoring, and for the harm that does eventually come, will all be extinguished. Fifty million users who may ultimately suffer the same condition from which George suffers will have no recourse.

The inadequacy of George's representation is critical at this settlement stage. The district court should have decertified the class until additional or different representatives could be appointed to review the settlement proposal.

Accordingly, the settlement is not fair, reasonable, or adequate under Rule 23(e), and the district court should neither have approved it nor have permitted the certification of the class to go forward without different representation.

3. Unnamed Class Members May Not be Bound.

In *Hansberry*, the Court held that class members are bound by a class judgment only if they were adequately represented. Those class members whose claims were not represented adequately by George are not likely to be bound by the class judgment.

Even those claims who were represented may not be bound if they were not properly provided adequate notice under Rule 23(c)(2), which requires notice for Rule 23(b)(3) classes. Similarly, those persons who were not properly notified may not be bound if California could not exercise personal jurisdiction over them. *See Phillips Petroleum v. Shutts*. Finally, class members who properly opted out of the class are not bound by the class judgment.

TOOLS FOR SELF-CRITICISM

Although the commonality, typicality, and adequacy requirements of Rule 23(a) "tend to merge," the facts here create some distinction between the efficiency-focused commonality requirement and the representation-focused typicality and adequacy requirements. Thus, you should not treat all three requirements together as one "merged" requirement. Nonetheless, because typicality and adequacy both address representative concerns, it would be more appropriate to discuss them together. Keeping the twin policy aims of Rule 23 (efficiency and representational quality) in mind should help you distinguish between the different requirements and identify when they are implicated.

Don't forget, though, that typicality and adequacy problems may be curable by substituting different class representatives or by adding class representatives. If you conclude that the proposed class has typicality or adequacy problems, you also should address whether these changes might alleviate those problems. In evaluating the propriety of George's status, you should focus on the legal requirements of adequacy and typicality, rather than the strategic consideration of whether George is a sympathetic plaintiff.

The sample essay reaches the initial conclusion that the class should not have been certified because it did not mean the prerequisites under Rule 23(a). Nevertheless, it continues to assess whether the case is eligible for class treatment under 23(b). Although it is true that if the court determined that the class did not meet the prerequisites it would likely refrain from analyzing any further, you should never stop there. As an attorney, you will never go to court unprepared to argue a viable alternative argument, no matter how certain you are that the judge will agree with your first argument. Similarly, on an exam answer, always finish out the analysis. Your professor may not agree with the conclusion that would allow you to stop where you are, and given the context, you should display as much relevant knowledge as you have to offer.

Were you tempted to characterize this class as a 23(b)(2) class because the defendant's conduct was directed to bald men as a class? The relief sought—exclusively damages—essentially prevents this from being a (b)(2) class, which is reserved for primarily declaratory or injunctive relief.

Rule 23(b)(3) classes have additional requirements. But, like the typicality and adequacy requirements of 23(a), the superiority and manageability requirements of 23(b)(3) can be ameliorated by creative judicial intervention. You should recognize those opportunities rather than simply evaluating the 23(b)(3) requirements with reference solely to the status quo.

Did you remember to discuss subject-matter jurisdiction? In the midst of the highly formalistic requirements of Rule 23, it would have been easy to forget this staple of civil procedure, but remember that jurisdiction pervades every single adversarial proceeding beginning with the complaint. Here, the hypothetical prompts you to discuss whether the court's actions were appropriate. Because the district court has an obligation to ensure that subject-matter jurisdiction is proper, you would be wise to address this issue.

Be careful to avoid discussing the merits of the claims unless they are relevant to certification. Certification is a procedural issue, not a substantive one. The certification determination may necessarily depend upon some merits issues and proof (e.g., a representative's weak individual claim may implicate adequacy and typicality concerns if class members' claims are far stronger) but merits questions that do not inform the certification requirements should not be considered, no matter how dispositive they may seem.

Notice how the second and third questions continue to test the twin aims of class actions—efficiency and representational quality—through the crucibles of settlement and preclusion. It bears repeating that keeping these aims in mind will give more depth and meaning to your analyses.

VARIATIONS ON THE THEME

Say an appellate court holds, as the sample answer does, and remands to the district court. What should the district court do on remand? What might the parties suggest? *See, e.g.*, FED. R. CIV. P. 23(c)(4) & (c)(5).

If two additional representatives were added—one who had not yet experienced any symptoms and one who had experienced only minor symptoms—how would that affect your analysis? What issues would still remain, and how might the court alleviate them?

Would it matter if George has initiated a separate individual lawsuit in state court for essentially the same claims?

Why might General Hair Products have opposed the motion for certification? Why might it have decided, as a strategic matter, *not* to oppose the motion? Indeed, could General Hair Products have sought class certification on the punitive damages issue, and if it did, should George have opposed it? Would those positions have been rational for the parties to take? How should the court decide such a motion?

Assume that the facts show that users who are symptom free for more than three years after the last usage are 99.9 percent likely to experience no adverse effects in the future. Would that fact justify the disparate treatment of the future-injury claimants in the settlement?

What if General Hair Products is threatened with bankruptcy and has essentially no assets of its own to pay any judgment, but does have a liability insurance policy that covers liability up to $25 million. Would that justify class certification and the fairness of the settlement? *Cf.* Ortiz v. Fibreboard Corp., 527 U.S. 815 (1999).

How might you draft a settlement notice to the class members in this case? What kind of information would you include, and how would you word it?

Say the case is not settled but is instead set for trial. During discovery, experts conclude that George's cancer and scalp problems were caused solely by the sun and not by FollicAll. General Hair Products successfully moves for summary judgment on George's claims, and the court dismisses him from the lawsuit. What happens to the class?

OPTIONAL READINGS

No other country in the world has the kind of commitment to aggregate civil litigation that the United States does. Indeed, class actions are unheard of in most foreign jurisdictions. Recently, however, some foreign countries have begun to experiment with class actions in civil matters. For more, see Antonio Gidi, *Class Actions in Brazil—A Model for Civil Law Countries*, 51 Am. J. Comp. L. 311, 312–13 & 313 n.1 (2003); Richard A. Nagareda, *Aggregate Litigation Across the Atlantic and the Future of American Exceptionalism*, 62 Vand. L. Rev. 1 (2009).

There is a split among the courts as to whether subclasses under Rule 23(c) may be used to retain a class action that cannot meet the requirements of Rule 23(a) or (b). For more, see Scott Dodson, *Subclassing*, 27 Cardozo L. Rev. 2351 (2006). The same controversy surrounds issue classes under Rule 23(c). *See* Laura J. Hines, *The Dangerous Allure of the Issue Class Action*, 79 Ind. L.J. 567 (2004); Laura J. Hines, *Challenging the Issue Class Action End-Run*, 52 Emory L.J. 709 (2003).

Although detailed study of CAFA is more appropriate for an advanced course rather than an introduction to civil procedure, it is worthwhile to understand the controversy surrounding CAFA and some of its early effects. For more, see Symposium, *Fairness to Whom? Perspectives on the Class Action Fairness Act of 2005*, 156 U. Pa. L. Rev. 1439–2160 (2008).

DISCOVERY AND PRIVILEGE

14

OPENING REMARKS

Liberal pleading (and, to some extent, liberal amendment and liberal joinder) requires liberal discovery. Why would a system that, based solely on allegations, allows plaintiffs broad access to the courts, and defendants broad latitude to assert defenses, limit the parties' opportunity to uncover factual support for those allegations?

By and large, the American system doesn't. (Query whether this should change after *Iqbal*.) The discovery rules allow for wide-ranging exchange of information. A party may discover any nonprivileged information relevant to a claim or defense of any party. Relevant evidence need not even be admissible evidence if it is reasonably calculated to lead to evidence that is admissible. In addition, for good cause, a party may discover information relevant to the subject matter of the lawsuit. In sum, discovery is broad.

There are some limitations. Privileged information is not discoverable. The most common privilege raised in civil procedure classes is the attorney-client privilege, which attaches to confidential communications made between an attorney and her client for the purpose of seeking or providing legal advice. A party who withholds information based on privilege must disclose sufficient details about the information being withheld to allow the opposing party to assess whether the privilege is being properly asserted. This disclosure is often called a "privilege log." It is important to remember that only the communication is privileged—the underlying facts are still discoverable through other means.

In addition, the Rules recognize that, under the circumstances of a particular case, discovery requests may be legitimately objectionable: if the request is unreasonably cumulative or duplicative, if the information sought is obtainable from some other source that is more convenient or less burdensome or expensive, if the requestor has had ample opportunity to obtain the information, or if the burden of production outweighs the information's likely benefit. The court may also limit disclosure in other ways, such as through redactions, confidentiality orders, or the purposeful structuring of discovery. Finally, work product—material prepared in anticipation of litigation or trial by a party or its representative—is protected from discovery, although fact work product may be discovered upon a showing of substantial need for the information and undue hardship obtaining it by other means.

There are several different discovery devices. Parties must make initial, mandatory disclosures under Rule 26(a) soon after discovery begins. Parties may also use interrogatories, requests for production or inspection of documents and other tangible things, oral depositions, written depositions, requests for admissions, and requests for examination. Of course, parties also may obtain information in lawful ways not specifically prescribed by the Rules, such as by interviewing witnesses, hiring an expert, or conducting one's own investigation.

Usually, parties serve discovery requests, respond to them, and work out discovery disputes on their own, without court involvement. (Discovery of nonparties, however, usually necessitates court involvement through a subpoena.) Rule 26(f) requires the parties to meet to construct a joint discovery plan for the litigation before discovery can begin. If a discovery dispute arises, parties generally meet to discuss the issue to try to work it out themselves. If they cannot, the requesting party may file a motion to compel, or the responding party may file a motion for a protective order, and the court will then resolve the dispute. The losing party then may be subject to sanctions.

The timing of discovery is rule based but flexible. Most discovery cannot occur until after the initial discovery conference. Discovery orders may or may not set out further time lines for specific discovery requests. If not, then those requests are largely subject to the decisions of the parties. Thus, the parties will get together to schedule depositions and will serve other discovery requests at their leisure. Responses usually are set at about 30 days, but the parties routinely allow for reasonable extensions unless otherwise set by the court. Importantly, in most cases, all of the discovery exchanges and disputes happen without involving the court at all—the parties drive the discovery and attempt to resolve any disputes. It is only when a party seeks court intervention, or when the court deems necessary to exert more control, that the court plays a role.

The discovery rules have changed over the years. Discovery was restricted under the Field Code but dramatically expanded upon adoption of the Federal Rules. Recent amendments have provided for mandatory disclosures, restricted the scope of discovery, provided for presumptive limits on discovery, and addressed the nettlesome issues of electronic discovery, just to name a few of the many changes in the discovery rules.

HYPOTHETICAL

Penny Pettigrew has brought a wrongful death action in federal court in the name of her 12-year-old son, Sam, against Darklords of Delaware, an online fantasy role-playing game. She alleges Sam killed himself as a result of playing Darklords. She states a claim for negligence on the ground that Darklords owed Sam a duty of care and that it breached that duty by failing to provide appropriate safeguards against the risks of psychological harm that the game can cause.

Penny sends a set of interrogatories and a request for production of documents to Darklords. Interrogatory 10 states:

> Please identify all persons who have ever registered to play your game, including their names, duration of registration, number of games played, ages, and whether they are current or former gamers.

Darklords answered:

> Darklords objects on the grounds that this interrogatory is irrelevant and unduly burdensome and seeks information that is both highly confidential to the gamers and proprietary to Darklords. Nevertheless, without waiving this objection, Darklords answers as follows: Sam Pettigrew, registration 1/1–9/1, 125 games, age 12, former gamer.

Penny's Request No. 6 in her request for documents sought:

> All documents relating to any potential harmful effects of playing
> Darklords, including any studies you have performed on such effects.

Darklords answered:

> Darklords objects on the grounds that this request seeks information that
> is privileged or protected from discovery. Darklords identifies all responsive
> but withheld documents in the following privilege log:

Type	From	To	Regarding	Privilege or Protection
Notes	Counsel	File	Interviews of gamers re: adverse effects of gaming	Work Product
Memo	Counsel	Board	Legal advice re: potential adverse effects of gaming	A/C Privilege
Report	Marketing	Board	Level of violence & realism for optimal marketability	A/C Privilege; Work Product

In a meet-and-confer teleconference, Penny explains to Darklords that she needs the gamers' information because she would like to interview them to determine what adverse effects, if any, gaming has had on them. She communicated her belief that the withheld documents are neither privileged nor protected and that, even if they are, she is entitled to them anyway.

Darklords counters that the interrogatory information is not relevant and would be unduly burdensome on Darklords because its collection of gamer identities is essentially a customer list that would subject it to a competitive disadvantage if disclosed to its gaming competitors. Darklords also says that gamers usually wish to keep their identity secret and that divulging their identities would impair their First Amendment right to freedom of association. Finally, Darklords asserts that the documents sought are privileged and protected as explained in its privilege log and explains specifically that the Report is privileged and protected because in-house counsel sat in on that particular Board meeting and received the Report. Thus, Darklords continues to adhere to its responses.

Penny, therefore, files a motion to compel seeking a complete response to Interrogatory 10 and the three documents listed on Darklords's privilege log. Darklords opposes the motion. Each asserts the same arguments made in the meet-and-confer. What should the judge do?

SUGGESTED READINGS

Fed. R. Civ. P. 26
Fed. R. Civ. P. 29
Fed. R. Civ. P. 30

FED. R. CIV. P. 31
FED. R. CIV. P. 32
FED. R. CIV. P. 33
FED. R. CIV. P. 34
FED. R. CIV. P. 35
FED. R. CIV. P. 36
FED. R. CIV. P. 37
FED. R. CIV. P. 45
Hickman v. Taylor, 329 U.S. 495, 497–514 (1947)
Upjohn Co. v. U.S., 449 U.S. 383, 386–402 (1981)
Mareese v. Am. Acad. of Orthopaedic Surgeons, 726 F.2d 1150, 1151–52, 1156–62 (7th Cir. 1984)

SAMPLE ESSAY

I. The Interrogatory

Rule 26 allows discovery of any nonprivileged, relevant information. Information is "relevant" if it is reasonably calculated to lead to admissible evidence. Here, the information sought in the interrogatory is nonprivileged (and Darklords has not asserted any privilege or protection over it). It is relevant because it bears upon the critical element of causation. Responsive information could lead Pettigrew to obtain relevant, admissible evidence from other gamers. She is therefore correct that the information is discoverable under Rule 26(b).

Rule 26(c), however, permits an objection if the burden of production outweighs its benefit, taking into account the needs of the case, the amount in controversy, party resources, and its importance to the issues. Here, Darklords asserts confidential and proprietary business interests and the gamers' significant First Amendment association rights. If the court did not have additional mechanisms to lessen these burdens, this would be a close call. However, the court has ample authority under the Rules and prevailing case law to structure discovery to alleviate Darklords's burdens.

For example, the court could delay disclosure of this information until the end of discovery to see if settlement or party preference obviates the need for it by that time. The court should consider the possible prejudice to the plaintiff of the delay in disclosure, however. That prejudice may be significant because Pettigrew wishes to use the information to contact the gamers and gather additional information from there. Thus, Pettigrew may need the time to gather the ultimate information she seeks. As a result, delaying disclosure might not be the most accommodating option.

The court also could issue a confidentiality order to prevent disclosure to anyone outside the scope of this lawsuit. That would protect Darklords's business interests. It also would protect the confidentiality of the gamers outside the scope of the lawsuit, although some gamers ultimately may be contacted and their information divulged to the parties.

The court also could limit the scope of the response. In other words, Pettigrew may not need *every* gamer's name. Pettigrew might be willing to begin with those most likely to lead to the information she seeks, such as gamers of the ages 10–14 who are no longer registered, or perhaps the gamers interviewed by Darklords's counsel as noted in the privilege log. Such a smaller subset would protect the confidentiality of the vast number of gamers while still giving

Pettigrew the most relevant information. If Pettigrew believes she needs the rest of the identities, she can try to show why the information she received from the subset is insufficient and why the other identities are likely to lead to more relevant information.

The court could order Darklords to seek consent of its gamers to divulge their personal information as a way of ameliorating the privacy concerns. One way would be for the parties jointly to draft a letter to gamers explaining the case and how the information would be used. Initially, only Darklords would contact the gamers and receive their responses in order to protect their privacy. Those gamers who willingly opted to divulge their information could then be disclosed to Pettigrew. The court should consider the burden on Darklords in such a case and the likely delay that the process would cause.

Finally, the court could sustain Darklords's objection based on burdensomeness but preclude Darklords from introducing evidence obtained from any other gamers out of fairness to Penny.

Thus, before ruling on the motion, the court should hear oral argument on the motion and ask the parties whether any of these creative solutions might obviate the need for a ruling by the court in the first instance.

II. The Documents

Whether these documents must be produced depends upon whether Darklords has met its burden of demonstrating that the documents are privileged or protected and whether Pettigrew has made a sufficient showing to overcome any protection. The two main issues here implicate attorney-client privilege and work product protection.

A. ATTORNEY-CLIENT PRIVILEGE

Attorney-client privilege, as explained in *Upjohn*, protects non-waived, confidential communications between an attorney and her client made for the purposes of seeking or providing legal advice.

The Memo is almost certainly privileged. It is between counsel and the company, and it pertains to legal advice. To be certain, the court could examine the memorandum *in camera*. If privileged, the only question would be whether the privilege has been waived in some way by disclosing the communication to others outside the circle of confidence. There is no evidence or intimation of that, so the document should be considered privileged and non-discoverable until such evidence is shown.

The Report is another story. The mere presence of counsel at discussions or as a recipient does not itself make a communication privileged. Here, the communication from the marketing department seems to be directed to the Board in its business capacity, not to counsel for purposes of obtaining legal advice. Again, the court should consider examining the document *in camera* to determine whether the document itself gives any clues as to its purpose, but it does not appear that, on the facts as given, Darklords has met its burden of establishing privilege over the Report. If Darklords has, however, then the Report will be privileged because there is no evidence of waiver and no exceptions apply.

Importantly, if attorney-client privilege applies, no exceptions such as substantial need and undue hardship will overcome the privilege—Pettigrew is out of luck.

B. WORK PRODUCT PROTECTION

Work product is governed by Rule 26(b)(3) and *Hickman v. Taylor*. The work product doctrine protects documents and tangible things prepared in anticipation of litigation or for trial by or for another party or its representative.

This standard leads to a number of questions. Were the Notes and Report prepared in anticipation of litigation? When were the documents prepared? Were they for a strategic business decision or for litigation? On the information given so far, Darklords probably has made an initial showing—albeit a circumstantial one—that the Notes are work product because they were created by counsel on an issue that is likely to give rise to litigation. Darklords probably has not made such a showing as to the Report because it appears to have been made for the purposes of marketability rather than litigation. It would be wise for the court to examine the documents *in camera* or order more detailed information on the privilege log before making a conclusive ruling.

Even if the work product doctrine applies, any fact work product in the Notes or Report may nevertheless be discovered upon a showing of substantial need and undue burden. On the other hand, "core" attorney work product—the mental impressions of attorneys and trial strategy—is highly protected under the Rules and *Hickman* and perhaps may not even be susceptible to discovery in any case.

Here, it is not clear that Pettigrew has a substantial need for the information. True, it may aid the development of Pettigrew's case for causation, but it is not clear whether other information would make Pettigrew's case without it. If so, then Pettigrew is unlikely to be able to show a substantial need. If not, then Pettigrew might in fact be able to make such a showing.

It also is unclear whether Pettigrew could not obtain the same information without undue hardship. It seems that there are other ways for Pettigrew to get the information. Indeed, if the court requires disclosure of some of the names of gamers in response to Pettigrew's interrogatory, those names may provide Pettigrew with the opportunity to conduct her own interviews of those gamers and to essentially replicate the very Notes that she seeks. Pettigrew also could hire her own industry expert to obtain information likely contained in the Report about the marketability of violence in games. One primary purpose of the work product protection is to prevent attorneys from free riding on the efforts of their adversaries; that purpose would be frustrated if Pettigrew's attorney were able to obtain Darklords's counsel's interview Notes if Pettigrew had access to the same interviewees or Reports by generating their substantial equivalent through her own efforts. Of course, the test is not "impossibility" but "undue hardship," and therefore if the costs were unreasonably high for Pettigrew to obtain the information in the documents by other means, then a court might nonetheless find Pettigrew entitled to them.

To the extent that the Notes are verbatim recitations of the interviewees, they may be primarily fact work product and thus subject to discovery upon a showing of substantial need and undue hardship. But any mental impressions of the attorney conducting the interviews will be core work product. Thus, if the attorney's line of questioning is apparent from the interviews, or if the attorney only wrote down certain facts that the attorney deemed important, then it might not be possible to separate the fact work product from the core work product, rendering the entire document core work product subject to heightened protection.

The Report, if it is even work product, is most likely fact work product rather than core work product. There may be core work product if counsel asked for the information in the Report and the Report divulges counsel's mental processes in asking for the information.

In each case, *in camera* inspection may be necessary to determine what type of work product is at issue. To the extent both exist, redaction may be an appropriate method of protecting core work product if Pettigrew is entitled to the fact work product.

III. Sanctions or Cost Shifting

Pettigrew filed a motion to compel under Rule 37 and, as such, the court should consider whether sanctions or cost shifting is appropriate. Rule 37(a)(3)(B) allows motions to compel answers to interrogatories and responses to requests for production. Accordingly, assuming Pettigrew included the required meet-and-confer certification, her motion is procedurally proper.

In addition, Rule 37(a)(5) requires or allows the court to shift costs associated with the expenses of the motion under certain circumstances. If the motion is granted or denied in full, the court must, after giving an opportunity to be heard, require the losing party to pay the prevailing party's reasonable expenses incurred in making the motion, including attorney's fees, unless the losing party's position was substantially justified or other circumstances make cost shifting unjust. If the motion is denied in part and granted in part, then the court may, after giving an opportunity to be heard, apportion the reasonable expenses for the motion.

Here, the facts given suggest that each party's position was substantially justified. Pettigrew has a right to the information sought in the interrogatory; Darklords had reasonable cause to seek protection from it. Similarly, Darklords has substantial justification to assert privilege or protection over the documents; Pettigrew has substantial justification to test the validity and applicability of the assertions. It may be that more information from *in camera* inspection will undermine one party's justification (such as Darklords's assertions of privilege and protection over the Report). If so, then the court should consider cost shifting. Otherwise, cost shifting and sanctions would be inappropriate.

TOOLS FOR SELF-CRITICISM

Did you pay attention to the cause of action in the hypothetical? Because a party may discover any nonprivileged information relevant to the claim or defense of any party, the basic inquiry into relevance will begin with the cause of action alleged. Here, Pettigrew sued Darklords under a negligence theory and must prove causation to make a successful claim. Interrogatory 10 requests the identity of registered players so that Pettigrew can interview them to determine what adverse effects gaming has had on them. As an initial matter, you should have recognized the connection between the information Pettigrew requested and the causation element of negligence.

With this type of question, you can be creative in coming up with possible courses of action for the court. The sample essay certainly does not provide all of the options available to the court. You might have been tempted to limit your answer to resolving the party's arguments in the hypothetical. But, the court has broad discretion in resolving discovery disputes, and the call of the question invited you to explore the parameters of that discretion in your answer. In exercising this discretion, as the sample essay reflects, the court will consider the interests of the parties. Thus, for example, by issuing a confidentiality order, the court could protect Darklords's business interests and the identity of the gamers, while simultaneously providing Pettigrew with needed information. Your answer should reflect, as the Seventh Circuit did in *Mareese*, the way in which the court can balance the parties' competing interests within the limits of the discovery rules.

In addition, think about the underlying issues of preserving efficiency and resources that will likely affect the court's decision. The court need not issue an order entitling Pettigrew to every gamer's name, because such discovery may be an undue intrusion on the privacy of certain gamers and may cost more in time and money than other options. Similarly, the court would be concerned with the delay caused by the parties drafting a letter to gamers to appease privacy concerns as opposed to merely requiring Darklords to hand over the information.

Did you take Darklords at its word that the documents in question were privileged? An assertion of attorney-client privilege by a party does not necessarily mean that the document is, in fact, privileged. In particular, the fact that the Report was prepared by Marketing for the Board should have clued you in to the likelihood that an attorney-client privilege assertion was invalid with respect to the Report. Of course, the actual contents of the Report in question were not made available by the hypothetical, so you should have addressed the lack of complete information and a way to obtain this information and resolve the ambiguity.

Likewise, you should have addressed the ambiguities with respect to Darklords's assertion of work-product protection. The sample essay questions whether the Notes and Report were prepared in anticipation of litigation, when they were prepared, as well as whether they were prepared as a strategic business decision. It is important to recognize when more information is needed, and to point out that the court may review the documents *in camera* to make the relevant determinations.

Did you get tripped up by the presence or absence of attorneys in the assertion of privilege or protection? Whereas the absence of an attorney is usually fatal to a claim of attorney-client privilege, attorneys need not be involved in creating protected work product. Work product protection extends to documents created in anticipation *by a party or a party's representative*. Thus, work product can be created by a party, a party's insurer, a party's fact expert, or other non-attorney persons (although it can also be created by an attorney).

Did you keep the exceptions to work product protection straight? The first important point is that there are no (at least not in most civil procedure courses) exceptions to attorney-client privilege. The privilege can be waived, of course, but if the privilege attaches, no showing of need or burden will vitiate it. Work product protection, however, does have a limited exception. A party can discovery otherwise protected work product upon a showing of substantial need and undue hardship. That exception, however, does not extend to "core" work product that encompasses the mental impressions and trial strategies of counsel. If you did not keep these exceptions straight in your answer, consider reviewing your materials again.

Finally, did you forget about costs? Discovery motions always have the opportunity for cost shifting (or other sanctions) under Rule 37. Remember that Rule 37 allows cost shifting against the losing party on a discovery motion if that party's position was not substantially justified.

VARIATIONS ON THE THEME

Would it change your answer if the Notes had been created by the Product Safety Department as part of a periodic assessment of the harmful effects of gaming? What if the Product Safety Department scheduled a routine assessment every six months, but this one was done after only three months from the date of the last assessment because of a sudden increase in tort claims against Darklords? Would it make a difference if counsel were involved?

What if Darklords intended to call one of its registered gamers as a witness in furtherance of its affirmative case at trial? *See* FED. R. CIV. P. 26(a)(1). If so, could Pettigrew force the gamer to submit to a psychological examination to assess what effects gaming had had on him? *See* FED. R. CIV. P. 35.

If Pettigrew had not attempted to meet and confer with Darklords before filing her motion to compel, could she still seek sanctions?

Say that Darklords had retained a consulting expert to assist with the defense but not to testify. The expert was an expert in sociological harm from gaming and was hired to assess causation in the case. If Darklords showed the expert all of the documents in its privilege log, would any privilege or protection covering them have been waived? What if Darklords asked the expert to testify about his conclusions? *See* FED. R. CIV. P. 26(a)(2).

As part of Darklords's system, a nonparty support company maintains data on gamers, including the information sought by Interrogatory 10. How might Pettigrew obtain the same information from that nonparty?

Could Darklords have objected to Interrogatory 10 on the grounds that the information, coming from Darklords in its answer, would be inadmissible hearsay? *See* FED. R. CIV. P. 26(b)(1).

Say Darklords later obtains a study that was done by a neutral third party that is neither privileged nor protected. If Darklords only came into possession of the study after answering the document request, must it now produce the study? *See* FED. R. CIV. P. 26(e).

OPTIONAL READINGS

Discovery implicates tensions between the adversarial system and the need for full disclosure to prepare for meaningful trial. Proponents of the adversarial system, for example, might balk at the notion of mandatory disclosures. For more, see *Amendments to the Federal Rules of Civil Procedure*, 146 F.R.D. 401, 507–13 (1993).

The judge has some latitude to tailor discovery to fit the needs of the case. Although discovery often is time consuming and expensive, not all cases involve massive discovery. For two views on discovery, compare Frank H. Easterbrook,

Discovery as Abuse, 69 B.U. L. Rev. 635 (1989), with Linda Mullenix, *The Pervasive Myth of Pervasive Discovery Abuse and the Consequences for Unfounded Rulemaking*, 46 Stan. L. Rev. 1393 (1994) (arguing that extensive discovery is not the norm).

Another controversy surrounding discovery is its scope, particularly in light of the costs attendant to broad discovery and the fact that no other country in the world has as broad discovery as the United States. *See* Richard L. Marcus, *Retooling American Discovery for the Twenty-First Century: Toward a New World Order?*, 7 Tul. J. Intl. & Comp. L. 153 (1999); Stephen N. Subrin, *Discovery in Global Perspective: Are We Nuts?*, 52 DePaul L. Rev. 299 (2002).

SUMMARY JUDGMENT

15

OPENING REMARKS

What if, after ample opportunity for discovery, it turns out that the evidence adduced reveals no genuine factual dispute between the parties? Must the parties still go to trial?

The short answer is no. Summary judgment is a procedure for short-circuiting the litigation in this circumstance. The crucible of trial is meant to resolve genuine disputes of fact that are material to the claims. If no genuine dispute remains, then trial is unnecessary, and the summary judgment procedure allows the court to enter judgment for a party rather than go to trial. The idea is this: If no rational jury could possibly find for Party A, then we ought to save the parties, court, and prospective jurors the time and expense of trial and simply end the matter right now.

Rule 56 captures this idea by providing for summary judgment if "there is no genuine issue as to any material fact and that the movant is entitled to judgment as a matter of law." The Rule further provides that when a movant shows entitlement to summary judgment, then the opposing party may not rely merely on its pleadings but rather must "set out specific facts showing a genuine issue for trial."

Rule 56 thus sets forth a burden-shifting mechanism for making and opposing summary judgment motions. First, the movant must show the absence of a genuine issue of material fact and entitlement to judgment as a matter of law. If the movant does not do so, then the court should deny the motion. If the movant does so, then the burden shifts to the nonmovant to come forward with specific facts that create a genuine issue of material fact. If the nonmovant does so, then summary judgment should be denied. If the nonmovant does not, then summary judgment should be granted.

With the exception of admissions in pleadings, the evidence considered on a summary judgment motion must be admissible at trial. This makes sense because summary judgment asks whether any jury could find for the nonmovant, and, at trial, any evidence that the jury hears would have to be admissible. Recall, however, that discovery allows for disclosure of both admissible and inadmissible evidence (as long as it could lead to the discovery of admissible evidence!). Thus, although you should think of summary judgment as a way of evaluating whether the case should continue in light of what discovery has revealed, you also should recognize that the universe of evidence that may be considered in a summary judgment motion may be narrower than that of discovery.

Paradoxically, the summary judgment universe of evidence may also be larger than that of formal discovery. Summary judgment evidence may be augmented by affidavits containing admissible evidence or testimony that was not disclosed during discovery. Affidavits are sworn statements based on personal knowledge. They can usefully fill in gaps left unfilled by the discovery process. As a practical matter, then, the prospect of moving for or opposing summary judgment affects discovery. A party anticipating that she will move for summary judgment will wish to be particularly thorough in her discovery requests and deposition questions to preclude the possibility that she might find her summary judgment motion opposed by an affidavit that adds new and unexpected information. Similarly, a party that expects to oppose a motion for summary judgment must answer formal discovery carefully and as narrowly as possible to preserve the ability to put forward helpful affidavit statements to fill those gaps later.

Because summary judgment tests the sufficiency of the evidence that is likely to be used at trial, a party opposing a summary judgment motion who believes that additional discovery will uncover evidence that would aid its opposition can oppose the motion on that ground. As a result, although Rule 56 allows summary judgment motions to be made relatively early in the litigation, most summary judgment motions are made only after the close of discovery (or at least after all discovery on that particular issue).

Because the goal of summary judgment is to avoid trial on essentially undisputed issues, summary judgment may be partial. In other words, a party need not move for summary judgment on all claims (although a party may certainly do so). Summary judgment may resolve just one claim or even as little as one issue of fact on one claim or defense. Thus, for example, if a plaintiff sues a defendant for negligence seeking compensatory damages and punitive damages, the defendant can move for summary judgment only on the issue of punitive damages. If successful, the case will proceed to trial only on the remaining issues. Similarly, the plaintiff might move for summary judgment on one of the defendants' affirmative defenses. If granted, the defendant will not be permitted to invoke that defense or present evidence of it at trial.

In practice, litigants (especially defendants) routinely move for summary judgment. Although the standard purports to be quite difficult to meet, and putting the motion together can involve much attorney time and costs, a summary judgment is a judgment—a win—for the party. For most defendants, the potential of avoiding the unpredictability and expense of trial is well worth the costs of the motion.

In conceptualizing summary judgment, it may be useful to contrast it with a motion to dismiss for failure to state a claim under Rule 12(b)(6). A motion to dismiss, which is based on the pleadings, tests whether there is any reason to proceed to discovery, and results in a dismissal (usually) without prejudice to refiling. By contrast, a motion for summary judgment is based on the evidence adduced in discovery, tests whether there is any reason to proceed to trial, and results in a judgment with preclusive effect.

HYPOTHETICAL

Pam and Dan were each driving cars that collided at an intersection controlled by a traffic light. Pam sued Dan in federal court based on diversity alleging negligence. The elements for negligence are duty of care, breach of that duty, causation of harm by the breach, and damages as a result. In a claim for negligence, the plaintiff bears the burden of proof by a preponderance of the evidence.

Pam sought both compensatory and punitive damages. State law allows punitive damages only if the plaintiff proves willful or wanton conduct by clear and convincing evidence. Punitive damages are not an independent claim but rather a form of relief.

Having returned a waiver of service, Dan has not yet answered the complaint. Nevertheless, 21 days after commencing the action, Pam files a motion for summary judgment. She attaches three affidavits in support of her motion.

First, Pam attaches her own affidavit. In it, she asserts that she was traveling at the speed limit of 30 miles per hour as she approached the intersection. She saw the light turn green 100 yards before she got to the intersection, and the light remained green as she entered the intersection. She said that while her light was green, Dan crossed into the intersection in front of her, and the front of her car crashed into the driver's side of Dan's car. Pam also said that her new car was damaged extensively in the accident and that she suffered a broken leg. She attaches two documents to her affidavit: her mechanic's bill for repair of her car for $10,000, and her medical bills for her leg totaling $70,000.

Second, Pam attaches the affidavit of Officer Oscar. He said that he was the police officer who responded to the accident. He confirmed Pam's description of the location of the cars in the intersection. He also said that he smelled alcohol on Dan's breath and gave him a breathalyzer test, which registered a .07 percent blood alcohol level, just under the legal limit of .08 percent. He said that he ticketed Dan for driving while his license was suspended for prior traffic infractions. A copy of the traffic citation is attached to the affidavit.

Third, Pam attaches the affidavit of her son, who said that he was riding as a passenger in Pam's car at the time of the accident. He confirmed that Pam had a green light at the time of the accident. He also said that, just after the collision, Dan apologized to him for the accident.

You represent Dan. Dan tells you that his light turned from green to yellow at the moment he entered the intersection, that he had consumed two beers about an hour before the accident but that his driving was not impaired by them, and that he did not "apologize" to Pam's son but rather merely expressed his concern for Pam and her son after the accident. He has no way to dispute the claimed compensatory damages. Nor does he have any affirmative defenses to impose. How will you oppose Pam's motion for summary judgment, and what cross-motion might you make? How is the court likely to rule?

Assume that the documents are all admissible into evidence, that the affidavits are based on personal knowledge, that they set out facts that would be admissible, and that the affiants are all competent to testify.

SUGGESTED READINGS

U.S. CONST. amend. VII
FED. R. CIV. P. 56
Adickes v. S.H. Kress & Co., 398 U.S. 144, 153–61 (1970)
Celotex Corp. v. Catrett, 477 U.S. 317, 319–28 (1986)
Anderson v. Liberty Lobby, 477 U.S. 242, 244–58 (1986)
Matsushita Elec. Indus. Co. v. Zenith Radio Corp., 475 U.S. 574, 576–99 (1986)
Scott v. Harris, 550 U.S. 372, 374–76, 378–81 (2007)

SAMPLE ESSAY

I. General Legal Standards

Rule 56 allows summary judgment to be granted if there is no genuine issue of material fact, and the movant is entitled to judgment as a matter of law. A material fact is one that will affect the outcome. According to *Anderson*, a genuine issue is one about which a reasonable jury could reach different conclusions. In addition, in determining whether a genuine issue exists, *Anderson* also instructs courts to consider the substantive burden of proof. All reasonable inferences must be resolved in favor of the nonmovant, though *Matsushita* instructs that an inference may not be reasonable if it is implausible.

The moving party bears the initial burden of establishing entitlement to summary judgment. The moving party must show the absence of a genuine issue of material fact and entitlement to judgment as a matter of law. If the moving party is successful, the burden shifts to the nonmovant to raise a genuine issue of material fact.

II. Dan's Opposition

As a preliminary matter, Dan cannot move to strike or otherwise oppose Pam's motion on grounds that it is not timely. Rule 56(b) specifically allows Pam to move for summary judgment on all or part of her claim at any time until 30 days after the close of discovery. The rule says nothing about waiting until the defendant has filed an answer. Accordingly, Dan cannot attack Pam's motion as too early (with the exception of the fourth argument below).

Nevertheless, Dan should oppose Pam's motion on four grounds.

First, Dan should argue that Pam has not met her initial burden of establishing entitlement to summary judgment. This would be a difficult argument for Dan to make, at least on the claim for liability and compensatory damages. Pam's affidavit establishes her substantive case of negligence, causation, and damages. Documentary evidence and the other witnesses' affidavits confirm her assertions. Dan could argue that Pam has the burden of proof at trial, and a jury might disbelieve the testimony and evidence that she proffers, even if Dan offers no contradictory evidence in rebuttal. If so, then a jury might find that she has not met her burden of proof at trial and render a verdict for Dan. Dan might also point out that at least one of the witnesses, Pam's son, is related to Pam and appears to have an inherent bias. Dan should argue that courts are reluctant to grant summary judgment for the party with the substantive burden of proof for these reasons.

Dan has a stronger case on punitive damages. Pam has no direct evidence of willful or wanton conduct. The citation is evidence of past driving infractions, which might lead to an inference of present reckless driving, but there is very little evidence (if any) of willful conduct by Dan. In addition, Pam's substantive burden is clear and convincing evidence of willful conduct—she would have to show that all rational juries would conclude that she has met her substantive standard. It is doubtful that Pam has met her burden of establishing entitlement to judgment as a matter of law on liability for punitive damages. Dan should argue all this and is likely to prevail.

Second, Dan should attach an affidavit detailing what he told me and argue that, even if Pam has met her initial burden, Dan has met his burden of creating a genuine issue of material fact. Dan's affidavit will call into question two elements:

breach and causation. His statement that his light was green directly contradicts Pam's affidavits, and would, if credited, cause a jury to find for Dan. The fact dispute is therefore genuine and material under *Anderson*. Its persuasiveness is irrelevant; that is for a jury to decide. A court is likely to find that Dan has met his burden to oppose summary judgment on liability for negligence.

Third, Dan should argue that, even if Pam has met her burden and Dan has not, the court should deny summary judgment. Rule 56 does not require a court to enter summary judgment. As the Advisory Committee Notes state, if there is a reasonable doubt about the credibility of affiants, then a court can deny summary judgment on the basis that appropriate resolution can only be had by evaluating live testimony. Here, Dan should argue that the only way to assess whether a jury could find for him or not would be based on live testimony as opposed to self-serving affidavits.

Fourth, Dan should argue that even if Pam has met her burden and Dan has not, the court should deny summary judgment or take the motion under advisement until discovery is complete. Rule 56(d) allows a party opposing a motion for summary judgment to show by affidavit that it cannot present facts essential to justify its opposition because discovery has not yet concluded. Dan ought to have a strong argument. In light of his own version of the facts, he should be entitled to depose Pam, Officer Oscar, and Pam's son to determine the nature and contours of their testimony. In addition, he may wish to seek discovery or information from other eyewitnesses who may have seen the accident and who can verify Dan's version of the events.

In light of all of the points that Dan should make in opposition, the court is likely to deny Pam's motion for summary judgment on issues of liability. However, on the issue of compensatory damages, Pam likely has met her burden while Dan likely has not met his. The evidence thus far shows no genuine issue of material fact as to Pam's claimed compensatory damages. Under Rule 56(a), summary judgment may be granted as to a particular issue. Thus, a court could issue an order establishing the existence or amount of the compensatory damages, unless Dan can convince the court that additional discovery would likely uncover contrary evidence. If the court does so, the court must issue an order specifying that compensatory damages are not genuinely at issue, and then those damages will be deemed to be established at trial.

III. Dan's Motion

A defendant may move for summary judgment on a plaintiff's claim in two ways: either by producing evidence that affirmatively negates an essential element of the claim or that conclusively establishes an affirmative defense; or, as *Celotex* confirms, by establishing that the record contains no evidence to support a contention on which the plaintiff bears the burden of proof.

Here, Dan should consider moving for summary judgment on all of Pam's claims, but he probably will prevail only on liability for the punitive damages. He should argue that Pam has insufficient evidence to allow a rational trier of fact to find in her favor on any issue. This argument is unlikely to be successful (and probably should not be made wholesale). As discussed above, Pam has ample evidence to support her claim for negligence and compensatory damages. It is entirely possible that a rational jury could credit her version of the events and find that she has established her case for negligence and compensatory damages by a preponderance of the evidence. Thus, Dan's motion on liability and compensatory damages is unlikely to be successful.

However, Dan has a strong change of obtaining an order establishing no genuine issue as to punitive damages. As discussed above, Pam must prove willful conduct by clear and convincing evidence. She has no (or almost no) evidence of willful conduct, and certainly no clear and convincing evidence of willful conduct. Dan should be able to meet his burden of establishing no genuine issue of material fact on punitive damages, unless Pam opposes his motion with either evidence that would allow a rational trier of fact to find clear and convincing evidence of willful conduct, or an affidavit justifying the need for additional discovery on the issue.

In sum, both motions for summary judgment likely will be denied. However, the court may issue an order deeming compensatory damages established and deeming punitive damages unavailable. In addition, rather than denying the motions, it is possible that the court will hold the motions under advisement to allow the completion of discovery.

TOOLS FOR SELF-CRITICISM

Summary judgment problems force you to be meticulous about the burden-shifting mechanism they entail. Thus, you should proceed stepwise. First, consider whether the movant has met her initial burden. If not, then the court need go no further—the motion should be denied. This first step is reflected in the sample answer as Dan's first line of defense. Only if the movant meets her initial burden need the court proceed to the nonmovant's opposition. Being careful about the burden-shifting mechanism will help ensure that you answer the question completely and properly demonstrate your knowledge of the legal standards.

Did you spot the other ways to oppose the motion besides the evidentiary arguments? Recognizing that summary judgments are discretionary and should be granted only after the nonmovant has had full opportunity to uncover opposing evidence is vital to Dan's opposition.

The substantive burden is also important to note. Here, Pam, the summary judgment movant, has the burden of proof on the merits. She therefore has a difficult summary judgment burden because she must convince a court that all reasonable juries would believe her. That is a difficult projection to make. As the sample answer shows, Dan should argue that the merits burden works against Pam's initial summary judgment burden.

Also, do not forget to incorporate any heightened merits burdens into the summary judgment standard. Punitive damages must be proven by clear and convincing evidence. Hence, if Pam is to obtain summary judgment on punitive damages, she must meet her summary judgment burden with that heightened merits standard in mind.

Remember that summary judgment may be partial. The court can resolve any undisputed issue. That is particularly important for the compensatory damages alleged here. Because there was no genuine dispute as to compensatory damages, summary judgment on that issue is appropriate, and you should have spotted that.

Did you get tripped up by the early nature of Pam's motion? Although summary judgment motions usually are made only after discovery, Rule 56 does not limit them to that time period. Here, Pam's motion was timely under the rule.

VARIATIONS ON THE THEME

What if the ticket issued to Dan had been for running the red light, and that such a ticket would be sufficient under state law to establish negligence as a matter of law?

Would your answer change if the complaint was filed on January 2, 2009, the accident occurred on January 1, 2006, and the undisputed applicable limitations period for Pam's claim is three years?

Assume that the court denies the motions and allows further discovery. Consider whether your analysis would change if discovery revealed either or both of the following pieces of evidence: (1) Pam and her son are very close and are in trouble financially—they have massive debt—and the hospital alleged to have treated her for her leg injury has no record of her as a patient; (2) the stoplight was equipped with a camera that took a photo showing Dan's light to be red as he crossed into the intersection. Might Scott v. Harris, 550 U.S. 372 (2007), then be of assistance?

OPTIONAL READINGS

Taking a case from a jury always implicates Seventh Amendment concerns. The Supreme Court long ago upheld the summary judgment procedure in the face of Seventh Amendment challenges, but the academic dispute has not gone away. *See* Suja A. Thomas, *Why Summary Judgment is Unconstitutional*, 93 Va. L. Rev. 139 (2007); Suja A. Thomas, *The Unconstitutionality of Summary Judgment: A Status Report*, 93 Iowa L. Rev. 1613 (2008); Edward Brunet, *Summary Judgment Is Constitutional*, 93 Iowa L. Rev. 1625 (2008); William E. Nelson, *Summary Judgment and the Progressive Constitution*, 93 Iowa L. Rev. 1653 (2008); Suja A. Thomas, *Why Summary Judgment Is Still Unconstitutional: A Reply to Professors Brunet and Nelson*, 93 Iowa L. Rev. 1667 (2008).

As noted above, summary judgment generally is based on admissible evidence. For more on the relationship between summary judgment and the rules of evidence, see James Duane, *The Four Greatest Myths About Summary Judgment*, 52 Wash. & Lee L. Rev. 1523 (1996).

The Supreme Court decided *Celotex, Anderson,* and *Matsushita* all on the same day in 1986. All three upheld the use of summary judgment for the defendants. They have been taken to suggest an invitation to litigants and the lower courts to use the summary judgment procedure more often and more readily. Because summary judgment is usually a tool for defendants, the trilogy was seen as a significant blow to the plaintiff's bar. For more, see Arthur Miller, *The Pretrial Rush to Judgment: Are the "Litigation Explosion," "Liability Crisis," and Efficiency Clichés Eroding Our Day in Court and Jury Trial Commitments?*, 78 N.Y.U. L. Rev. 982 (2003).

16

JUDGMENT AS A MATTER OF LAW

OPENING REMARKS

The plaintiff has survived summary judgment, and the case proceeds to trial. At trial, the parties present evidence and proffer testimony in stages, usually first by the plaintiff and then by the defendant. If the evidence presented virtually assures one party of victory, is there a mechanism for entering judgment immediately rather than requiring a jury to render a verdict?

Yes. The legal mechanism is called judgment as a matter of law. Think of judgments as a matter of law as akin to summary judgments. They have a similar legal standard—whether any rational trier of fact could find in favor of the nonmovant. But they have two important differences. First, motions for judgment as a matter of law are made during or after trial, rather than before trial. Second, they are based on evidence and testimony that actually is admitted into evidence at trial, rather than any evidence that may be admissible. Thus, a court can deny a motion for summary judgment because, based on the evidence adduced in discovery, a genuine issue of material fact exists but could later grant judgment as a matter of law if the evidence and testimony presented at trial do not dispute that issue.

Rule 50 deals with judgments as a matter of law. Note that there are two types. Rule 50(a) addresses judgments as a matter of law that are entered before the jury deliberates. These types also have been called "directed verdicts"—in essence, the court enters the verdict without involvement of the jury. Either party may move for a judgment under Rule 50(a), but only after the nonmoving party has been fully heard on the issue. Generally, then, the defendant will move for a judgment as a matter of law under Rule 50(a) at the close of the plaintiff's case, and then the plaintiff (and perhaps the defendant as well) will move for a judgment as a matter of law under Rule 50(a) at the close of the defendant's case.

Rule 50(b) addresses judgments as a matter of law that are entered after the jury returns a verdict (and essentially override the jury's decision). These also have been called judgments notwithstanding the verdict (or, JNOV). Rule 50(b) judgments can only be granted if the movant previously moved for a judgment as a matter of law under Rule 50(a) before the jury returned a verdict. The reason is that the Seventh Amendment prohibits district courts from reexamining facts determined by juries. Accordingly, Rule 50(b) motions are considered to be "renewed" Rule 50(a) motions originally made before submission to the jury.

HYPOTHETICAL

Peter and Donna were each driving cars that collided on a highway. Peter sued Donna in federal court based on diversity, alleging negligence. The elements for negligence are duty of care, breach of that duty, causation of harm by the breach, and damages as a result. In a claim for negligence, the plaintiff bears the burden of proof by a preponderance of the evidence. In addition, under the applicable state law, the plaintiff is barred from recovery if the defendant can prove the affirmative defense of contributory negligence, which means that the plaintiff's own negligence contributed to his injuries.

Discovery commenced and concluded. Neither party moved for summary judgment, and the case went to trial.

At trial, Peter testified. He asserted that he was driving on Interstate 95 when Donna's car unexpectedly swerved into his lane. Peter immediately hit his brakes but could not avoid a collision. Donna's car clipped his front bumper and sent Peter's car crashing into a guard rail. Peter testified that his car was damaged and that he suffers from chronic neck pain as a result. He offered, and the court admitted into evidence, a mechanic's bill for repair of his car for $10,000, and medical bills for his neck totaling $70,000.

At the close of Peter's case, outside the presence of the jury, Donna moved for judgment as a matter of law, arguing that Peter's evidence was insufficient as a matter of law to prove the legal elements of the claim. The court responded, "Peter's testimony was very convincing, and I believe him. A reasonable jury could find for him. Donna's motion is therefore denied."

Donna then presented her case. She testified that she was driving at about the speed limit when Peter's car came up behind very fast. Donna estimated that Peter was driving at least 15 miles per hour over the speed limit. Donna explained that she was so startled by Peter's fast approach that she did not notice a broken glass in her lane. The glass caused her tire to explode, which caused her to swerve slightly into Peter's lane. She testified that she did not swerve completely into Peter's lane and that a cautious driver in Peter's position going a safe speed could have avoided her car. Nevertheless, Peter failed to avoid the collision and hit the side of her rear bumper. Donna did not dispute the damages.

At the close of Donna's case, outside the presence of the jury, Peter moved for judgment as a matter of law on both liability and damages, seeking the full $80,000. Donna also renewed her motion for judgment as a matter of law based on the insufficiency of Peter's evidence. The court denied both motions and was particularly harsh with Donna, saying, "I already denied your motion once. I'm denying it again now. Don't make me deny it a third time."

The case was submitted to a jury, which returned a verdict for Peter on liability but awarded him only $10,000 in damages. The court immediately entered judgment on the verdict. The next day, Donna moved for judgment as a matter of law on the issue of liability, asserting two grounds. First, she renewed her argument that Peter's evidence is legally insufficient to prove her negligence. Second, she argued that her testimony established Peter's contributory negligence, that no testimony or evidence disputed Peter's negligence, and that therefore Peter was barred from recovery as a matter of law by the defense of contributory negligence. Thirty days later, Peter opposed Donna's motion and also submitted his own motion for judgment as a matter of law on damages, arguing that the full $80,000 was adequately supported and not disputed, and that therefore the full amount should be awarded notwithstanding the jury's verdict.

A. Was the court correct in denying the pre-submission motions? Why or why not?
B. How should the court rule on the post-verdict motions and why? Do not discuss the possibility of ordering a new trial.

SUGGESTED READINGS

U.S. Const. amend. VII

Fed. R. Civ. P. 50

Anderson v. Liberty Lobby, 477 U.S. 242, 251–52 (1986)

Lavender v. Kurn, 327 U.S. 645, 646–54 (1946)

Reeves v. Sanderson Plumbing Prods., Inc., 530 U.S. 133, 137–40, 149–54 (2000)

Galloway v. United States, 319 U.S. 372, 388–96 (1943)

Neely v. Martin K. Eby Constr. Co., 386 U.S. 317, 318–30 (1967)

Unitherm Food Sys., Inc. v. Swift-Eckrich, Inc., 546 U.S. 394, 396–407 (2006)

Garrison v. United States, 62 F.2d 41, 42 (4th Cir. 1932)

SAMPLE ESSAY

A. Pre-Submission Motions

The standard for judgment as a matter of law under Rule 50 is whether the evidence proffered at trial is not legally sufficient for a jury to find for a party. Although older cases suggest that any scintilla of evidence in favor of a party will require denial of a judgment as a matter of law against that party (*see Lavender*), more recent cases suggest that the standard for Rule 50 is the same as the standard for summary judgment (*see Anderson*). In deciding a Rule 50 motion, the court should consider all of the evidence that is available at the time of the ruling. *See Reeves v. Sanderson Plumbing.*

Under this standard, the court correctly denied Donna's pre-submission motions. Both times, Donna moved for judgment as a matter of law for Peter's failure to meet his burden of proving negligence. But Peter testified that Donna swerved into his lane and hit his car. Taking all inferences and credibility determinations in Peter's favor, a reasonable jury could find that Donna owed Peter a duty to stay in her lane, that she failed to do so, and that her failure caused Peter's injuries. Accordingly, the court properly denied Donna's first motion.

The court did comment on Peter's evidence. In ruling on a Rule 50(a) motion, a court is not permitted to make credibility calls or pick inferences that it seems most likely. Instead, a court must construe all reasonable inferences credibility determinations in favor of the nonmoving party. *Reeves.* It is not clear if the court's opinions improperly influenced its decision to deny Donna's motion, but even if they did, the court's error was harmless because the court should have construed the evidence in the light most favorable to Peter and, as a result, denied Donna's motion anyway.

Despite Donna's testimony, the court also properly denied her second motion. Donna's testimony explained why she swerved, but a reasonable jury could still find that she breached a duty to Peter. And, a reasonable jury could disbelieve her testimony. Donna could have moved for judgment as a matter of law based upon her affirmative defense of contributory negligence, but she did not do so; instead, she moved only on the insufficiency of Peter's own case. Peter's testimony, if believed, could have allowed a reasonable jury to find for him, even after Donna's testimony. Accordingly, the court properly denied Donna's motion.

Peter's motion is more difficult. The court properly denied the portion of the motion seeking judgment as a matter of law on the issue of liability. Donna's testimony provided ample evidence to allow a jury to find Peter contributorily negligent and thus bar him from recovery. But no evidence of testimony disputed Peter's damages of $80,000. The court could have found that no reasonable trier of fact could have awarded less than $80,000 in damages. This is a difficult question because Peter's evidence would have to conclusively establish all of the elements entitling him to the $80,000, including causation. If he did, though, the court probably could have granted Peter's motion as to the damages amount and submitted only the issue of liability to the jury.

That does not mean that the court's denial of Peter's motion was in error, however. Courts routinely deny motions for judgment as a matter of law (or at least take them under advisement) to avoid taking the fact-finding function away from the jury. It may be that the jury will find as the evidence directs anyway. Also, erroneously entering a judgment as a matter of law after the verdict may be more efficient than entering it before verdict because, if the judgment is reversed on appeal, no new trial would be required. In addition, Peter bears the burden of proof on the issue of damages, and it may be that the jury could find Peter incredible. Finally, Rule 50(a) says that a court "may" resolve an issue against a party in ruling on a motion for judgment as a matter of law—it does not say "must." Denying Peter's motion, then, was within the discretion of the court. Indeed, the Supreme Court has encouraged district courts to submit cases to the jury instead of granting Rule 50(a) motions. *Unitherm*. Based on the interest in protecting the jury function and on the burden of proof that Peter bears, the court did not err in denying Peter's motion.

B. Post-Verdict Motions

The court should deny both post-verdict motions. Donna's motion was based on two theories: (1) insufficiency of Peter's evidence of her negligence, and (2) unrefuted evidence of Peter's contributory negligence. As to the second ground, Donna's motion must be denied because the Seventh Amendment prevents reexamination of the fact issue of contributory negligence. Although Rule 50(b) motions may be granted after a jury verdict notwithstanding the Seventh Amendment, they may be granted only if they are renewals of Rule 50(a) motions made *before* submission to the jury. Donna never moved for judgment as a matter of law on her affirmative defense of contributory negligence before submission to the jury. As a result, the Seventh Amendment bars the court from granting her Rule 50(b) motion now.

As to the first ground, Donna's motion should be denied as well, for two reasons. First, Donna's motion fails for the same reason that her pre-submission Rule 50(a) motions failed: Peter's evidence is not legally insufficient. Second, Donna's motion may run into Seventh Amendment problems on this ground as well. Although Rule 50(b) states that a court that does not grant a Rule 50(a) motion is considered to have submitted the action to the jury subject to the court's power later to decide the motion, that consideration may be inapplicable here. The court said, in denying Donna's Rule 50(a) motion, "I already denied your motion once. I'm denying it again now. Don't make me deny it a third time." That statement could be considered to be a flat-out denial of her Rule 50(a) motion, without the possibility of renewal. It is unclear whether Rule 50(b)'s "is considered to have" language trumps all emphatic denials. If not, then Donna's Rule 50(b) motion on insufficient evidence grounds has Seventh Amendment problems. If so, then Donna's motion still has merits problems. In either case, it should be denied.

The court also should deny Peter's motion. Although Peter's motion is strong on the merits, as discussed above in the context of his Rule 50(a) motion, similar counterarguments apply. In addition, Peter's Rule 50(b) renewal is untimely. Rule 50(b) requires such a motion to be made within 28 days after the entry of judgment. Here, Peter renewed his Rule 50(a) motion 30 days after the entry of judgment. Rule 6(b) prevents a court from extending the 14-day window. Accordingly, Peter's Rule 50(b) motion should be denied as untimely.

TOOLS FOR SELF-CRITICISM

This problem requires you to know both the substantive standards of Rule 50 and the technical requirements for making appropriate motions. Did you keep both in mind?

You first should have evaluated the pre-submission motions. They all were technically proper because they were all made after the nonmoving party had been heard on the issue. You should not have been tripped up by the fact that Donna moved under Rule 50(a) twice. Nothing prevents her from moving first at the close of the plaintiff's case and then again at the close of her own case.

Of course, you should have caught Donna's tactical error in not moving for judgment as a matter of law on her affirmative defense (which she only could have done after the close of her own case). That was a critical omission by Donna because it prevented her from properly moving on that ground under Rule 50(b).

On the merits, Peter's pre-submission motion was most difficult. Although it is possible that the court could have granted the motion as to damages, several policy and practical reasons justified the court's denial. Did you discuss those? Particularly in light of the Supreme Court's admonition in *Unitherm*, you should have.

How did you deal with the judge's opinion of Peter's evidence? That should have triggered a red flag for you—usually, the judge's own opinions of evidence and credibility are appropriate for new trial orders but not for judgments as a matter of law. Thus, you should have recognized the issue. Nevertheless, you also should have realized that not every error is harmful. Here, the judge's opinions may or may not have affected her decision making, but the decision making was still correct.

The Rule 50(b) motions tested your knowledge of the technicalities of the procedure for making them. Thus, Donna's motion based on her affirmative defense was improper because she failed to make a Rule 50(a) motion on the same grounds. And Peter's motion was improper because he failed to make it within 28 days of judgment.

VARIATIONS ON THE THEME

Could Peter have made his Rule 50(a) motion at the close of his case? Why not?

Suppose that applicable state law required the plaintiff, as part of his affirmative case, to establish that he was not contributorily negligent. Would that change your response to any of the motions that were made?

Would it have been proper for the court to grant Peter's pre-submission motion as to damages? If you were an appellate court reviewing such a grant, what would you do?

Say Donna moved under Rule 50(a) for judgment as a matter of law on the issue of contributory negligence at the close of Peter's case, but she fails to move again at the close of her own case. How would that change your answer to her Rule 50(b) motion?

What if the judge had said, "Donna, your Rule 50(a) motion is meritless and always will be. Rule 50(b) says that if I don't grant it, it will be considered to be open for renewal after the jury's verdict. But let me tell you now that I do not consider it open for renewal. I am denying it unconditionally and unreservedly." What kinds of Seventh Amendment implications would Donna's Rule 50(b) attempt to renew that motion then have?

OPTIONAL READINGS

For a similar fact pattern from a real case, see Denman v. Spain, 135 So. 2d 195 (Miss. 1961).

Empirical evidence suggests that juries and judges agree in the result of the vast majority of cases. *See, e.g.,* Valerie P. Hans & Stephanie Albertson, *Empirical Research and Civil Jury Reform*, 78 Notre Dame L. Rev. 1497, 1500–03 (2003); Harry Kalven Jr. & Jans Zeisel, The American Jury 63–65 (1966). Thus, Rule 50 only matters in fringe cases.

For a discussion of in-the-trenches Rule 50 practice, see 9 Moore's Federal Practice § 50 (3d ed. 2008).

17 NEW TRIALS

OPENING REMARKS

Judgments as a matter of law take the case away from the jury, which implicates substantial Seventh Amendment and system-acceptance concerns. New trials, by contrast, are far more palatable on these terms because they do not involve lodging the decision with a judge. On the other hand, they entail significant waste of resources, for an entire trial must be redone.

Losing parties almost always move for them, usually in conjunction with a renewed motion for judgment as a matter of law. New trial motions must be made within 28 days of the entry of judgment and state the grounds for the new trial. In addition, a court may order a new trial on its own during that same time period.

New trials may be ordered for any reason historically accepted as a basis for a new trial in actions at law in federal court, which generally means for any reason that calls into question the propriety of the verdict. Juror misconduct is one common basis. Another is that the verdict is against the weight of the evidence. Newly discovered evidence may also be the basis for a new trial. A fourth is clear legal error, which will enable the judge to correct herself instead of being reversed on appeal. Of course, if any of these reasons is harmless—that is, if it did not affect the outcome—then a new trial should not be held.

New trials can be partial, in that the court orders a new trial only on certain issues, while other issues remain established by the first trial. In addition, new trials can be conditional, such as with remittitur. Remittitur is when a court, believing an award of damages is too high, orders a new trial as to damages unless the plaintiff consents to a lower figure. The converse, additur, is not currently permitted in federal court.

HYPOTHETICAL

Paulette was fired from her job as a telemarketer with PhoneU, Inc. After exhausting her administrative remedies, she timely and properly sued PhoneU in federal court under federal law for gender discrimination.

During jury selection, the jury was asked whether any juror or any member of a juror's family had ever been subject to discrimination of any form. Gerald Gottfried stated that he believed he had been discriminated against several years ago on the basis of his race when he applied for and was denied a position as a server in a restaurant. The court refused to strike him for cause. PhoneU nevertheless struck Gerald Gottfried on a peremptory challenge. No other jurors mentioned any discrimination.

At the two-day trial, Paulette testified that she worked at PhoneU for only two months. While she worked at PhoneU, she overheard her supervisors making remarks about her gender. Paulette testified that her direct supervisor, Harvey Mint, told her that PhoneU was for "good old boys" and that "pretty ladies have no reason to work here." She testified that she was fired one month later. She testified that she was always polite on the phone with her customers. She also testified that she performed her job adequately by getting about 25 percent of her callers to sign up for the products and services PhoneU was charged with selling. She presented evidence that the average sales percentage for telemarketers in her division was 23 percent. She also presented evidence that PhoneU hired a man to replace her.

Paulette testified that she earned $400 per week working for PhoneU and that she intended to work there indefinitely. The day after she was fired, she was hired by another telemarketing company, but she only earns $300 per week there. She testified she has not been able to find a job that pays as much as she made at PhoneU. She also testified that she suffers from emotional damages as a result of the stigma of being terminated because of her gender.

Paulette called as a witness Manny Fortas, a former coworker at PhoneU, who testified that he also overheard Harvey Mint making gender-based comments about Paulette. Paulette wanted to call another coworker from PhoneU to testify similarly, but the judge, over Paulette's objections, prevented the witness from testifying, reasoning that the testimony would be merely duplicative and a waste of time.

Harvey Mint testified for PhoneU. He admitted making comments about Paulette's gender but testified that he terminated Paulette only because a customer complained to him that Paulette was abusive and aggressive on the phone. On cross-examination, Harvey admitted that neither he nor the company had any record of the customer or the customer's complaint.

Both parties moved for judgment as a matter of law prior to submission of the case to the jury. The court denied both motions. The court then instructed the jury that a gender discrimination claim requires proof of intent to discriminate because of gender. The court also instructed the jury that it did not need direct evidence of intent but could infer an intent to discriminate based on circumstantial evidence. The jury returned a verdict for the defendant.

Although neither party ever renewed its motion for judgment as a matter of law, 27 days after the entry of judgment, Paulette moved for a new trial under Rule 59. She argued that the foreman of the jury failed to properly answer questions during jury selection. Apparently, the foreman had once been discharged from the Army after suffering slight loss of peripheral vision in his right eye. The foreman said, "Well, sometimes the Army just has to do what the Army has to do." The court set a hearing on the motion for several weeks later.

At the hearing, Paulette argued in support of her motion based on the foreman's failure to answer truthfully. She also made a second motion for a new trial on the ground that the exclusion of her second PhoneU witness was legal error. She argued that his testimony would not have been cumulative and should have been allowed. She argued that the exclusion of this witness warranted a new trial as well.

After the hearing, the judge turns to you, her clerk. She asks you to draft a bench memo recommending a ruling and opinion on question of whether a new trial should be granted. She also tells you that she was very, very surprised that the jury found for PhoneU because she found Harvey Mint's testimony not credible and because she found Paulette's testimony and evidence compelling, though she did not believe any damages for emotional harm were warranted. She also asks you if she could offer Paulette the choice between a new trial and a judgment for $5,200 (representing $100/wk for 52 weeks, which the judge believed was the amount of time that Paulette reasonably would have to work at $300/wk until she could find a better paying job). Do not address any Rule 60 issues.

SUGGESTED READINGS

U.S. CONST. amend. VII.
FED. R. CIV. P. 6
FED. R. CIV. P. 50
FED. R. CIV. P. 59
FED. R. CIV. P. 61
Hetzel v. Prince William County, 523 U.S. 208, 208–12 (1998) (per curiam)
Dimick v. Scheidt, 293 U.S. 474, 475–76, 484–88 (1935)
McDonough Power Equip., Inc. v. Greenwood, 464 U.S. 548, 549–56 (1984)
Aetna Cas. & Surety Co. v. Yeatts, 122 F.2d 350, 352–55 (4th Cir. 1941)
Hulson v. Atchison, Topeka & Santa Fe Ry. Co., 289 F.2d 726, 727–31 (7th Cir. 1961)
Great Am. Indem. Co. v. Brown, 307 F.2d 306, 307, 309–10 (5th Cir. 1962)

SAMPLE ESSAY

BENCH MEMORANDUM

To: Judge
From: Clerk
Re: New Trial Issues in *Paulette v. PhoneU*

ISSUE

Can or should a new trial be granted in *Paulette v. PhoneU*? If so, can the court offer Paulette the choice between a new trial and a judgment of $5,200?

SHORT ANSWER

A new trial can be granted, but only on the ground that the verdict is against the weight of the evidence, and only after the court gives the parties notice and an opportunity to be heard on the issue. The court cannot offer Paulette the choice between a new trial and a judgment of $5,200 because the Seventh Amendment prohibits the judgment.

DISCUSSION

There are three possible grounds for a new trial and one option for a judgment. Each will be discussed in turn.

A. Juror Misconduct

Under Rule 59, a motion for a new trial must be made within 28 days of judgment. Paulette's motion was made in 27 days and thus is timely.

Juror misconduct, including the failure of a juror to answer truthfully during voir dire, can be the basis for a new trial. The standard for new trials based on juror answers is whether a correct answer would have resulted in the juror being stricken for cause. In *McDonough Power Equipment v. Greenwood*, a juror whose son had broken his leg in a truck fire remained silent when asked whether any immediate family members had sustained any severe injuries. The Supreme Court stated that to invalidate the trial on the basis of a juror's honest but mistaken response is to insist on something closer to perfection than our judicial system can be expected to give. According to the Court, to obtain a new trial in such a situation, the party must demonstrate both that the juror failed to answer honestly a material question and that an honest answer would have provided a valid basis for a challenge for cause.

This case is similar to *McDonough Power*. As there, the foreman's silence here may not have been incorrect. Being discharged from the Army based on a disability is not commonly thought of as discrimination. Further, the Army did not act unlawfully in discharging the foreman. And the only juror who spoke up alluded to more typical discrimination. Thus, it is entirely possible that the foreman's silence was completely honest. In addition, a full answer probably would not have led him to be stricken for cause. The foreman's experience may not have any bearing on his views of unlawful employment discrimination in the private sector. In short, Paulette has made no showing that the foreman was biased against her in any way or that his experience would have led him to be stricken for cause.

B. Exclusion of Testimony

Paulette's motion for a new trial based on legal error in excluding her witness is untimely. Rule 59 requires a motion for a new trial to be filed no later than 28 days after entry of judgment. That time bar is rigid under Rule 6 and cannot be extended. *Hulson v. Atchison, Topeka & Santa Fe Ry. Co.* Here, Paulette's motion was made more than two weeks after entry of judgment and is therefore untimely.

Nevertheless, the court can and should consider Paulette's arguments anyway. There are two possible ways around the time bar. First, there is no question that Paulette filed at least one timely motion for a new trial. Rule 59(b) does not address whether the time bar applies to successive motions after a timely motion is in fact made. Nor does Rule 59(b) appear to apply to amended motions. It is possible that Rule 59(b) might not bar consideration of the second but untimely motion as either a motion or an amendment to the timely motion. More research would need to be done to determine whether case law would support such a reading of Rule 59(b). Second, even if the second motion is barred under Rule 59(b), the court can grant a timely motion for a new trial for a reason not stated in the motion under Rule 59(d). In other words, because Paulette made one timely motion, any grounds that could support a new trial would support the granting of the motion. Those grounds could include the legal error asserted here.

Nevertheless, the legal error asserted here does not support the awarding of a new trial. The testimony that was excluded would be cumulative. Both Paulette and one coworker testified about Harvey's comments. Harvey admitted that he made the comments. Having a third witness testify about the same matter would simply be cumulative. Other cases have held similarly. In *Great Am. Indem. Co. v. Brown*, for example, the defendant's new trial motion was denied even though it came forward with new evidence mitigating the plaintiff's injuries because the defendant had already presented similar evidence in mitigation at trial, and the new evidence would merely have been cumulative. The same principle applies to Paulette's evidence.

In fact, Paulette has an even harder road ahead, for the issue of Harvey's comments was not really in dispute because Harvey admitted that he made the statements. Thus, even had it been legal error to exclude the testimony, the error would have been harmless under Rule 61, for the admission of the testimony could not have changed the outcome. As a result, this ground does not warrant a new trial.

C. Weight of the Evidence

Paulette did not move for a new trial based on the weight of the evidence. However, if a timely motion was made, Rule 59(d) authorizes a district court to grant a new trial on a ground not stated in the motion. Here, Paulette made a timely motion for a new trial. The court therefore could grant the motion on a ground not stated in the motion if it complies with Rule 59(d).

A judge may grant a new trial if she is of the opinion that the verdict is against the clear weight of the evidence or will result in a miscarriage of justice, even though substantial evidence supports the verdict. *Aetna Cas. & Surety Co. v. Yeatts*. There are two important points. First, unlike a motion for judgment as a matter of law, the judge can take her own views of the evidence and credibility of the witnesses into account. Second, it is not sufficient that the judge merely disagree with the verdict; rather, the verdict must represent to the judge a serious error in judgment. The court must also take into consideration the expense of a new trial.

Here, the evidence strongly favors Paulette. She demonstrated without dispute that Harvey made disparaging comments about her gender. She was terminated under circumstances that give rise to an inference of discrimination in that she was proficient at her job (exceeding the average performance of her peers), and a man was hired to replace her. Harvey offered a legitimate reason for terminating Paulette, but he was not credible and offered no evidence to back his reason up, and his reason was disputed by Paulette. Under these circumstances, it could be found that the clear weight of the evidence is against the verdict. The expense of a new trial is unfortunate, but with only a two-day trial, the expense is relatively minor.

Accordingly, at this stage, it appears that a new trial may be warranted. Before the court decides, however, Rule 59(d) requires the court to give the parties notice and an opportunity to be heard. It may be that the parties' submissions and arguments will either convince the court that a new trial is warranted or convince the court that a new trial is not warranted. If the court ultimately grants a new trial on this ground, it must specify the reasons in its order. Rule 59(d).

D. Option for Judgment

Neither party moved to renew its motion for judgment as a matter of law. And, even though the verdict appears to be against the weight of the evidence, substantial evidence (namely, Harvey's testimony) does support it. Accordingly, judgment as a matter of law cannot be entered.

Such a judgment would violate PhoneU's Seventh Amendment jury trial right. Additurs violate the Seventh Amendment. *Dimick v. Scheidt*. Offering the plaintiff judgment is like an additur because it increases the damages from $0 to $5,200. Indeed, the judgment is even more offensive because not even the liability of the defendant has been established by a jury. In either case, the Seventh Amendment would bar the entry of a judgment against PhoneU unless based upon a valid jury verdict or upon evidence that was conclusive as a matter of law and part of a properly made motion for such judgment.

In conclusion, a new trial can be granted after providing the parties with notice and an opportunity to be heard on the weight of the evidence issue, but the court does not have the power to enter judgment for the plaintiff.

TOOLS FOR SELF-CRITICISM

You should begin this problem with the time deadline for new trials. Rule 59(b)'s 28-day window is rigid. Thus, timeliness is a critical fact. However, there are several ways a court can consider grounds not raised in a timely motion—do not overlook them! The problem forces you to apply Rule 59(b) and to think creatively about the application of the rule.

The first substantive ground is juror misconduct. Note that *McDonough Power* sets a high bar for new trials based on incorrect answers during voir dire. Paulette must do more than what she has to meet this standard.

The second substantive ground implicated evidentiary issues and harmless error rules. Did you catch the Rule 61 implications of the excluded testimony? When faced with such a question, ask yourself whether the evidence, if admitted, could have changed a reasonable juror's mind. If it could not have, then a new trial is not warranted.

The third substantive ground is the hardest one. That is partly because the standard is not easy to apply. The posture of the question—a judge giving you a clue as to how she viewed the evidence but putting on you the onus of applying a vague legal standard to that view—is not dissimilar from a judge having to view the evidence through a jury's eyes. Did you catch the significance of the judge's assessment of the evidence and witnesses? That's fair game on a new trial motion. But, it is cabined by the "clear" weight of the evidence standard that sets a relatively high burden. How did you balance these two competing factors of weight-of-the-evidence new trials?

The option for judgment fails on a number of grounds, but it is hard to characterize it as a remittitur or additur. How did you analogize the facts to those legal paradigms?

VARIATIONS ON THE THEME

Could the court have granted a new trial before the hearing? How so? *See* Rule 59(d) (allowing the court to grant a new trial sua sponte for any reason that would justify one on motion if the order for a new trial is issued within 28 days of judgment).

Consider how your memorandum might change if this was the third retrial of the same case, each previous iteration of which resulted in a verdict for the defendant and then an order for a new trial based on the weight of the evidence.

Could the court order a new trial but exclude evidence of emotional damages? Could the court condition the award of a new trial on Paulette's consent to a take-nothing judgment on emotional damages?

What else would Paulette need to show to meet the *McDonough Power* standard for a new trial based on the foreman's answers?

What if Paulette admitted that a customer complained about her abusive and aggressive demeanor on the phone? How would that change your answer?

Assume instead that the jury awarded judgment for Paulette for $150,000. If PhoneU moves for a new trial based on excessive damages, what can the court do? If PhoneU does not move for a new trial, can the court act sua sponte? How?

Say the coworker who was excluded from testifying would have testified that he heard Harvey say that when he fires a caller, he always tells the caller that customers complained about the caller's abusive and aggressive demeanor. What might that change about your answer?

What if Paulette, instead of moving for a new trial, instead moved for a renewed judgment as a matter of law (but not expressly for a new trial). What could the court do?

OPTIONAL READINGS

Remittitur and additur are subjects of much commentary. *See, e.g.*, Suja A. Thomas, *Re-examining the Constitutionality of Remittitur Under the Seventh Amendment*, 64 OHIO ST. L.J. 731 (2003). Although federal law does not currently permit additur, *see* Dimick v. Scheidt, 293 U.S. 474, 484–88 (1935), some state courts permit it, *see, e.g.*, Freeman v. Wood, 401 N.E.2d 108 (Mass. 1980).

How should a trial court determine what the "proper" amount of damages should be in a remittitur? *Compare* Earl v. Bouchard Transp. Co., 917 F.2d 1320 (2d Cir. 1990) ("only to the maximum amount that would be upheld by the district court as not excessive"), *with* Meissner v. Papas, 35 F. Supp. 676 (E.D. Wis. 1940) (to the lowest amount that could properly be found by a jury), *aff'd*, 124 F.2d 720 (7th Cir. 1941), *and with* CAL. CIV. PROC. CODE § 662.5(b) (an amount that "the court in its independent judgment determines from the evidence to be fair and reasonable").

Should there be a different standard for erroneous admissions of evidence in a bench trial as opposed to a jury trial? *See* Builders Steel Co. v. Comm'r, 179 F.2d 377 (8th Cir. 1950).

Motions for new trials and judgments notwithstanding the verdict are often made together. Rule 50 addresses their interrelations, as has the Supreme Court. *See* Montgomery Ward & Co. v. Duncan, 311 U.S. 243 (1940). Expect to analyze both new trial issues and judgment as a matter of law issues after a judgment has been entered.

RELIEF FROM JUDGMENT

18

OPENING REMARKS

Rule 60 allows a party to apply for relief from a judgment or order. "Relief" usually takes the form of an order that sets aside the previous judgment or order. Rule 60 specifies two categories of grounds justifying such relief.

The first category is clerical mistakes and oversights under Rule 60(a). A court may correct clerical mistakes and oversights on motion or sua sponte, with or without notice, although it may do so while an appeal is pending only with the appellate court's leave. The errors contemplated by this subsection are those in which the judgment must be corrected to reflect the court's true intent. An example is changing the name of a party when that name was erroneously altered in the judgment.

The second is a set of six other grounds for relief under Rule 60(b). These are grounds that might convince a court to change its mind. They include (1) mistake, inadvertence, surprise, or excusable neglect; (2) newly discovered evidence that, with reasonable diligence, could not have been discovered in time to move for a new trial; (3) fraud, misrepresentation, or misconduct by an opposing party; (4) the judgment is void because, for example, the court lacked personal or subject-matter jurisdiction; (5) the judgment has been satisfied or discharged, is based on an earlier judgment that has been reversed or vacated, or applying it prospectively is no longer equitable; and (6) any other reason that justifies relief.

Rule 60(b)(6) is a catchall provision. Most courts hold that it applies only when none of the other grounds applies. In addition, the moving party must show exceptional (sometimes termed "extraordinary") circumstances justifying relief.

Relief under Rule 60(b) must be on motion and upon just terms. Just terms usually require the movant to make a showing that, but for one of the enumerated conditions, the outcome might have been different. The decision to grant relief, with the exception of void judgments, is within the discretion of the trial court. In addition, the motion must be made within a reasonable time, and, for any of the first three reasons, no more than one year from the date of the judgment or order from which relief is sought.

Part of the reason for these restrictions is the interest in finality of judgments. As a policy matter, parties and the legal system ought to be able to rely on judgments relatively soon after they are entered. Rule 60 relief obviously counteracts judgment finality and, as a result, is narrowly applicable.

HYPOTHETICAL

ShopU is a regional grocery store in the tri-state area. On January 1, 2000, a customer named Rachel Rey slipped in an aisle of a ShopU store in Connecticut, fell, and was injured. She sued ShopU for negligence in state court. Rachel sought compensatory damages.

ShopU removed on grounds of diversity, claiming that Rachel was a citizen of Connecticut, while ShopU was corporation incorporated in Delaware with its principal place of business in New York. Rachel did not oppose the removal and never moved for remand.

During discovery, ShopU sought all medical records relating to injuries allegedly caused by Rachel's fall. Rachel produced medical records from a Dr. Frank Fender. Those records indicated that Rachel suffered internal injuries to her lower abdomen that permanently damaged her uterus, making it nearly impossible (99.9 percent certainty) for her ever to carry a child or produce viable eggs. Rachel also produced medical records from Dr. Elizabeth Eddy, a psychologist. Those records indicated that Rachel suffered extensive emotional damage as a result of the inability to carry a child or produce viable eggs. Rachel did not produce any medical records from any other doctor.

At trial, ShopU objected to the introduction of evidence concerning its net worth, arguing that punitive damages were not sought and that the evidence thus was irrelevant and prejudicial. The court overruled the objection and allowed the evidence. The court allowed the medical records into evidence. Rachel testified repeatedly that she had never had children, that she had always wanted a child, and that she was devastated that she no longer could have one.

The case was submitted to a jury on January 1, 2002, which returned a general verdict for Rachel in the amount of $1.5 million. ShopU prepared a motion for a new trial based on the court's erroneous admission into evidence of ShopU's net worth. Twenty-five days after the judgment was entered, ShopU's attorney handed a messenger service the motion and instructed the messenger to file it in the federal court that day. The messenger misunderstood the instructions and, instead, filed it in the state court, which was across the street from the federal court. A week later, the state court informed ShopU of the mistake. ShopU then filed the motion in the proper court, but the judge denied the motion as untimely and never reached the merits of the motion.

ShopU's attorney in charge of the case, Malcolm McCoy, feeling guilty about the incorrect filing, immediately went into a period of deep despair. Though not apparent to ShopU at first, Malcolm was unable to focus on his work. ShopU believed that Malcolm was diligently working on an appeal, and Malcolm himself made that seem true. A day before the appeal was due, however, Malcolm checked himself into a psychiatric facility for severe clinical depression.

ShopU, frantic, immediately assigns you to the case. When you look for Malcolm's files, you find nothing. Unable to file an appeal within the allotted time period, you seek an extension from the Court of Appeals, which is denied. Believing the case to be over, you turn to other matters.

A month later, a colleague comes into your office with all of Malcolm's office files and other effects. Buried in a mislabeled file are Malcolm's notes on the Rachel Rey case. You peruse them and discover a notation from Malcolm on removal. The notation suggests that Malcolm removed on the basis of diversity but wasn't sure whether ShopU's principal place of business was actually in New York.

You decide to do a little research and conclude that, for diversity purposes, ShopU's principal place of business is actually Connecticut. This piques your interest, and so, over the next few months, you decide to investigate the case more closely. You call up the opposing counsel on the case, who says she no longer represents Rachel Rey and has no idea where Rachel Rey is now. You Google Rachel and find her Facebook page. On it are pictures of a very pregnant Rachel and comments indicating that the fetus is biologically hers. It appears Rachel became pregnant in January 2002.

Now very interested, you find Rachel's new attorney and send him a letter asking for all medical records in Rachel's possession relating to her accident. The attorney sends you copies of the medical records received in discovery, plus an additional file from Dr. Dimitri Donorov, a psychologist whom Rachel apparently saw before Dr. Eddy. Dr. Donorov's notes suggest that Rachel never actually wanted to have a child and, frankly, was relieved to hear that the accident left her unable to have children. Upon questioning Rachel's new attorney, you learn that Rachel apparently gave this file to her former attorney and did not know that the former attorney failed to turn it over to ShopU.

It now has been 11 months since judgment was entered. Please discuss what Rule 60 options you have and what the likely success of each will be.

SUGGESTED READINGS

Fed. R. Civ. P. 60

Jones v. Aero/Chem Corp., 921 F.2d 875, 876–79 (9th Cir. 1990) (per curiam)

Schultz v. Butcher, 24 F.3d 626, 628–31 (4th Cir. 1994)

Pioneer Inv. Servs. Co. v. Brunswick Assocs. LP, 507 U.S. 380, 393–94 (1993)

Lowe v. McGraw-Hill Co., 361 F.3d 335, 337–43 (7th Cir. 2004)

Pierce v. Cook, 518 F.2d 720, 721–24 (10th Cir. 1975)

Ackerman v. United States, 340 U.S. 193, 194–202 (1950)

SAMPLE ESSAY

Rule 60 allows relief from a judgment or order under certain circumstances. There do not appear to be any issues pertaining to clerical mistakes or oversights under Rule 60(a). Those kinds of mistakes represent judgments that, as issued, do not reflect the true intent of the court. *Lowe v. McGraw-Hill.* All of the Rule 60 issues discussed below implicate corrections that would change the intent of the court. Thus, they are Rule 60(b) issues, not Rule 60(a) issues.

Rule 60(b) allows for relief "[o]n motion and just terms" for any of six reasons. Thus, the first thing I must do is file a motion seeking relief under Rule 60(b). The motion would argue the following grounds for relief.

1. Excusable Neglect under Rule 60(b)(1).

ShopU may have an argument for relief from judgment based on excusable neglect under Rule 60(b)(1). There are several issues involved in such an argument.

I have a decent argument on the merits. ShopU clearly intended to file a timely motion for a new trial based on the erroneous ruling of admitting evidence of ShopU's net worth into evidence despite the lack of a punitive damages claim. ShopU's attorney in fact delivered the motion to a messenger service before the 28-day window expired, but the messenger service failed to file the motion in the proper court. ShopU believed the motion to have been filed timely and properly. It was not, however, and because the 28-day window is a rigid bar, no excusable neglect argument would have been successful in making the motion timely.

When the new trial motion was denied as untimely, ShopU intended to proceed with an appeal, but ShopU's attorney did not file the appeal in a timely fashion. ShopU was unaware that the attorney was suffering from depression and was not prepared to file the appeal. Although ShopU chose Malcolm McCoy as its attorney and is bound by McCoy's failings, this might be the case where those failings amount to excusable neglect under Rule 60(b)(1).

However, to justify relief under Rule 60(b)(1), I will have to show that, absent the neglect, the outcome might have been different. Here, the basis for the new trial was that the district court erred in admitting evidence of ShopU's net worth absent a claim for punitive damages. So, I will have to show that the new trial motion would have been granted if it had been filed properly; or, had the appeal been filed timely, it would have resulted in an order vacating the judgment. In either case, I will have to show that the erroneous ruling admitting the evidence led the jury to award higher damages than otherwise were warranted. Because the jury returned a general verdict, that will be difficult. I may wish to try to get information from the jurors about their deliberations and views of the evidence to determine whether any of them deemed ShopU's net worth to be relevant. Without such information, it will be difficult for me to justify the relief.

Another problem with the motion will be timing. The motion must be made within a reasonable time and no more than one year after entry of judgment. Rule 60(c)(1). Under the one-year provision, the motion must be filed in the next month, which I could do. But filing within the next month so as to be under the one-year limitation period does not necessarily make the motion timely. The one-year bar is an outer limit; the motion must still be made in a reasonable time.

Here, the excusable neglect for which I am arguing—ShopU's failure to file a timely motion for a new trial or a timely appeal on the grounds that evidence of ShopU's net worth was allowed into evidence despite the lack of a punitive damages claim—was discovered when I was first assigned the case several months ago. Although I tried to remedy the situation by seeking an extension from the Court of Appeals to file an appeal, that motion was denied. I then "turn[ed] to other matters" for several months.

My problem will be that I could have filed a Rule 60(b)(1) motion immediately instead of turning to other matters for several months. Unless I have some other reason for the delay, aside from an erroneous belief that the case was over, a judge probably would not find it reasonable that I filed the Rule 60 motion after waiting for several months.

2. Newly Discovered Evidence under Rule 60(b)(2).

ShopU also may have an argument for relief from judgment based on newly discovered evidence under Rule 60(b)(2). There are two issues involved.

One is of timing. Like a Rule 60(b)(1) motion, a Rule 60(b)(2) motion must be made within a reasonable time and not more than one year after judgment. Accordingly, I must file in the next month and also make the argument that the timing is reasonable. Here, the argument is likely to be successful because the newly discovered evidence—that Rachel can carry and have children—was only discovered a few months ago, and I have worked diligently toward filing a motion since then. Thus, the motion probably will be deemed timely.

The other is on the merits. For a motion for relief based on newly discovered evidence, I must show that the evidence existed at the time, could not have been discovered with reasonable diligence, and was so important that it likely would have changed the outcome. *Jones v. Aero/Chem Corp.* My biggest problem here is that the evidence did not exist at the time of trial—Rachel became pregnant after the judgment was entered. In addition, it is arguably cumulative: Rachel's witness testified that it was "nearly impossible (99.9 percent certainty)" for her to become pregnant. That she actually did so just means she is the one of a thousand. Accordingly, although timely, a motion under Rule 60(b)(2) is unlikely to be successful. Fortunately, if I can succeed on any one motion for relief resulting in a new trial, I may be able to use this evidence on retrial.

3. Misconduct by Opposing Party under Rule 60(b)(3).

ShopU also may have an argument for relief from judgment based on misconduct under Rule 60(b)(3). Again, there are two issues involved: timing and merits.

Like the Rule 60(b)(2) issue, timing under Rule 60(b)(3) is unlikely to pose a problem. A Rule 60(b)(3) motion must be made within a reasonable time and not more than one year after judgment. Accordingly, I must file in the next month and also make the argument that the timing is reasonable. Here, the argument is likely to be successful because the misconduct—that Rachel's attorney filed to turn over highly relevant documents requested during discovery—was only discovered a few months ago, and I have worked diligently toward filing a motion since then. Thus, the motion probably will be deemed timely.

A motion for relief based on party misconduct need not necessarily show that the outcome likely would have been different without the misconduct. The idea is not that the judgment was rendered in error but rather that the party did not have a full and fair opportunity to present his case. The failure to produce requested documents in a party's possession generally qualifies as misconduct within Rule 60(b)(3). The court must balance the competing policies of finality and fairness, but finality can give way when the misconduct impeded the fair trial process. *Schultz v. Butcher.* For discovery requests, the movant must show due diligence in requesting the information and that the nonmovant had constructive knowledge of the information and failed to produce it. *Jones v. Aero/Chem.* The decision to grant relief is within the discretion of the trial court.

Here, ShopU requested all medical records relating to injuries allegedly caused by Rachel's fall. In response, Rachel's attorney produced records from Dr. Eddy but not from Dr. Donorov, despite the fact that her attorney had both records in possession. The failure to produce Dr. Donorov's records is suspicious because Dr. Donorov's conclusions undermine Rachel's case, while Dr. Eddy's conclusions support her case. At a minimum, though, Dr. Donorov's records were discoverable and should have been disclosed.

It is unclear whether there were any objections imposed in the discovery response by Rachel that might justify the withholding of Dr. Donorov's records. If so, then I would need additional information as to whether ShopU exercised due diligence in pursuing avenues to discover them, such as meeting and conferring or filing a motion to compel discovery. If, however, no objections were made, or Rachel's attorney misrepresented the existence of Dr. Donorov's records, then I have a strong argument for misconduct here.

The misconduct prejudiced ShopU's trial preparation and defense. The records would have impeached Rachel's testimony that she always wanted a child and was devastated not to be able to bear one. The records also may have resulted in a lesser damage award. In sum, I have a strong argument for seeking relief from judgment and a new trial on the ground that Rachel's attorney's failure to provide these highly relevant records to me in discovery amounted to misconduct within the meaning of Rule 60(b)(3).

4. Void Judgment under Rule 60(b)(4).

I also may move for relief under Rule 60(b)(4) based on the argument that the district court's lack of subject-matter jurisdiction rendered the judgment void. The other reasons for granting Rule 60(b) relief are within the discretion of the court, but if a judgment is void, the court must award relief. Nevertheless, the motion must be made within a reasonable time, though the one-year bar applicable to the previous conditions does not apply to void judgments.

Here, I have concluded that ShopU is not (and, presumably, never was) diverse from Rachel. Rachel's failure to contest the removal is irrelevant because subject-matter jurisdiction cannot be consented to, waived, or forfeited. Assuming that no other ground for federal jurisdiction applies, the district court lacked subject-matter jurisdiction to enter the judgment, and, therefore, the judgment is void.

Such a motion likely would be timely because I have worked diligently toward filing a Rule 60(b) motion since discovering the possibility of nondiversity. It is possible that a court could rule that the motion is not timely because ShopU should know its own principal place of business at all times, including at the time judgment was entered, and therefore such a motion is not made in a reasonable time if made several months after that. But principal place of business determinations are often difficult. That seems to be the case here, where Malcolm "wasn't sure" about it himself. And, a party's own determination of citizenship is not determinative—the court must make an independent assessment. Accordingly, it seems likely that a court would consider the motion to be timely.

Thus, if I move for relief on Rule 60(b)(4) grounds, and if I am correct in my assessment that ShopU was, in fact, not diverse from Rachel, then my motion will be granted. The district court would set aside the judgment and remand to the state court.

Whether or not I should so move is a different question. Relief from a void judgment cannot result in a new trial in federal court; instead, it likely would result in a remand to state court for lack of subject-matter jurisdiction. ShopU must have preferred federal court at the time it removed the case. Thus, if I believe that my other bases for relief are meritorious, I might consider moving solely for relief on those grounds rather than for relief based on a void judgment. Of course, if I do so and lose on retrial, any subsequent motion for relief based on a void judgment at that time may be considered to be untimely. The same untimeliness argument could be made if I made the other Rule 60(b) motions first, waited until they were denied, and then made the Rule 60(b)(4) motion as a fallback option.

5. Exceptional Circumstances under Rule 60(b)(6).

In the alternative to moving for relief under Rule 60(b)(1)–(3), I should consider moving for relief under Rule 60(b)(6). Rule 60(b)(6) allows for relief for "any other reason that justifies relief." Courts have construed this provision narrowly, allowing relief only under exceptional or extraordinary circumstances that were not created by the party's own free and deliberate choice. *Ackerman v. U.S.* Thus, a party's litigation choices and strategies cannot create the exceptional circumstances justifying Rule 60(b)(6) relief. Rather, the exceptional circumstances must be beyond the party's reasonable control. *Pioneer v. Brunswick.*

There are four potential bases for relief under Rule 60(b)(6): the legal error by the court in admitting evidence of ShopU's net worth, the neglect by ShopU's attorney in failing to file timely a motion for a new trial and an appeal, the discovery of Rachel's pregnancy, and the misconduct by Rachel's former attorney.

Legal error is almost never an appropriate basis for Rule 60(b)(6) relief, though it can be in unusual circumstances, such as when legal error implicates an unconstitutional course that a court took. *Pierce v. Cook.* Here, however, the legal error of erroneous admission of evidence was not exceptional, does not implicate any unconstitutional course of conduct by the court, and does not warrant Rule 60(b)(6) relief.

The neglect also probably does not warrant Rule 60(b)(6) relief. Generally, the movant must show that the circumstances were not caused by her own conduct but instead were beyond her reasonable control. *Pioneer v. Brunswick.* Thus, for example, a party who chooses not to appeal cannot use that free and deliberate choice as a basis for exceptional circumstances. *Ackerman v. U.S.* It may be that in gross negligence cases, an attorney's negligence can serve as the basis for a party's motion for Rule 60(b)(6) relief, but ShopU's attorney's negligence in failing to ensure proper filing of the new trial motion probably does not rise to that level. ShopU's attorney's negligence in failing to file a timely appeal might be a stronger argument because it appears that ShopU's attorney intentionally misled ShopU about the status of the appellate filing. But even if so, making the argument under Rule 60(b)(6) would still run into the same timeliness and outcome-determinative problems discussed above. Accordingly, making this argument under Rule 60(b)(6) is weaker than making the neglect argument under Rule 60(b)(1).

The discovery of Rachel's pregnancy is another matter. As discussed above, the main hindrance to pursuing this argument under Rule 60(b)(2) is that courts generally require the evidence to have existed at the time. Rule 60(6)(6), however, does not have that requirement; rather, what is required is exceptional circumstances. I could argue that the fact that Rachel became pregnant days after the entry of a judgment that awarded her damages largely based on the belief that she could not become pregnant manifests exceptional circumstances that warrant relief to avoid the unjust result of allowing Rachel to receive a substantial windfall. On the other hand, it could be argued that the possibility that Rachel could become pregnant was always there, that the jury appropriately considered it, and that subsequent events that prove Rachel's injury less than anticipated should not qualify as exceptional circumstances. I would have to research this in more depth to determine if any case law supports one argument over the other.

The misconduct of Rachel's attorney is already adequately addressed by the Rule 60(b)(3) arguments above and is unlikely to be stronger in the Rule 60(b)(6) context.

* * * * * * * * * *

In conclusion, I have a number of avenues through which to seek relief under Rule 60.

TOOLS FOR SELF-CRITICISM

This question is all about Rule 60. The first organizational track to take is to differentiate between Rule 60(a) and Rule 60(b). Did you catch the difference? *Lowe* contains a good description of how to distinguish the two grounds for relief.

In addition to the enumerated grounds for relief in Rule 60(b), the rule also requires a timely motion and just terms. Did you remember to address those additional requirements? Just terms usually means that the outcome would have been different, but that need not be the case for void judgments or party misconduct. In addition, grounds (1)–(3) have an outer window of one year, but the other grounds do not. It is important to keep the different requirements for the different grounds straight.

Did you note that the one-year time bar is an outer limit rather than a threshold? In other words, the test is always that the motion must be filed within a reasonable time period—it is just that motions filed beyond a year are per se unreasonable for certain grounds. Motions filed within a year may still be outside what constitutes a reasonable time. That was an important legal point to know, and it implicated the timeliness issues that you should have spotted in the facts.

The newly discovered evidence ground seems tailor-made for the facts of the hypothetical, and you should have latched onto that issue right away. However, on close inspection, you should also have realized that a critical component of that ground—that the evidence existed at the time (why is that a critical ground, by the way?)—was missing. Note, though, that the inability to get a new trial on the basis of newly discovered evidence does not necessarily make the evidence valueless—if you get a new trial via another ground, you may be able to the use the new evidence on retrial to substantially reduce the liability exposure on the second go-around.

Unlike newly discovered evidence, misconduct goes to the integrity of the trial process rather than the likelihood of error. Our procedural system values system integrity more highly than individualized error. As a result, it is somewhat easier to get a new trial for misconduct than for newly discovered evidence. You should recognize the differences between Rules 60(b)(2) and (b)(3) and their underlying policies. Note that if ShopU was not diligent in requesting the information, the misconduct ground becomes substantially weaker.

Void judgments are different creatures. The idea is that the district court's entry of judgment was itself ultra vires. On the facts, this is the easiest motion to make. There is some doubt as to how the court will determine citizenship, but, if the court finds that ShopU is not diverse, there is only one result—remand. (Did you catch that the result would be a remand rather than a dismissal or a new trial, by the way?) Be sure to consider the strategic implications, too. After all, winning the motion may put ShopU in a worse position of having to completely relitigate in a more hostile forum with an entire case's worth of new costs. There may be benefits to winning (or at least making) the motion, but they should be considered strategically, particularly in light of other options. Do not rush to file every motion that you can, just because you can!

Rule 60(b)(6) is the catchall provision. Remember that the key to it is "exceptional" (sometimes "extraordinary") circumstances. That is a narrow and highly fact-dependent standard. It is unlikely to provide relief already covered by a specifically enumerated ground, but it might for relief that falls outside of those grounds. Here, the newly discovered evidence of Rachel's pregnancy is the best shot at Rule 60(b)(6) relief because it likely fell outside of Rule 60(b)(2) and yet has great equitable appeal.

VARIATIONS ON THE THEME

What if you discovered evidence (that could not have been discovered with reasonable diligence) that Rachel previously had had an abortion?

How might you analyze the competing policies of justice and finality in each of the grounds above if asked to do so during oral argument by the judge?

OPTIONAL READINGS

Courts are split over whether certain legal errors can constitute "mistakes" under Rule 60(b)(1). *Compare, e.g.,* Int'l Controls Corp. v. Vesco, 556 F.2d 665, 669 (2d Cir. 1977) (allowing the motion), *with, e.g.,* Parke-Chaptley Constr. Co. v. Cherrington, 865 F.2d 907 (7th Cir. 1989) (disallowing the motion), *and* Page v. Schweiker, 786 F.2d 150 (3d Cir. 1986) (same).

Although most courts do not allow a party's attorney's simple negligence to be the basis for Rule 60(b)(1) relief for the party, courts also are split over whether the gross negligence of a party's attorney can be an appropriate ground for relief. *Compare, e.g.,* Dickerson v. Bd. of Educ., 32 F.3d 1114 (7th Cir. 1994) (no relief), *and* Heim v. Comm'r, 872 F.2d 245 (8th Cir. 1989) (same), *with, e.g.,* Community Dental Servs. v. Tani, 282 F.3d 1164 (9th Cir. 2002) (allowing relief).

19 APPELLATE REVIEW

OPENING REMARKS

Sadly, you have lost in the district court, and now it is time to consider whether you wish to appeal. There is no constitutional right to appeal in federal court, but Congress has authorized appeals by statute. The first level of appeal is from district courts to courts of appeals, called circuits. From the circuit courts, a party can seek discretionary review, called certiorari review, to the Supreme Court. In limited circumstances, a party may be able to appeal to the Supreme Court, either from a district court or from a court of appeals.

Section 1291 of title 28 of the U.S. Code allows appeals only from "final decisions" of district courts. Final decisions are those that resolve the entire case (like an order granting full summary judgment), while "interlocutory" orders are those that do not (like the denial of a motion to dismiss or an order compelling discovery). The final judgment rule exists to prevent piecemeal appeals. Consider what litigation would be like without the rule: Every order you lose, no matter how minor, you could appeal! It is far better, in most cases, to wait until the end, when the losing party can then consolidate all her points of appeal in one brief. And, by that time, the chance is good that many of the potential errors will have been rendered moot.

There are two wrinkles to the final judgment rule. One is Rule 54 of the Federal Rules of Civil Procedure, which allows an appeal from a judgment that finally resolves one claim or party even though it does not finally resolve other claims or parties. The second is the judicially created "collateral order" doctrine, which gives "final" a functional rather than a formalist interpretation. It deems an interlocutory order "final" when the order implicates a legally significant issue that is not an ingredient of the cause of action but that has finally been decided by the trial court, and waiting for a final judgment will effectively deny appellate review of the issue.

There are several exceptions to the final judgment rule. Section 1292(a) permits appeals from three types of interlocutory orders: injunctive orders, receivership orders, and certain admiralty orders. These orders are deemed too important to wait until final judgment for appeal. For immediate appeal of injunctive relief, the order must create the risk of serious consequences for the appellant and must be essentially unreviewable if the parties must await final judgment. Section 1292(b) permits appeals from interlocutory orders if both the trial and appellate courts agree that the order involves a controlling question of law on which there is a substantial difference of opinion and where the appeal may materially advance the ultimate termination of the litigation. Finally, Rule 23(f) grants courts of appeals the discretion to review a district court order either granting or denying a motion for class certification.

The procedure for appealing is contained in the Federal Rules of Appellate Procedure and federal statute. Rule 3(a) requires an appellant to file a notice of appeal in the district court. The notice explains which party is taking the appeal and what order is being appealed. The district court then serves a copy of the notice on all counsel. With limited exceptions, the notice must be filed within 30 days after entry of the appealable order. This time bar is jurisdictional. The appellant then transfers the notice and district court record to the appropriate court of appeals (usually the court of appeals in which the district court sits). The appellee may file a cross-appeal, if she wishes. The court of appeals will then set a schedule for motions, briefing, and (usually) oral argument.

On appeal, the court of appeals must determine the appropriate standard of review. On issues of law, the appellate court reviews de novo, meaning that it looks at the issue without deference to how the district court resolved it. On issues of fact, the appellate court defers to the district court's resolution of the issue and will only overturn it if clearly erroneous. Matters committed to the discretion of the trial judge are reviewed under an abuse of discretion standard.

You may find that introductory civil procedure courses omit much of this material or cover it relatively quickly and superficially. The hypothetical that follows assumes some in-depth coverage. Nevertheless, the readings that follow the hypothetical, coupled with your practice of civil procedure issues in general in the preceding chapters, should provide you with adequate materials and coverage to be able to answer the hypothetical and the challenging issues that it raises.

HYPOTHETICAL

Question 1:
Patty is injured when her car tire explodes on the highway. She sues the tire manufacturer, Delaware Tires, in federal court on diversity for products liability, claiming that the tire was defectively manufactured. She also seeks to represent a class of similarly situated purchasers of the tire who subsequently were injured in accidents. She seeks individual compensatory damages of $150,000. The class seeks over $10 million in compensatory damages. In addition, the class alleges recklessness on the part of Delaware, alleging that Delaware knew of the defect but chose to sell the tires anyway because the profits were so strong. Accordingly, the class also seeks $10 million in punitive damages.

Delaware files a motion to dismiss all the claims. Patty files a motion for class certification under Rule 23. The district court grants the motion to dismiss as to the punitive damages, concluding that state law does not permit punitive damages in these circumstances. The district court denies the rest of the motion to dismiss. The district court also denies class certification, concluding that Patty has not shown that the class meets the requirements of Rule 23(b). Can anyone appeal from either order now? Why or why not?

Question 2:
Say instead that the court denies the motion to dismiss entirely and certifies the class. No appeals are taken from any of the orders. Discovery commences. During discovery, Patty seeks all documents relating to Delaware's knowledge of the defect. Delaware withholds certain documents as privileged or protected by the work product doctrine. Patty files a motion to compel all existing

documents. The court decides to review the withheld documents in camera. The withheld documents are minutes of meetings, attended by in-house counsel, that record discussions about the defects among high-ranking officials, the costs of recalling the defective tires, the likely liability exposure of leaving them on the market, and the prospective profit margin. The court concludes that the documents are neither privileged nor entitled to work product protection and therefore grants the motion to compel and orders Delaware to produce the documents.

Delaware believes that the court is wrong on the law. In addition, Delaware believes that if the withheld documents become public, immeasurable damage to the company will follow. It would rather settle the case than have the withheld documents be produced to Patty. Can Delaware appeal the discovery order now? Do not address the possibility of mandamus.

Question 3:

The case proceeds through discovery, and settlement discussions begin. The parties agree to a settlement. The district court holds a fairness hearing, at which several class members object to the settlement as unfair. The district court nevertheless approves of the settlement and enters an order on January 1.

On January 2, the class (which still includes the objectors) files a motion for costs under Rule 54(d). On February 10, the court decides the motion for costs and denies the award of costs to the class, reasoning that the settlement always includes a provision for costs.

On February 15, the class files a notice of appeal from the order denying costs. The next day, the objectors file a notice of appeal from the approval of the settlement. In the class's appeal, the objectors are not specifically identified as appellants in the notice of appeal, although they are separately identified as "objectors" in the style of the case. Should the appellate court hear the appeals?

SUGGESTED READINGS

28 U.S.C. § 2107

28 U.S.C. § 1291

28 U.S.C. § 1292

FED. R. CIV. P. 23

FED. R. CIV. P. 54

FED. R. CIV. P. 58

FED. R. APP. P. 3

FED. R. APP. P. 4

FED. R. APP. P. 5

Curtiss-Wright Corp. v. G.E. Corp., 446 U.S. 1, 3–13 (1980)

Coopers & Lybrand v. Livesay, 437 U.S. 463, 464–77 (1978)

Firestone Tire & Rubber Co. v. Risjord, 449 U.S. 368, 369–78 (1981)

Cunningham v. Hamilton County, 527 U.S. 198, 200–10 (1999)

Will v. Hallock, 546 U.S. 345, 347–55 (2006)

Carson v. Am. Brands, Inc., 450 U.S. 79, 80–90 (1981)

Torres v. Oakland Scavenger Co., 487 U.S. 312, 313–18 (1988)

Mohawk Indus., Inc. v. Carpenter, 558 U.S. _ (2009)

SAMPLE ESSAY

Question 1

A. THE DISMISSAL ORDER.

Section 1291 permits appeals only from "final" orders. Ordinarily the denial of a motion to dismiss is not final because it does not end the litigation. There are limited exceptions, *see Will v. Hallock*, but this is a run-of-the-mill motion to dismiss that does not fit into them. Accordingly, Delaware cannot appeal its denial.

Patty may be able to appeal the grant of the motion to dismiss as to punitive damages, though. Rule 54(b) states that a district court may direct entry of a final judgment as to a claim so as to allow an appeal on that claim. This requires two things. First, the judgment must actually be final. Second, the judgment must be on a claim.

The first requirement is met. The dismissal disposes of the punitive damages issue and, because it was based on a matter of law, does not allow repleading. Thus, the order finally resolves the punitive damages claim.

The second requirement is more difficult. Whether punitive damages are a separate "claim" is a question that is not clear from the case law. Rule 54(b) allows judgment on traditional claims, such as cross-claims and counterclaims. Thus, it would not permit final judgment on, say, a particular *defense* to a claim. Likewise, it would not permit final judgment on a particularly *theory* of proof on a claim if alternate theories are available.

Punitive damages are similar to a species of relief. The same acts and omissions that give rise to punitive damages also give rise to compensatory damages, and, in many cases, punitive are not available if compensable damages did not result. In this way, punitives are not really a separate "claim."

On the other hand, punitives are often styled as a separate claim, and they do encompass, as commonly phrased, a separate "claim for relief." Punitives require more proof than claims for ordinary compensatory damages. And, courts often dispose of punitive damage "claims" separately or independently from compensatory damages claims.

More research would be needed to determine whether dismissing punitive damage claims may be treated as separate claims under Rule 54(b). If the answer is no, then the dismissal could not be appealable under Rule 54(b).

Even if the answer to that question is "yes," however, that does not mean that the punitive damages claim here is appealable as a final judgment under Rule 54(b). To be appealable under Rule 54(b), the district court must conclude that there is no just reason for delay of the appeal. In *Curtiss-Wright v. G.E.*, the Supreme Court stated that that decision must be with consideration of sound judicial administration, taking into account judicial administrative interests and the equities involved. Permissible factors to consider include whether the claims still under review are separable from the adjudicated claims, whether piecemeal appeal could be avoided, and whether the equities confronting the parties would be furthered by immediate review.

Here, the punitive damages claim is substantially related to the underlying claim for compensatory damages. Thus, a determination that the facts do not support the underlying claim for liability will be dispositive of the punitive damages claim as well. On the other hand, the punitive damages were dismissed on a legal basis not applicable to the underlying claim for compensatory damages;

thus, the decision itself is completely separate from the adjudication of the compensatory claim.

Allowing the punitive claim to be appealed separately would provide certainty for the parties going forward. Punitive damages are either allowed under the law or they are not. Resolving that issue would allow the parties better to structure their discovery requests, arguments, and settlement negotiations. Allowing the appeal would not have to delay the litigation; the other claims can proceed without the punitive damages claim pending appellate resolution, and any burdensome discovery requests pertaining only to punitive damages can be delayed until the court of appeals addresses them. Although there may reach a point in time at which the district court must halt the proceedings to await the determination from the court of appeals, the parties likely to be most burdened by that decision would be Patty and the class, the very parties that produced the delay by appealing in the first place.

Finally, if the class certification order is appealable (see below), then judicial resources may be conserved by allowing the punitives determination also to be appealed. For all these reasons, it is likely that a district court would find no just reason to delay an appeal.

If the court's order dismissing the punitive damages claim does qualify for final judgment treatment under Rule 54(b), then it will be appealable only if the district court enters final judgment on the claim and expressly determines that there is no just reason for delay. Accordingly, if Patty wishes to appeal the order, she should immediately ask the court to enter final judgment on the punitive damages claim and to expressly determine in the judgment the reasons why there is no just reason to delay an appeal.

B. THE ORDER DENYING CLASS CERTIFICATION.

Patty also may be able to appeal the denial of class certification. Until Rule 23 was amended, such as denial was not appealable. *See Coopers & Lybrand v. Livesay*. But Rule 23(f) now allows a court of appeals to permit an appeal from an order denying certification if a petition for permission to appeal is filed with the circuit clerk within 14 days after the order is entered. FRAP 5 restates this requirement. Thus, Patty must file, within 14 days of the order denying certification, a petition with the court of appeals for permission to appeal the order. If the court of appeals grants the petition, then Patty may file an appeal.

Question 2

Section 1291 permits appeals only from "final" orders. The discovery order is not "final" in the usual sense of the word because the litigation will continue. However, interlocutory orders may be appealed if they are "collateral orders" or if they are appealable under § 1292(a) or § 1292(b).

A. COLLATERAL ORDER DOCTRINE

The collateral order doctrine allows immediate appeals from orders that, though not final, should be treated as such to achieve a healthy legal system. An order is immediately appealable under the collateral order doctrine if it (a) conclusively resolves the disputed question, (b) resolves an important issue completely separate from the merits of the action, and (c) is effectively unreviewable on appeal from a final judgment. The order to compel conclusively resolves the issue, so only the last two factors are at issue.

Before 2010, courts were split on whether orders to compel discovery claimed as privileged were appealable under the collateral order doctrine. On the one hand, the information in the contested documents is factually relevant to the merits, and the Supreme Court has stated that a discovery sanctions order is not normally sufficiently divorced from the merits to qualify for collateral order treatment. *See Cunningham v. Hamilton*. And, it might be useful for an appellate court, in assessing the privilege on review, to have the benefit of hindsight with additional facts and evidence adduced after full discovery. The Court itself has suggested that issues best assessed after a full record should not qualify for collateral order treatment. *See Firestone v. Risjord*.

In addition, the underlying policies of appellate jurisdiction—the need to promote judicial efficiency by avoiding piecemeal appeals and avoiding intrusion into the pretrial process—support restricting collateral orders to those for which an immediate appeal would not delay the pretrial process for the merits.

On the other hand, the issues of privilege and work product are legally distinct from the substantive cause of action at hand. They concern the need, grounded in public policy, for keeping certain documents and communications from discovery. Those issues—the need for effective communication between client and counsel and for a zone of protection against interference from adverse counsel—are divorced from the substantive merits.

And, unlike other routine discovery orders, the specific conduct at issue is not the admissibility of the documents but the decision to disclose them to the other side. This is the crucial feature of orders to produce documents protected from discovery by privilege or work product doctrines. The whole point of the doctrines is to keep the documents from being produced to the other side in discovery, not just to keep them inadmissible in court. Once produced to an adversary, the damage is done, and one cannot later unring the bell. Thus, an order to produce privileged documents is different than an order denying a disqualification motion, as was the case in *Firestone v. Risjord*, for the latter order could be determined after final judgment through the granting of a new trial with different counsel.

The Supreme Court resolved this issue, though, in *Mohawk Industries*, holding that orders compelling production of potentially privileged information are not within the scope of the collateral order doctrine. Thus, Delaware will not be able to appeal the order on that ground.

Delaware could defy the compel order, suffer contempt sanctions, and then challenge the compel order while appealing the sanctions order. *Mohawk Industries* specifically suggested this possibility.

B. INJUNCTION EXCEPTION

The injunction exception is codified in § 1292(a), which allows for an immediate appeal of any order pertaining to injunctions. Orders to compel are not primarily thought of as injunctive orders. They do not relate to substantive relief; rather, they pertain only to the district court's authority to control the procedural case development before the court. And, motions to compel are filed in many cases. To allow immediate appeal from either the granting or denying of a motion to compel (or even just the granting) would wreck havoc on appellate dockets and district court pretrial litigation. It seems unlikely that the injunction exception applies to run-of-the-mill orders to compel.

There are arguments to the contrary. Although not thought of as injunctions, orders to compel do have that effect. The court's order is to force, under penalty of contempt sanctions, a party to do something: here, to disclose documents in its possession. The Supreme Court in *Carson v. American Brands* has suggested that the injunction exception should apply pragmatically rather than formalistically.

Carson, however, addressed a consent decree that would have, in effect, permanently enjoined the defendants from discriminating against certain employees. That effect was similar to the injunctive relief actually sought in the complaint. Here, the order to compel does not affect substantive conduct, nor does it extend beyond the confines of pretrial litigation. And, *Mohawk Industries*, considering the available avenues for review of just the kind of compel order here, did not mention the injunction exception as a possible vehicle for review. As a result, it seems unlikely that the compel order could be appealable as an injunction under § 1292(a).

If for some reason the motion to compel can be treated like an injunction for purposes of § 1292(a), then *Carson* still requires that the putative appellant show that the appeal will further the statutory purpose of permitting litigants to effectually challenge interlocutory orders of serious, perhaps irreparable, consequence. Thus, for example, as explained in *Carson*, the denial of a motion for summary judgment by plaintiffs seeking injunctive relief was not immediately appealable because the plaintiffs still could have obtained the injunctive relief at trial and, if they failed to do so then, an appeal could be had at that time.

Many discovery orders are effectively unreviewable on appeal. For most discovery orders, though, there is no harm. The exchange of documents has little bearing on the ultimate resolution of the case. But, as discussed above, privilege questions are somewhat different. An order compelling the production of documents privileged or protected from discovery not only is effectively unreviewable on appeal but also can impose serious harm on the producing party, harm that stems from the disclosure itself as opposed to any admissibility questions. Privilege and work product protection documents are not discoverable—independent of admissibility questions—for a reason: their disclosure would confer an unjust advantage on the requesting party or would invade the client-counsel zone of confidence. Thus, in some instances, an order to compel disclosure of documents protected or privileged from discovery might be immediately appealable under § 1292(a).

Here, there is at least an argument that the order compelling the production of the meeting minutes would impose serious and perhaps irreparable harm on Delaware. First, the information in the documents may allow the plaintiffs to piggy-back on investigative efforts of Delaware and its counsel, a primary justification for the work product doctrine. Second, the disclosure would breach the attorney-client confidence and chill frank discussions of liability with corporate counsel, a primary justification for the privilege. Third, the information in the documents would put enormous pressure on Delaware to settle the case on unfavorable terms, both because of the damning nature of the information to the case but also because of the harm to Delaware's broader business if the information because publicly available. And, once the information is disseminated, no appeal will mitigate the harm. For these reasons, it is possible that Delaware could meet *Carson*'s serious and perhaps irreparable harm test.

There are counterarguments. Delaware may not yet have exhausted its options for minimizing the harm. Delaware could, for example, seek a confidentiality order preventing dissemination of the information beyond the litigation. Delaware could challenge its admissibility in court on other grounds. In other words, it is not certain that Delaware will suffer harm just because the documents are disclosed to Patty.

On balance, it is likely that the compel order will not be immediately appealable because it is not an injunction within the meaning of § 1292(a), though arguments to the contrary are not without some merit.

C. SECTION 1292(b).

Section 1292(b) permits appeals from orders which the district court states in writing involve a controlling question of law as to which there is a substantial ground for difference of opinion and that an immediate appeal may materially advance the ultimate termination of the litigation.

Here, it is not clear whether the compel order satisfies these requirements. Whether the documents are in fact privileged or protected from discovery is a controlling question of law, but the legal issues of privilege and work product are fairly well settled. That the district court may have gotten the law completely wrong is not a basis for discretionary appeal; rather, there must be substantial ground for disagreement on the law. It does not appear that the privilege and work product protection issues involved raise unsettled questions of law. Finally, it is not clear whether an immediate appeal will materially advance the litigation. Even if produced in discovery, the documents may not be used at trial. It is possible that the appeal would materially advance the litigation if, say, Patty's case would lack sufficient evidence to proceed to trial without the documents. But that is not suggested in the facts. To the contrary, rejecting an appeal of the compel order might technically advance the ultimate termination of the litigation by facilitating settlement. For these reasons, a discretionary appeal under § 1292(b) seems like a difficult case for Delaware to make.

If Delaware does make the case, however, it will first need to ask the district court to certify the question and make specific findings satisfying each of the conditions of § 1292(b). Then, Delaware must petition the court of appeals within 14 days of that order for leave to appeal. Both the district court's and the appellate court's decisions are within their discretion.

Question 3

A. THE COSTS APPEAL.

No. The class filed its notice of appeal five days after the order to be appealed, which was timely. The notice of appeal failed to mention the objectors specifically, and this might have been fatal to the objectors' appeal of costs under previous case law. *See Torres v. Oakland Scavenger*. However, FRAP 3(c) now states that an appeal should not be dismissed for failure to name a party whose intent to appeal is otherwise clear from the notice. Even if the styling of the objectors was separate on the notice of appeal, their continuing status as class members, coupled with their opportunity to obtain costs, suggests that they intended to appeal as well.

FRAP 3(c) also states that in a class action, the notice of appeal is sufficient if it names one person qualified to bring the appeal as representative of the class. Thus, ordinarily the failure to mention class members specifically should not deprive them of their right to appeal.

B. THE SETTLEMENT APPEAL.

Maybe. The objectors are appealing the settlement approval order, which was entered more than 30 days before the appeal. FRAP 4(a) and § 2107(a) require a notice of appeal to be filed within 30 days of the entry of the order to be appealed. This deadline is jurisdictional under *Bowles v. Russell*.

There are several ways around this deadline, though. First, FRAP 4(a)(3) states that if a party files a timely notice of appeal, any other party may file a notice of appeal within 14 days of the first notice. It is unclear from the Rule whether the two appeals must be from the same order. It would seem likely that they must, for otherwise co-parties could eviscerate the 30-day deadline by filing one timely appeal on one issue and then joining all the untimely appeals with it. Thus, this is not likely to be a viable mechanism for the objectors' appeal.

Second, the objectors' appeal may be timely if the Rule 54(d) motion tolled the time to appeal. Rule 58(e) states that a district court may order that a Rule 54(d) motion toll the time to appeal as a new trial motion would under Rule 59. FRAP 4(a)(4) states that a new trial motion under Rule 59 tolls the time to file an appeal until the entry of an order disposing of the motion. It is not clear from the facts whether the district court ordered that the Rule 54(d) motion tolled the time to appeal. If so, then the objectors' appeal is timely. If not, then it is not.

Third, the time period could have been extended by motion by the objectors made within the 30-day window. *See* FRAP 4(a)(5)(A)(i). Again, it is not clear from the facts whether the objectors made this motion or not. If so, and the court granted it, then the objectors' appeal may be timely. If not, then it would not.

Fourth, the objectors can move for an extension of the appeal deadline even now. FRAP 4(a)(5)(A)(ii) and § 2107(c) allow a court to extend the time period if a party moves within 30 days of the expiration of the deadline and shows excusable neglect or good cause for missing the original deadline. Objectors are within the second 30-day window and thus could file a motion to extend the deadline, which may be granted if the objectors show excusable neglect or good cause.

Fifth, the objectors could move to reopen the time period to file a notice of appeal under FRAP 4(a)(6) and § 2107(c) if the objectors failed to receive notice of the order within 21 days of its entry, and no party would be prejudiced by reopening the time to appeal. The facts do not disclose whether the objectors received notice of the order within 21 days or not. If so, then this option is not available to them. If not, then this option may be available to them.

TOOLS FOR SELF-CRITICISM

This chapter raises many issues, and the hypothetical attempts to capture many of them. You should keep in mind that there are a variety of appellate doctrines and question whether each applies to each issue.

Question 1 focuses on finality. The first part asks for an analysis of whether the punitive damages "claim" is eligible for final judgment treatment under Rule 54. Did you catch the ambiguity in the word "claim"? How did you resolve it?

Using analogies to defenses or theories, as the sample answer does, may be helpful. Did you spot the need for Rule 54? Remember that grants of motions to dismiss are often appealable, while denials of motions to dismiss usually are not. Thus, if a motion to dismiss is granted in part and denied in part, then Rule 54 probably will govern any appealable issues.

Did you analyze whether there is no just reason for delay of an appeal under Rule 54? If Patty wants an appeal, she must convince the district court to so state.

The denial of class certification is an easier issue. Although the Supreme Court previously held that such a denial was not appealable, and, ordinarily, it would not seem to fit comfortably into the appealability doctrines, Rule 23(f) specifically allows such an appeal under the discretion of the court of appeals. Rule 23(f) does not, however, explain what standards the court of appeals should use to guide its discretion.

Did you catch that Rule 23(f) does not allow an immediate appeal but, rather, allows a party to *petition* for leave to appeal? There is a difference, and it involves a separate motion and different timeframes.

Question 2 addresses the collateral order doctrine and statutory exceptions to the final judgment rule. An order granting a motion to compel is clearly not a final judgment, and therefore you should have recognized the availability of these mechanisms and analyzed each of them.

The first is the collateral order doctrine. There are creative arguments to be had here, but *Mohawk Industries* essentially forecloses them.

The injunction exception presents similar hazards and opportunities for the appealability of the order. Note that it is not enough that the order be about an injunction or not. Case law establishes that some orders are injunction-like enough to qualify, and some orders that are injunction orders are not sufficiently meaningful to be appealable. So, simply calling the compel order injunctive or not is not enough. This question presents an opportunity for you to demonstrate your ability to reason through the law, facts, and underlying policies.

Question 3 focuses on the mechanics of filing an appeal and the timing issues involved. Timing issues are critically important, particularly after *Bowles v. Russell* held them to be jurisdictional. Contrast the timing issues with other technical noncompliance, which generally is not fatal to an appeal. Did you distinguish between the timing issues and the naming issues?

In addition to the initial timing calculations, there are a number of ways to avoid the timing deadlines. Be sure that you think creatively about them and exhaust all options. Here, the Rules hold the keys, though not all the keys are in Rule 4.

VARIATIONS ON THE THEME

Would your answer change if the cause of action arose under federal law?

What if the district court granted the motion to dismiss but only because Patty had not alleged the appropriate facts showing entitlement to punitive damages, and the court gave Patty leave to amend her complaint to do so. Would the order be immediately appealable? What might Patty's options be?

Instead of a compel order for privilege documents, say the documents contain valuable trade secrets. Would that change your analysis? What fact scenario can you come up with that most strongly justifies immediate appeal of a discovery order?

Say Delaware moved for recusal based on its belief that the judge was biased against it. The judge denies the motion. Is that denial immediately appealable?

If the plaintiffs had sought injunctive relief in their complaint, and, after discovery, the court had denied the defendant's motion to for summary judgment on the injunctive relief claims, would that order have been appealable under § 1292(a)? *See* Cunningham v. Hamilton County, 527 U.S. 198 (1999); Switzerland Cheese Ass'n v. East Horne's Market, Inc., 385 U.S. 23 (1966).

Say the district court refused to approve the class action settlement. Is that order immediately appealable? *Compare* Seigal v. Merrick, 590 F.2d 35 (2d Cir. 1978) (no), *with* Norman v. McKee, 431 F.2d 769 (9th Cir. 1970) (yes).

OPTIONAL READINGS

Are temporary restraining orders immediately appealable under § 1292(a)? The general rule is no, because TROs are of such limited duration that the issue would become moot by the time the appeal was decided. *See, e.g.,* Bd. of Governors v. DLG Fin. Corp., 29 F.3d 993 (5th Cir. 1994).

Mandamus is a vehicle for review of a district court order that is not necessarily conscribed by the rules regarding appeals. Some courts have allowed mandamus to review privilege decisions. *See, e.g., In re* Occidental Petroleum Corp., 217 F.3d 293, 295 (5th Cir. 2000).

For more on appellate jurisdiction generally, see Adam N. Steinman, *Reinventing Appellate Jurisdiction*, 48 B.C. L. Rev. 1237 (2007).

PRECLUSION

20

OPENING REMARKS

Sadly, there is an end to all things, including (perhaps not so sadly) litigation. The preclusion doctrines allow for this finality. Without them, the losing party could simply try again (and again, and again) until obtaining her desired result. This result, in turn, is likely to be a fleeting one, for there would be a new loser to try again. It is easy to see that the important policy interests driving the preclusion doctrines are a need for finality and a desire to avoid wasting judicial resources.

There are two types of preclusion doctrines. The first is claim preclusion, also known as res judicata. The idea is that the parties only get one shot at litigating their claims and defenses. The second is issue preclusion, also known as collateral estoppel. The idea there is that once an issue has been resolved, it should not be relitigated. Both preclusion doctrines are affirmative defenses under Rule 8(c).

Claim preclusion has several requirements. The first is "mutuality"—parties who litigated against each other in one case generally must be litigating against each other in a second case. In limited cases, nonparties to the first case might be subject to claim preclusion in a subsequent case if they are in privity with a party from the first case. Second, the second case must raise the same claim between the parties as the first case. "Claim" can be quite broad here. Generally speaking, any claim that should have been brought in the first case will be deemed to have been resolved. Thus, a compulsory counterclaim that is not asserted in the first case will be precluded in a subsequent case. Third, the claim in the first case must have been resolved by a valid final judgment on the merits.

Issue preclusion is both broader and narrower than claim preclusion. It is broader because it is not necessarily restricted to the same parties or the same claim. It is narrower because it pertains only to an issue rather than a claim for relief. Thus, for example, a determination in one case that a tire was defectively manufactured can be used to establish that issue in other cases involving other circumstances and other parties.

Issue preclusion requires an issue that was actually litigated and determined and was essential to a final judgment on the merits. The determination of that issue usually will be determinative of the same issue presented in a second case against a party who was a party to (or in privity with a party to) the first case.

There are exceptions to the application of the preclusion doctrines. For example, a party that lacked a full and fair opportunity to litigate the claim or issue in the first case generally will not be subject to preclusion.

HYPOTHETICAL

Pablo Pérez works in the mail delivery room of Daisy Industries, a large Delaware corporation with its principal place of business in New York. After three years of working there, he applies for a promotion to assistant manager and is turned down. A colleague, a non-Hispanic female, is given the promotion instead, even though she had worked in the mail room for only two years. Pablo has noticed that Hispanic men have routinely been turned down for promotions in a variety of positions.

Pablo therefore sues Daisy for race and gender discrimination, claiming that Daisy discriminates against Hispanic men in promotions. He also seeks to represent a class of Hispanic men denied promotions on the basis of race and gender, and he alleges a pattern or practice of such discrimination. Pablo also asserts a claim under the same statute for hostile work environment based upon racial slurs directed at him by his direct supervisor while he was working there.

Pablo sues in New York state court under New York state antidiscrimination laws only. Because Pablo commutes into work from New Jersey, Daisy timely removes the case on the basis of diversity jurisdiction.

In federal court, Daisy asserts a number of defenses, including the two-year statute of limitations governing claims under the state statute. Daisy does not assert any counterclaims.

Pablo moves for class certification on the promotion claims. The district court denies the motion, finding insufficient evidence of a pattern or practice of discrimination. After discovery, Daisy moves for summary judgment on the hostile work environment claim, asserting that the alleged statements all were made more than two years prior to the lawsuit and thus is barred by the statute of limitations. The court grants summary judgment on the hostile work environment claim on that basis.

Pablo's individual discrimination claim then goes to trial before a judge. Pablo elects not to put on any evidence of mental anguish and instead proceeds solely with damages evidence of lost wages. The trial judge finds that Daisy discriminated against Pablo based on his race. The trial judge finds no discrimination based on gender. The trial judge finds damages in lost wages of $4,000 and enters judgment in that amount. Both parties appeal.

While the appeal is pending, Pablo files a second lawsuit against Daisy in New Jersey federal court. He sues for both race and gender discrimination in promotions, and for hostile work environment, under both the state and federal antidiscrimination statutes. The federal antidiscrimination statute has the same scope, requirements, protections, and remedies as the state antidiscrimination statute. He seeks damages for both mental anguish and lost wages in excess of the $4,000 awarded in the first lawsuit. He is joined by Pedro Pujols. Pedro was a member of the putative class in the first lawsuit. Pedro alleges an individual claim of race and gender discrimination under both federal and state antidiscrimination laws. Daisy asserts the same affirmative defenses as it did in the first lawsuit. In addition, Daisy asserts a counterclaim against both Pablo and Pedro for conversion, contending that they stole supplies from the mail room while they worked there.

Please identify and discuss all issues relating to claim and issue preclusion that may arise in this second lawsuit.

SUGGESTED READINGS

Fed. R. Civ. P. 8
Restatement (Second) of Judgments §§ 24–29
Federated Dep't Stores, Inc. v. Moitie, 452 U.S. 394, 395–401 (1981)

Allen v. McCurry, 449 U.S. 90, 91–96, 102–05 (1980)

Cooper v. Fed. Res. Bank of Richmond, 467 U.S. 867, 869–80 (1984)

Cromwell v. County of Sac, 94 U.S. 351, 353 (1877)

Montana v. United States, 440 U.S. 147, 149–64 (1979)

Parklane Hosiery Co. v. Shore, 439 U.S. 322, 324–33 (1979)

Semtek Int'l, Inc. v. Lockheed Martin Corp., 531 U.S. 497, 499–500, 506–09 (2001)

Taylor v. Sturgell, 128 S. Ct. 2161, 2166–67, 2171–80 (2008)

United States v. Mendoza, 464 U.S. 154, 155–64 (1984)

SAMPLE ESSAY

A few preliminary issues should be addressed at the outset. First, the fact that the first judgment is pending on appeal does not alter its finality or its preclusive effect. Second, preclusion is itself an affirmative defense that must be asserted in a timely fashion. If the party seeking preclusion does not do so, the court can adjudicate the claim or issue that otherwise would have been precluded. The party seeking preclusion also has the burden of proving it. Third, under *Semtek*, the preclusive force of the first federal judgment is determined by resort to federal common law even though it was a diversity case. Fourth, each of the conclusions below that preclusion applies is dependent upon the prior adjudication providing a full and fair opportunity for litigation. No evidence in the facts indicates otherwise, but it is worth noting that the party seeking to avoid preclusion may be able to do so if he can make the argument that he did not have a full or fair opportunity to litigate in the prior lawsuit. With that said, I will discuss both claim preclusion and issue preclusion.

Claim Preclusion

Claim preclusion prevents relitigation of claims if the prior litigation was between the same parties and resolved the claims by a valid final judgment on the merits. There are at least four potential opportunities for claim preclusion.

1. PABLO'S STATE CLAIMS

Pablo litigated his state claims in his original lawsuit against the same defendant. He had three claims: race discrimination, gender discrimination, and hostile work environment.

I assume the court had diversity jurisdiction because the parties were diverse, although the fact pattern does not indicate whether the amount-in-controversy requirement was met. If the requirement was not met, then the judgment may be void and thus not "valid." Assuming otherwise, however, the discrimination claims were resolved by a valid final judgment on the merits after trial. As a result, claim preclusion attaches: Pablo may not relitigate those claims in a successive lawsuit.

The hostile work environment claim was resolved by valid summary judgment on statute of limitations grounds. The question here is whether the applicability of the defense of statute of limitations is a decision on the merits that justifies claim preclusion. Under *Semtek*, the preclusive effect of a federal court diversity judgment is a matter of federal law, but it is determined by incorporation of the law of the state in which that court sits. Thus, if New York state courts would give preclusive effect to a judgment based on the state statute of limitations, then Pablo's claim is barred. If not, then Pablo's claim is not precluded. The fact pattern does not disclose what the applicable state law is, so I would need to do more research to make that determination.

If claim preclusion applies, the Restatement directs that it apply even if Pablo seeks to present different evidence, grounds, theories, or forms of relief. Thus, Pablo cannot avoid preclusion just because he is now prepared to pursue damages for mental anguish, or he has new evidence, or he wishes to pursue a new argument that might avoid the applicable statute of limitations.

2. PABLO'S FEDERAL CLAIMS

Pablo did not assert any federal claims in his original lawsuit. However, his federal claims may now be precluded if he could have joined them in his original lawsuit. The idea here is that a litigant ought to get one full and fair opportunity to assert his claims; if he does not assert them, but should have, then he should be barred from doing so outside of the original lawsuit. The Restatement takes this approach. The claims precluded include all rights of the plaintiff with respect to all or any part of the transaction or series of transactions out of which the action arose.

Here, Pablo is pursuing a federal claim founded upon the exact same facts (and providing identical rights) as the state claim. Nothing indicates that Pablo could not have joined his federal claims with his state claims in the previous lawsuit. He should have done so—he likely is now barred from asserting his federal claims in the second lawsuit. However, it will be Daisy's burden to assert and establish claim preclusion.

3. PEDRO'S DISCRIMINATION CLAIMS

Pedro did not assert any individual discrimination claims in Pablo's original lawsuit. There are two ways his individual discrimination claims might be precluded now, though neither is likely.

First, because Pedro was a member of the class in the first lawsuit, those class claims might preclude his individual claims in the second lawsuit. But this is very unlikely. Class claims can be preclusive of successive class or individual claims, but only if they are resolved on the merits. Here, the class failed to meet the certification requirements of Rule 23, a non-merits determination. As a result, the ruling likely is not preclusive of anything.

Second, Pablo's individual claims might preclude Pedro's individual claims. Generally, only judgments between parties to the same lawsuit can have preclusive effect. In *Taylor v. Sturgell*, the Supreme Court disapproved of "virtual representation" between non-mutual parties. Certain exceptions do apply, such as a special relationship like bailee or assignee, adequate representation via class actions or trust fiduciaries, or if the party essentially assumed control over the previous litigation as in *U.S. v. Montana*. But none of those exceptions appears to apply here, and *Taylor* is against expanding those exceptions beyond their limited applicability.

4. DAISY'S COUNTERCLAIMS

Daisy did not assert any counterclaims in the first lawsuit. However, its counterclaims against Pablo may now be precluded if it could have asserted them in the first lawsuit and failed to do so.

The Restatement makes clear that claim preclusion can extinguish claims that were *not* asserted in the first lawsuit if they arose out of the same transaction or series of transactions as the claims that *were* asserted in the first lawsuit. The Restatement states that this test is to be applied pragmatically, giving consideration to whether the facts are related in time, space, origin, or motivation; whether they form a convenient trial unit; and whether their treatment as a unit conforms to the parties' expectations or business understanding or usage. The Restatement is not binding on courts, but it is in accord with the general policies behind claim preclusion: parties ought to get one—but only one—opportunity to litigate their claims (and their related claims). Compulsory counterclaims should count, too.

Here, Daisy's counterclaims arise from the same employment relationship and time frame as Pablo's discrimination claims. In addition, if Daisy were to defend the discrimination lawsuit on the ground that Pablo was fired for theft as opposed to discriminatory animus, then the counterclaims might form a convenient trial unit with Pablo's claims. There are counterarguments—for example, discrimination is entirely separate and unrelated to theft, involving divergent witnesses and evidence—but they seem weaker. On balance, claim preclusion probably should apply, though Pablo will have the burden of proving that it should.

Daisy's counterclaims against Pedro are not barred. Pedro was not a party to the original action. Hence, claim preclusion cannot apply to the counterclaims against him.

Issue Preclusion

For issue preclusion to attach, the issue must have been actually litigated, decided, and essential to a valid final judgment. There are at least four issues squarely implicated by the facts of this case.

1. PATTERN OR PRACTICE OF DISCRIMINATION

The first lawsuit alleged, as part of its class allegations, a pattern or practice of discrimination. The court found insufficient evidence of such a pattern or practice and refused to certify the class. It is unlikely that issue preclusion would attach here. Although the issue was contested, and the court made a finding that was essential to the denial of class certification, the denial of certification is not typically considered to be a final judgment on the merits, which is a requirement for issue preclusion.

Even if the determination were entitled to issue preclusion, it is unclear whether it would have much value. A finding of no pattern or practice of discrimination in class claims is preclusive only of the issue of pattern or practice of discrimination. *See Cooper.* Individual discrimination may manifest itself in a variety of ways. Thus, even if issue preclusion attaches, Pablo and Pedro may still pursue their discrimination claims, as long as they do not rely solely on a pattern or practice of discrimination.

2. STATUTE OF LIMITATIONS

Assuming the first lawsuit's judgment based on the statute of limitations was on the merits, findings essential to that judgment are entitled to issue preclusive effect in the New Jersey lawsuit. Thus, if the court determined that a hostile work environment occurred before a certain date, or if the court determined that certain alleged acts actually did *not* occur, those findings would have issue preclusive effect in the New Jersey lawsuit for any claims for which they would be relevant, including, for example, Pablo's federal hostile work environment claims.

3. FINDINGS ON DISCRIMINATION

The court found that Daisy discriminated against Pablo based on race. That issue was essential to the valid final judgment against Daisy. There is no indication that the issues were not fully, fairly, and adequately litigated. As a result, that issue of race discrimination against Pablo is deemed to be established in the second lawsuit. Pablo can use that finding as determinative in the second lawsuit in his claims against Daisy for discrimination under both state and federal law.

The court found that Daisy did not discriminate against Pablo based on gender. That issue was essential to the valid final judgment against Pablo on that issue. As a result, the finding of no gender discrimination against Pablo is deemed to be established in the second lawsuit. Daisy can use that finding as determinative against the claims by Pablo under both state and federal law.

It is possible that these findings could have issue preclusive effect in the claims asserted by Pedro. Discrimination claims are often individualized. But, to the extent the factual disputes actually litigated and determined in Pablo's claims in the first lawsuit are sought to be relitigated by Pedro or Daisy in the second lawsuit, they could have issue preclusive effect. Specifically, Daisy can seek preclusive effect under *Blonder-Tongue*, which allows for non-mutual defensive issue preclusion; and Pedro can seek preclusive effect under *Parklane Hosiery*, which allows for offensive non-mutual issue preclusion. Pedro may only do so, however, if it would not reward Pedro for failing to join the first lawsuit and where it would not be unfair to Daisy. In particular, if it appears that Pedro intentionally declined to join Pablo's first lawsuit so that Pedro could get a free look at what might happen, he probably will not be able to use issue preclusion against Daisy in the second lawsuit. Similarly, if Pablo's claims were relatively small compared to Pedro's, it might be unfair to allow preclusion of issues established by Pablo.

4. MENTAL ANGUISH

Assuming the entire claim is not precluded, the issue of mental anguish will not be precluded. Issue preclusion only attaches to issues that are actually litigated and determined. In the first suit, Pablo simply declined to pursue his claims for mental anguish damages. Accordingly, he is not barred by issue preclusion principles from pursuing them in a second lawsuit.

TOOLS FOR SELF-CRITICISM

There is a lot going on in this problem. Be sure to keep the parties, claims, and lawsuits clear. Consider using a diagram to keep your facts straight.

The preclusion doctrines can be bifurcated into their two principal parts: claim preclusion and issue preclusion. Keeping that in mind may help you identify the issues. Spot each claim and ask: Could this be subject to or cause claim preclusion? Then, spot each issue actually litigated and decided, and ask whether it could cause issue preclusion. Don't forget to analyze which parties are entitled to pursue which, and which parties may be subject to which!

The sample answer tackled claim preclusion first, and so we will start there as well. You should have isolated all the claims in the second lawsuit. There are 12 of them, so keep them all straight. Then, you should have asked whether any of them are precluded by claims from the first lawsuit. There were only 4 of those, but do not be mislead by that figure. Claim preclusion can attach even from claims that were *not* asserted in the first lawsuit if those claims *should* have been asserted there. So you should carefully determine which claims were previously asserted and which claims should have been previously asserted.

For those claims that were previously asserted, you will have to determine which resulted in a valid, final judgment on the merits. (Don't get sidetracked by the appeal—appeals do not negate preclusive effects!) Certainly the discrimination claims resulted in a valid, final judgment on the merits. Did the hostile work environment claim that was subject to a statute of limitations defense? Did the class claims that were never certified? Those were less clear but still worthy of discussion.

Then, you should have considered whether preclusion would apply. Recall that claim preclusion requires, with very few exceptions, mutuality. Thus, claims between Pablo and Daisy ordinarily could not preclude claims between Pedro and Daisy. The class action claims in the first lawsuit complicate that normally bright-line prerequisite for claim preclusion because class claims can be preclusive of individual claims. But, here, the class claims were not adjudicated on their merits.

Acknowledging mutuality reduces the complexity a bit, but you still must consider whether the failure to assert claims in the first lawsuit precludes their later assertion in the second lawsuit. That principle of claim preclusion implicates Pablo's federal discrimination claims and Daisy's counterclaim against him.

After exhausting claim preclusion, you should turn to issue preclusion. Unlike claim preclusion, issue preclusion bars only issues. Thus, the class claims are only preclusive, if at all, on the particular issue of pattern and practice of discrimination. They would not preclude claims founded on other issues.

Issue preclusion need not be confined to the same claims, though. Thus, issues established in the state claims between Pablo and Daisy may preclude relitigation of the same issues in the federal claims between them. Indeed, because the state and federal statutes are very similar, the issues established in the state claim are likely to be preclusive in the federal claim.

Also, issue preclusion is not bound by mutuality as claim preclusion is. Thus, issues established in the claims between Pablo and Daisy may preclude relitigation of the same issues in the claims between Pedro and Daisy. There are some limitations on non-mutual preclusion, however. Take care to acknowledge and deal with those.

Finally, do not forget that issue preclusion only applies to issues that are actually litigated and decided. Pablo's reassertion of mental anguish damages may be barred by claim preclusion, but it cannot be barred by issue preclusion, for he never litigated them to an adjudication.

VARIATIONS ON THE THEME

Say Daisy had failed to answer the first lawsuit and had a default judgment entered against it as to all of Pablo's state law claims. Would those state law claims be preclusive in the second lawsuit? *See* Morris v. Jones, 329 U.S. 545 (1947) (holding a default judgment to be on the merits and entitled to claim preclusion). Would the allegations that supported them be entitled to issue preclusion?

Assume that Pablo is a citizen of New York and, thus, the first lawsuit lacks diversity. Pablo wishes to preserve his state forum for his state claims, but he knows that if he joins his federal discrimination claims in the state lawsuit, Daisy can remove the case to federal court. Must he nevertheless do so to avoid subsequent preclusion of those claims? Should he have to? Would issue preclusion apply?

Suppose that, in the New Jersey lawsuit, Daisy argued that federal antidiscrimination statute was unconstitutional. Pablo argued otherwise, but the court agreed with Daisy. Say that the Equal Employment Opportunity Commission (EEOC), a federal agency charged with remedying discrimination, then sues Daisy for related discrimination under the same law. Can Daisy assert issue preclusion? What if the EEOC had intervened in the first lawsuit in support of Pablo?

Suppose that, in the time between the New York court's judgment and the New Jersey lawsuit, the New York legislature changes the statute of limitations of its antidiscrimination statute from two years to four years. Are the claims and issues related to the old statute of limitations and decided by the New York court preclusive in the New Jersey court? What if it was not a legislative change but a New York Court of Appeals ruling that "corrected" an erroneous lower court interpretation of the statute of limitations as two years?

OPTIONAL READINGS

Although federal law is moving toward a more robust use of non-mutual offensive issue preclusion, *see* Parklane Hosiery Co. v. Shore, 439 U.S. 322 (1979), most states have not, *see, e.g.,* Beaty v. McGraw, 15 S.W.3d 819 (Tenn. App. 1998); Trappell v. Sysco Food Servs., 850 S.W.2d 529 (Tex. App. 1992). For the back-and-forth history of non-mutual estoppel, see Berhard v. Bank of Am. Nat'l Trust & Sav. Ass'n, 122 P.2d 892 (Cal. 1942); Brainerd Currie, *Mutuality of Collateral Estoppel: Limits of the* Berhard *Doctrine*, 9 STAN. L. REV. 281 (1957); James Wm. Moore & Thomas S. Currier, *Mutuality and Conclusiveness of Judgments*, 35 TUL. L. REV. 301 (1961); Albernaz v. City of Fall River, 191 N.E.2d 771 (Mass. 1963); Michael J. Waggoner, *Fifty Years of* Bernhard v. Bank of America *is Enough: Collateral Estoppel Should Require Mutuality but Res Judicata Should Not*, 12 REV. LITIG. 391 (1993).

For more on the preclusive effects on compulsory counterclaims, see Kevin M. Clermont, *Common-Law Compulsory Counterclaim Rule: Creative Effective and Elegant Res Judicata Doctrine*, 79 NOTRE DAME L. REV. 1745 (2004).

Should preclusion cross the civil-criminal divide? *See, e.g.,* David L. Shapiro, *Should a Guilty Plea Have Preclusive Effect?*, 70 IOWA L. REV. 27 (1984).

TABLE OF CASES AND MATERIALS

Cases

Eggleton v. Plasser & Theurer Export von Bahnbaumaschinen Gesellscaft, MBH, 495 F.3d 582 (8th Cir. 2007)

Empire HealthChoice Assur., Inc. v. McVeigh, 547 U.S. 677 (2006)

Erie R.R. Co. v. Tompkins, 304 U.S. 64 (1938)

Exxon Mobile Corp. v. Allapattah Servs., 545 U.S. 546 (2005)

Federated Dep't Stores, Inc. v. Moitie, 452 U.S. 394 (1981)

Ferens v. John Deere Co., 494 U.S. 516 (1990)

Firestone Tire & Rubber Co. v. Risjord, 449 U.S. 368 (1981)

First Am. Corp. v. Price Waterhouse LLP, 154 F.3d 16 (2d Cir. 1998)

Foman v. Davis, 371 U.S. 178 (1962)

Freeman v. Wood, 401 N.E.2d 108 (Mass. 1980)

Fuentes v. Shevin, 407 U.S. 67 (1972)

Galloway v. United States, 319 U.S. 372 (1943)

Garrison v. United States, 62 F.2d 41 (4th Cir. 1932)

Gasperini v. Ctr. for Humanities, Inc., 518 U.S. 415 (1996)

Gen. Tel. Co. of the S.W. v. Falcon, 457 U.S. 147 (1982)

Goodyear Dunlop Tires Operations, S.A. v. Brown, 564 U.S. __ (2011)

Goodyear Tire & Rubber Co. v. Chiles Power Supply, Inc., 332 F.3d 976 (6th Cir. 2003)

Great Am. Indem. Co. v. Brown, 307 F.2d 306 (5th Cir. 1962)

Greene v. Lindsey, 456 U.S. 444 (1982)

Grable & Sons Metal Prods., Inc. v. Darue Eng'g & Mfg., 545 U.S. 308 (2005)

Grupo Dataflux v. Atlas Global Group, L.P., 541 U.S. 567 (2004)

Guaranty Trust Co. v. York, 326 U.S. 99 (1945)

Hanna v. Plumer, 380 U.S. 460 (1965)

Hansberry v. Lee, 311 U.S. 32 (1940)

HC Servs., Inc. v. Hiller Inv., Inc., No. 2:06cv160KS-MTP (S.D. Miss. Mar. 30, 2007)

Heim v. Comm'r, 872 F.2d 245 (8th Cir. 1989)

Hertz Corp. v. Friend, 559 U.S. _ (2010)

Hetzel v. Prince William County, 523 U.S. 208 (1998) (per curiam)

Hickman v. Taylor, 329 U.S. 495 (1947)

Hoagland v. Sandberg, 385 F.3d 737 (7th Cir. 2004)

Hoffman v. Blaski, 363 U.S. 335 (1960)

Holstrom v. Peterson, 492 F.3d 833 (7th Cir. 2007)

Hulson v. Atchison, Topeka & Santa Fe Ry. Co., 289 F.2d 726 (7th Cir. 1961)

Hurt v. Dow Chem. Co., 963 F.2d 1142 (8th Cir. 1992)

Intec USA, LLC v. Engle, 467 F.3d 1038 (7th Cir. 2006)

Int'l Controls Corp. v. Vesco, 556 F.2d 665 (2d Cir. 1977)

Int'l Shoe Co. v. Washington, 326 U.S. 310 (1945)

James-Dickinson Farm Mortgage v. Harry, 273 U.S. 119 (1927)

J.A. Olson Co. v. City of Winona, 818 F.2d 401 (5th Cir. 1987)

J. McIntyre Machinery, Ltd. v. Nicastro, 564 U.S. _(2011)

Jones v. Aero/Chem Corp., 921 F.2d 875 (9th Cir. 1990)

Jones v. Flowers, 547 U.S. 220 (2006)

Jones v. Ford Motor Credit Co., 358 F.3d 205 (2d Cir. 2004)

Krupski v. Costa Crociere S.p.A, 560 U.S. _ (U.S. 2010)

Lafferty v. St. Riel, 495 F.3d 72 (3d Cir. 2007)

Lavender v. Kurn, 327 U.S. 645 (1946)

Lively v. Wild Oats Markets, Inc., 456 F.3d 933 (9th Cir. 2006)

Louisville & Nashville R.R. Co. v. Mottley, 211 U.S. 149 (1908)

Lowe v. McGraw-Hill Co., 361 F.3d 335 (7th Cir. 2004)

Magnuson v. Video Yesteryear, 85 F.3d 1424 (9th Cir. 1996)

Mareese v. Am. Acad. of Orthopaedic Surgeons, 726 F.2d 1150 (7th Cir. 1984)

Marks v. United States, 430 U.S. 188 (1977)

Martino v. McDonald's Sys., Inc., 598 F.2d 1079 (7th Cir. 1979)

Mas v. Perry, 489 F.2d 1396 (5th Cir. 1974)

Matsushita Elec. Indus. Co. v. Zenith Radio Corp., 475 U.S. 574 (1986)

McDonough Power Equip., Inc. v. Greenwood, 464 U.S. 548 (1984)

CONSTITUTIONS, STATUTES, RULES, AND TREATIES

U.S. Const. art. III, § 2
U.S. Const. art. VI, cl. 2
U.S. Const. amend. VII
U.S. Const. amend. XIV, § 1
15 U.S.C. § 78u–4(b)
28 U.S.C. § 1291
28 U.S.C. § 1292
28 U.S.C. § 1331
28 U.S.C. § 1332
28 U.S.C. § 1367
28 U.S.C. § 1391
28 U.S.C. § 1404
28 U.S.C. § 1406
28 U.S.C. § 1441
28 U.S.C. § 1446
28 U.S.C. § 1447
28 U.S.C. § 1652
28 U.S.C. § 2072
28 U.S.C. § 2107
Fed. R. App. P. 3
Fed. R. App. P. 4
Fed. R. App. P. 5
Fed. R. Civ. P. 3
Fed. R. Civ. P. 4
Fed. R. Civ. P. 5
Fed. R. Civ. P. 6
Fed. R. Civ. P. 8
Fed. R. Civ. P. 9
Fed. R. Civ. P. 10
Fed. R. Civ. P. 11
Fed. R. Civ. P. 12
Fed. R. Civ. P. 13
Fed. R. Civ. P. 14
Fed. R. Civ. P. 15
Fed. R. Civ. P. 16
Fed. R. Civ. P. 18
Fed. R. Civ. P. 19
Fed. R. Civ. P. 20
Fed. R. Civ. P. 21
Fed. R. Civ. P. 23
Fed. R. Civ. P. 24
Fed. R. Civ. P. 26
Fed. R. Civ. P. 29
Fed. R. Civ. P. 30
Fed. R. Civ. P. 31
Fed. R. Civ. P. 32
Fed. R. Civ. P. 33
Fed. R. Civ. P. 34
Fed. R. Civ. P. 35
Fed. R. Civ. P. 36
Fed. R. Civ. P. 37
Fed. R. Civ. P. 41
Fed. R. Civ. P. 42
Fed. R. Civ. P. 45

Fed. R. Civ. P. 50

Fed. R. Civ. P. 54

Fed. R. Civ. P. 56

Fed. R. Civ. P. 58

Fed. R. Civ. P. 59

Fed. R. Civ. P. 60

Fed. R. Civ. P. 61

Fed. R. Civ. P. Form 5

Fed. R. Civ. P. Form 11

Cal. Civ. Proc. Code § 662.5(b)

Restatement (Second) of Judgments §§ 24–29

Convention on the Service Abroad of Judicial and Extrajudicial Documents in Civil or Commercial Matters, The Hague, 1965, 20 U.S.T. 361, T.I.A.S. No. 6638, 658 U.N.T.S. 163

OTHER MATERIALS

Amendments to the Federal Rules of Civil Procedure, 146 F.R.D. 401 (1993)

Thomas J. André, Jr., *The Final Judgment Rule and Party Appeals of Civil Contempt Orders: Time for a Change*, 55 N.Y.U. L. REV. 1041 (1980)

Samuel P. Baumgartner, *Is Transnational Litigation Different?*, 25 U. PA. J. INT'L ECON. L. 1297 (2004)

Edward Brunet, *Summary Judgment Is Constitutional*, 93 IOWA L. REV. 1625 (2008)

Stephen P. Burbank, Semtek, *Forum Shopping, and Federal Common Law*, 77 NOTRE DAME L. REV. 1027 (2002)

OSCAR G. CHASE ET AL., CIVIL LITIGATION IN COMPARATIVE CONTEXT (West 2007)

Kevin M. Clermont, *Common-Law Compulsory Counterclaim Rule: Creative Effective and Elegant Res Judicata Doctrine*, 79 NOTRE DAME L. REV. 1745 (2004)

Jeremy A. Colby, *You've Got Mail: The Modern Trend toward Universal Electronic Service of Process*, 51 BUFF. L. REV. 337 (2003)

Brainerd Currie, *Mutuality of Collateral Estoppel: Limits of the* Berhard *Doctrine*, 9 STAN. L. REV. 281 (1957)

Scott Dodson, *Beyond* Twombly, CIVIL PROCEDURE PROF BLOG (May 18, 2009)

Scott Dodson, *Comparative Convergences in Pleading Standards*, 158 U. PA. L. REV. 441 (2010)

Scott Dodson, *In Search of Removal Jurisdiction*, 102 NW. U. L. REV. 55 (2008)

Scott Dodson, *The Mystery of* Twombly *Continues*, PRAWFSBLAWG (Feb. 5, 2008)

Scott Dodson, *Subclassing*, 27 CARDOZO L. REV. 2351 (2006)

Donald Doernberg, *There's No Reason for It; It's Just Our Policy: Why the Well-Pleaded Complaint Rule Sabotages the Purposes of Federal Question Jurisdiction*, 38 HASTINGS L.J. 597 (1987)

James Duane, *The Four Greatest Myths About Summary Judgment*, 52 WASH. & LEE L. REV. 1523 (1996)

Frank H. Easterbrook, *Discovery as Abuse*, 69 B.U. L. REV. 635 (1989)

Stephen D. Easton, Note, *Doe Defendants and Other State Relation Back Doctrines in Federal Diversity Cases*, 35 STAN. L. REV. 297 (1983)

Rebecca S. Engrav, Comment, *Relation Back of Amendments Naming Previously Unnamed Defendants under Federal Rule of Civil Procedure 15(c)*, 89 CAL. L. REV. 1549 (2001)

William A. Fletcher, *"Common Nucleus of Operative Fact" and Defensive Set-Off: Beyond the* Gibbs *Test*, 74 IND. L.J. 171 (1998)

Katherine Florey, *Making Sovereigns Indispensable:* Pimentel *and the Evolution of Rule 19*, 58 UCLA L. REV. 667 (2011)

Richard D. Freer, *Avoiding Duplicative Litigation: Rethinking Plaintiff Autonomy and the Court's Role in Defining the Litigative Unit*, 50 U. PITT. L. REV. 809 (1989)

Richard D. Freer, *Compounding Confusion and Hampering Diversity: Life after* Finley *and the Supplemental Jurisdiction Statute*, 40 EMORY L.J. 445 (1991)

RICHARD D. FREER, INTRODUCTION TO CIVIL PROCEDURE (2006)

Richard D. Freer, *Some Thoughts on the State of* Erie *After* Gasperini, 76 TEX. L. REV. 1637 (1998)

Antonio Gidi, *Class Actions in Brazil—A Model for Civil Law Countries*, 51 Am. J. Comp. L. 311 (2003)

Batya Goodman, *Honey, I Shrink-Wrapped the Consumer: The Shrink-Wrap Agreement as an Adhesion Contract*, 21 Cardozo L. Rev. 319 (1999)

Michael Steven Green, *Horizontal* Erie *and the Presumption of Forum Law*, 109 Mich. L. Rev. 1237 (2011)

Valerie P. Hans & Stephanie Albertson, *Empirical Research and Civil Jury Reform*, 78 Notre Dame L. Rev. 1497 (2003)

Peter Hay, Comment, *Transient Jurisdiction, Especially Over International Defendants: Critical Comments on* Burnham v. Superior Court of California, 1990 U. Ill. L. Rev. 593 (1990)

Laura J. Hines, *Challenging the Issue Class Action End-Run*, 52 Emory L.J. 709 (2003)

Laura J. Hines, *The Dangerous Allure of the Issue Class Action*, 79 Ind. L.J. 567 (2004)

Harry Kalven Jr. & Jans Zeisel, The American Jury (1966)

Mary Kay Kane, *The Golden Wedding Year:* Erie Railroad Company v. Tomkins *and the Federal Rules*, 63 Notre Dame L. Rev. 671 (1986)

Larry Kramer, *Diversity Jurisdiction*, 1990 B.Y.U. L. Rev. 97

Legal papers served via Facebook, BBC News (Dec. 16, 2008), *available at* http://news.bbc.co.uk/2/hi/asia-pacific/7785004.stm

Comment, *Lis Pendens and Procedural Due Process: A Closer Look after Connecticut v. Doehr*, 51 Md. L. Rev. 1054 (1992)

Ian Llewellyn, *NZ court papers can be served via Facebook, judge rules*, New Zealand Herald (Mar. 16, 2009), *available at* http://www.nzherald.co.nz/world/news/article.cfm?c_id=2&objectid=10561970

Richard L. Marcus, *Retooling American Discovery for the Twenty-First Century: Toward a New World Order?*, 7 Tul. J. Intl. & Comp. L. 153 (1999)

St. Claire McKelway, *Profiles—Place and Leave With I*, New Yorker 23 (Aug. 24, 1935)

St. Claire McKelway, *Profiles—Place and Leave With II*, New Yorker 21 (Aug. 31, 1935)

Arthur Miller, *Artful Pleading: A Doctrine in Search of Definition*, 76 Tex. L. Rev. 1781 (1998)

Arthur Miller, *The Pretrial Rush to Judgment: Are the "Litigation Explosion," "Liability Crisis," and Efficiency Clichés Eroding Our Day in Court and Jury Trial Commitments?*, 78 N.Y.U. L. Rev. 982 (2003)

James Wm. Moore & Thomas S. Currier, *Mutuality and Conclusiveness of Judgments*, 35 Tul. L. Rev. 301 (1961)

9 Moore's Federal Practice § 50 (3d ed. 2008)

Linda Mullenix, *The Pervasive Myth of Pervasive Discovery Abuse and the Consequences for Unfounded Rulemaking*, 46 Stan. L. Rev. 1393 (1994)

John M. Murphy III, Note, *From Snail Mail to E-Mail: The Steady Evolution of Service of Process*, 19 St. John's J. Legal Comment. 73 (2004)

Richard A. Nagareda, *Aggregate Litigation Across the Atlantic and the Future of American Exceptionalism*, 62 Vand. L. Rev. 1 (2009)

William E. Nelson, *Summary Judgment and the Progressive Constitution*, 93 Iowa L. Rev. 1653 (2008)

John B. Oakley, Kroger *Redux*, 51 Duke L.J. 663 (2001)

Todd David Peterson, *The Timing of Minimum Contacts*, 80 Geo. Wash. L. Rev. 202 (2010)

Edward Purcell, Jr., Litigation and Inequality: Federal Diversity Jurisdiction in Industrial America, 1870–1958 (1992)

Restatement (Second) of Conflict of Laws § 40 (1971)

Thomas D. Rowe, Jr., *Not Bad for Government Work: Does Anyone Else Think the Supreme Court is Doing a Halfway Decent Job in its* Erie-Hanna *Jurisprudence?*, 73 Notre Dame L. Rev. 963 (1998)

Thomas D. Rowe Jr. et al., 40 Emory L.J. 943 (1991)

Hilary A. Sale, *Heightened Pleading and Discovery Stays: An Analysis of the Effect of the PSLRA's Internal-Information Standard on '33 and '34 Act Claims*, 76 Wash. U. L.Q. 537 (1998)

David L. Shapiro, *Should a Guilty Plea Have Preclusive Effect?*, 70 Iowa L. Rev. 27 (1984)

Brittain Shaw, *The $75,000 Question: What is the Value of Injunctive Relief?*, 6 Geo. Mason L. Rev. 1013 (1998)

Adam N. Steinman, *Reinventing Appellate Jurisdiction*, 48 B.C. L. Rev. 1237 (2007)

Stephen N. Subrin, *Discovery in Global Perspective: Are We Nuts?*, 52 DePaul L. Rev. 299 (2002)

Suja A. Thomas, *Why Summary Judgment is Unconstitutional*, 93 Va. L. Rev. 139 (2007)

Suja A. Thomas, *The Unconstitutionality of Summary Judgment: A Status Report*, 93 Iowa L. Rev. 1613 (2008)

Suja A. Thomas, *Why Summary Judgment is Still Unconstitutional: A Reply to Professors Brunet and Nelson*, 93 Iowa L. Rev. 1667 (2008)

Suja A. Thomas, *Why the Motion to Dismiss Is Now Unconstitutional*, 92 Minn. L. Rev. 1851 (2008)

Suja A. Thomas, *Re-examining the Constitutionality of Remittitur Under the Seventh Amendment*, 64 Ohio St. L.J. 731 (2003)

Symposium, 74 Ind. L.J. 1–250 (1998)

Symposium, *Fairness to Whom? Perspectives on the Class Action Fairness Act of 2005*, 156 U. Pa. L. Rev. 1439 (2008)

Carl Tobias, *The 1993 Revision to Federal Rule 11*, 70 Ind. L.J. 171 (1994)

Roger Transgrud, *Joinder Alternatives in Mass Tort Litigation*, 70 Cornell L. Rev. 779 (1985)

Michael J. Waggoner, *Fifty Years of* Bernhard v. Bank of America *I2001: 362-70s Enough: Collateral Estoppel Should Require Mutuality but Res Judicata Should Not*, 12 Rev. Litig. 391 (1993)

Irving Younger, *What Happened in* Erie, 56 Tex. L. Rev. 1011 (1978)

CPSIA information can be obtained
at www.ICGtesting.com
Printed in the USA
BVHW07s1119300818
525907BV00006B/33/P